HEROINES

OF THE

RESTORATION

May 1997

Dear Deila,

Happy Mother's Day.
I hope you will
enjoy the story of
"Little Sister Higgs,"
your great great
grandmother!

Love,
Jeri

HEROINES OF THE RESTORATION

EDITED BY

BARBARA B. SMITH & BLYTHE DARLYN THATCHER

ILLUSTRATIONS BY

MELISSA LOWE

BOOKCRAFT
SALT LAKE CITY, UTAH

Library of Congress Catalog Card Number: 97–70854
ISBN 1–57008–307–X

First Printing, 1997

Printed in the United States of America

Contents

To the Writers Bringing Past Heroines to Life:

You all are arranged in your own light
like mirrors of who you came as,
women of faith accustomed to motion.

Mirrored too are who came with you,
generous landscapes of heroines
clearly awake in your sites and standings,
now in mine.

You have brought mothers, grandmothers,
pages of passersby with their joy
resonant as their pain.
You have ladled the gold of memory,
you have rediscovered childhood
and told the stories
that never forget.

You have made the women who made you
come to life by heart.

I loved them all and the incredible hope
of who you are and have been, will be
with them inside you.

The waves of witnesses
to the great exhilaration
that breathes in the gathering
of pioneers and history and words offered
like a scattering of stars
acquainted with the generous hand of God.

Thank you, my friends, for being there.
With love, of course, with love.

Emma Lou Thayne

Foreword

This volume recognizes the heroic contributions of vital women who helped pioneer the building up of The Church of Jesus Christ of Latter-day Saints—its programs, homes, people, professions, and faith—in the Restoration years.

The exodus of the Latter-day Saints from Nauvoo began in February of 1846 as the first wagon trains left on the westward trek, to be followed by thousands more wagons, handcarts, and approximately 80,000 Saints over the next 23 years, all making their way to the other side of the Rockies in search of religious freedom and the establishment of Zion. All who came were firmly rooted in the belief that, as Elder Henry B. Eyring stated, theirs was "a rare privilege to be called out of the world" to assist in this divine design of the Restoration.[1] For a fortunate few, this was a comparatively pleasant journey with good weather and sufficient provisions. For others, it cost everything they had, sometimes including limb or life.

Regarding such crucibles of human suffering, Elder Orson F. Whitney provided the following counsel: "Adversity and affliction, when patiently borne, purify the heart, broaden the mind, and make the soul more tender and charitable." He further explained: " 'Sweet are the uses of adversity,' for when rightly used it becomes the parent of wisdom, and such precious qualities as patience, faith, fortitude and humility spring from it as naturally as flowers from fertile soil. Tragedy, not comedy, is the great educator; pain, not pleasure, the leading part in the drama of human development."[2]

He also said that "our greatest blessings often come in disguise."[3] Each chapter in this book reveals that these early heroines understood that, as part of that disguise, "to try our faith is not simply to test it but to strengthen it."[4] These women who headed west with the Saints "saw more safety going forward to unknown service in the kingdom than to stay with the known and the comfortable."[5] They were women of lifelong, stalwart faith and commitment to Christ, his Church, and his gospel. And they are but representative of thousands who each played a role in the latter-day restoration of the kingdom.

Herein you will read of the "deep disguise" found in the heroines' "tribulations, [their] losses and disappointments, [their] blighted hopes and thwarted ambitions, [their] sorrow, sickness, and even death," as Elder Whitney wrote.[6] But "there is a great and wise purpose in all that we are called upon to endure. . . . It is by opposition that we progress, and by contrasts that we become wise. Wisdom grows upon the tree of Experience, planted in the soil of human suffering."[7]

Elder Eyring's great-grandmother, Mary Bommeli, was a teenage convert from Switzerland when she walked across the plains without incident, later stating that it was one of the happiest times of her life. Her "trials began in the promised land"—another story of heartache and suffering, and faith, in itself. Said Elder Eyring of his progenitor (which can be said of each heroine of the Restoration): "Mary's story is worth telling not because it is exceptional but because it isn't. The growth of her faith seemed as constant in times of deliverance as it was in times of trial." Then he continues with pivotal insight. For every heroines' story:

> It seems to me that was true because their faith was based in an understanding of why God allows us to pass into such close places and how he delivers us. The "how" springs from the "why." The "why" is that our loving Heavenly Father and his Son, Jesus Christ, wish for us to be sanctified that we may have

eternal life with them. That requires our being cleansed through faith in Jesus Christ, repenting because of that faith, and proving ourselves faithful to the covenants they offer us. . . . Knowing their loving purpose makes it easier to understand both why they allow trials and how they deliver us.[8]

The "disguise" now no longer obscuring reality, Elder James E. Faust summarizes: "Here then is a great truth. In the pain, the agony, and the heroic endeavors of life, we pass through a refiner's fire, and the insignificant and the unimportant in our lives can melt away like dross and make our faith bright, intact, and strong. In this way the divine image can be mirrored from the soul. It is part of the purging toll exacted of some to become acquainted with God. In the agonies of life, we seem to listen better to the faint, godly whisperings of the Divine Shepherd."[9]

The heroines of this book led lives that mirrored the divine image. Having made sweet the "uses of adversity," evident in their lives are those precious qualities which "spring from it as naturally as flowers from fertile soil." Theirs is a legacy of wisdom, patience, faith, fortitude, and humility, an endowment to every Saint who follows after them, a sacred trust to pass on to each succeeding generation.

Our authors were selected from a cadre of the Church's premier women writers; each wrote a chapter on her heroine of choice. The writers provide the contemporary reader uplifting, insightful, enlightening accounts of these significant early feminine exemplars in Church history, whether they were chosen because of blood line or heart line.

While the writers themselves may not have walked the 1,300 miles as did the heroines who have taught them, they have crossed other perilous trails and endured other wrenching trials. Knowing the eternal perspective, they realize that in this life "times of peace [will] be temporary," as Elder Eyring has taught, so they make of them "times of gratitude and of boldness to go forward with the work" in full faith and testimony.[10]

This book is part of that bold endeavor of indebtedness. It is our sesquicentennial legacy to those who value the heritage of faith, believing the promise "that the tender mercies of the Lord are over all those whom he hath chosen, because of their faith, to make them mighty even unto the power of deliverance," sanctification, and eternal life (1 Nephi 1:20). This book is testament to that truth.

NOTES

1. Henry B. Eyring, "Faith of Our Fathers," Church Educational System Campus Education Week Devotional, 20 August 1996 (Salt Lake City: The Church of Jesus Christ of Latter-day Saints, 1996), p. 1.

2. Orson F. Whitney, "Blessings in Disguise," *Relief Society Magazine,* November 1924, p. 547.

3. Ibid.

4. Eyring, "Faith," p. 4.

5. Ibid., p. 3.

6. Whitney, "Blessings," p. 549.

7. Ibid., pp. 549, 550.

8. Eyring, "Faith," p. 4.

9. James E. Faust, "The Refiner's Fire," *Ensign,* May 1979, p. 53.

10. Eyring, "Faith," p. 3.

1

"If You Consider Me a Mother in Israel"
Lucy Mack Smith
1775–1856

*A*t the October 1845 general conference of the Church, a 70-year-old woman speaker had inspired the congregation with her particular style of moralizing. As she described rearing her large family to be God-fearing, she pointedly reminded the Saints that they were accountable for their children's conduct. Parents should take control of their own posterity, she said, rearing them in righteousness, warning them never to do in secret what they would not do in the presence of millions. Then suddenly, unabashedly, Lucy said, "If you consider me a mother in Israel I want you to say so." Immediately President Brigham Young arose and invited all who considered Lucy Mack Smith a mother in Israel to signify it by saying yea. Loud outbursts of support filled the Nauvoo Temple, which, although not yet completed, had been opened for congregational worship several days before this conference meeting.[1]

A "mother in Israel" has come to mean an exemplary mother within the Church in mortality and in the company of exalted beings in eternity, for whom the family unit continues.[2]

Lucy Mack Smith

Israel is often used to mean "one who prevails with God," or is a
true believer regardless of lineage.[3] For Lucy this was an incredible,
confirming tribute. People loved as well as revered her.

Or was the rousing shout an act of condescension to age? Not
many survived so long in the rugged life of a besieged Latter-day
Saint in America's frontier. Perhaps the enthusiastic response was
because the majority present hadn't known this woman's family
since their beginning. Many had come into the Church later and
were awestruck in the presence of the martyred Prophet's mother. It
had been about 25 years since young Joseph's first vision and the
subsequent total involvement of his mother as a defender of the
faith. Likely the response for the feisty little lady who stood before
them was because she was the mother who had nurtured their
beloved and still bereaved Prophet.

Lucy probably did not ask for public opinion at the conference
because she wanted reassurance of who she was, but rather because
she had a deeply rooted need to prod the Saints into practicing
Christian principles more diligently, using herself and her family as
an example. She always had taken every opportunity to remind
people of Joseph's role in serving the Savior and of the Saints' work
yet to be done on earth.

As a professional writer all my life I have been interested in
quality people and how, with a particular set of guiding principles,
their lives play out against the backdrop of events and conditions in
their day. It has been with keen curiosity that I have looked deeper
into the personality and the eternal spirit that dictated the choices
of Lucy Mack Smith. I found her worth the work! I had considered
her important because of the role she filled on earth as the mother
of Joseph Smith, the Prophet. But now I find her a marvel and one
worth emulating. She juggled her life happenings and her skills
with amazing grace. You see, not only was Lucy a leader among her
associates but she was a resourceful and passionately loving mother
as well. Lucy was an activist, but she needed no particular revelation to remind her how to honor her husband, being meek and
quick with consoling words.

Lucy was a working woman—she labored inside her home and

out, for love and also for recompense. Her life was full not of murmuring but of adventure and enthusiasm for the challenge ahead. She was close to God and reminiscent of the finest women the world has ever honored. I call her indomitable because of her attitude of courage in the face of the Martyrdom. Mothers are supposed to die before their children, aren't they? I've buried some of my own and was deeply touched that Lucy, Mother of Martyrs, set about becoming the biographer of the slain.

Lucy Mack Smith has been described with several titles of honor—Mother Smith, a mother in Israel, a most singular woman, mother of Joseph, the "matriarch of a Church patriarchy," a dynamic contributor to the infant Church, the first woman of the Church.[4] In truth Lucy holds the uncontested role of First Woman of the Restoration. Mother Smith prepared Joseph from infancy and taught him the virtue of knowing, believing, and trusting in God, of the possibility of visions and spiritual experiences, and of the need to continue the relentless search for God's will and his way instead of following the fabrications and suppositions of man. Lucy was first on record to speak to her son following his vision revealing that God the Father and his Son Jesus Christ were two separate beings and that they had appeared again on the earth. She was among the first to embrace all that was brought forth by Joseph, and it is significant that Lucy was decisive in her loyalty to the Restoration movement in every instance.

In spite of opinion to the contrary among strident women in recent years, careful scrutiny of history through all ages reveals that God indeed values his daughters on earth. The impact of experience upon the character of a woman is the same, though societal situations may differ. This is in the sense that God's principles are eternal for his creations in every generation of time. It follows that growth and even glory for a woman as a human being are dependent upon her own core reaction to what happens to her, and how she applies God's principles to her life events. Her worth as a person, her power for good, her enduring honor—or the opposite—come not because of or in spite of the fact that she is a woman. These shining qualities develop because of her grasp of life as she processes her challenges.

Lucy's Background and Family Life

It is distinctly stunning to study key women of all time who have been, still are, and will continue to be examples to all females. We view such women with wonder, hoping they will be type and shadow to our own quality of being. However else they may be limited at any given moment, women make their choices in the sanctity of their hearts. Such decisions of action and reaction make all the difference.

Lucy's life indicates that she was always God-fearing, seeking the Holy Ghost as she meshed the new religion with her own careful reasoning of what was good for a person. Lucy was a woman of her day, born to help the Restoration emerge for the great blessing of mankind. She learned the sacred role of women from her own mother, Lydia Gates Mack, a Congregational deacon's daughter. Lucy's grandfather was a man of means who saw that his daughter had a fine education. Lydia in turn furthered the culture and education of her own daughter, Lucy Mack. Lucy's father, Solomon Mack, was a hero in the French and Indian Wars. Reared in an atmosphere of religion and adventure, education and fine-tuned family relationships, Lucy's noble spirit was enhanced in ways suitable for her place as the mother of the Prophet of the momentous Restoration.

On 24 January 1796 Lucy married Joseph Smith Sr. About six years later, after miraculously being blessed to recover from a serious illness, Lucy increasingly turned her attention toward religion. She prayed about her husband's unwillingness to affiliate with one of the religious institutions in the community. Lucy put God first and was faithful to him. Her husband couldn't see much truth in what was being practiced in the name of Christianity. Even though Lucy was patient and loyal to her husband, she chose to be baptized by a minister who agreed to leave her free to join any church. On one occasion, after earnestly praying in behalf of her husband, she at last was given in a dream a spiritual answer that her husband would grow like a "pliant tree" in responding to God's Spirit.[5] Ultimately he did, accepting wholeheartedly every revealed truth that his son, the Prophet Joseph, later taught him.

In the midst of ridicule from neighbors, heartbreak, illness, fresh failures, and new starts, Lucy's home was permeated with charity and disciplined living. There was obvious affection among husband, wife, and children. Relationships in the family of Mother and Father Smith were based on Biblical charity and loyalty. Thus the twigs were trained by the pliant tree and his lively, religious wife. Such a family provided a protective cocoon for a young Prophet increasingly unpopular with those stirred up by the adversary to thwart God's work.

The Smiths seem a rare example for today's many dysfunctional families. How did they do it? We look to heritage. Both Lucy and Joseph were nurtured in large families with traditions of depending upon each other and seeking God's help in solving problems, preserving health and life itself, and providing joy in daily duties and pleasures. Lucy's father, Solomon Mack, was a daring military man who credited his wife, Lydia, with creating a home atmosphere of piety, gentleness, and reflection. In Lucy's own home with Joseph Smith Sr., all sought truth and strove to behave as Christians.

Lucy had three daughters and eight sons, including two who died in their infancy. Of the six sons she reared to manhood, five of them preceded her in death. One daughter was miraculously spared by Lucy's incredible fortitude and faith. Sophronia had been ill for many weeks, and finally she stopped breathing. Those present called Lucy crazy for pacing back and forth holding the child against her chest. In remembering this experience Lucy later wrote, "Are you a mother who has been bereft of a child? Feel for your heart-strings, and then tell me how I felt with my expiring child pressed to my bosom! Would you at this trying moment feel to deny that God had 'power to save to the uttermost all who call on him'! I did not then, neither do I now." At length the child sobbed. Lucy still pressed her to her breast and continued to walk the floor. This Lucy did until the child sobbed again and finally breathed normally. Lucy explained that her soul was satisfied but her own body was weakened, "completely overpowered by the intensity of my feelings."[6]

Lucy, a Working Woman

At various times in the struggle to make a living the Smiths were in merchandising, farmed, ran a coopering business to repair or make wooden barrels and tubs, kept a small shop, planted orchards, managed a maple sugar operation, and even painted patterns on oil-cloth with which to cover furniture. When they all had to work together, ages and abilities varying, Lucy saw to it that chores were done diligently and amicably, with some laughter and games, and frequently to the accompaniment of their own hymns. This amazing mother recalled, "Whilst we worked with our hands we endeavored to remember the service of [God] and the Welfare of our souls."[7]

Lucy was a working woman. There was rarely a time when she was not earning some sum of money. She worked alongside Joseph Sr. at whatever his trade for their keep. When he died she moved into the Mansion House with Joseph and Emma, where, with Joseph's blessing, she established a small museum in a lower room. People usually paid a quarter to see the curiosities she had collected with $6,000 of her own money, such as four ancient mummies that were kept in a cabinet.[8]

Lucy and God

Lucy's realization of her dependence on God was focused when, as mentioned, she was a critically ill young mother. She spent a frightening night near death. During this crisis she made a vow with God that if he would extend her life so that she could be a "comfort to her husband" and rear their family together, she would serve him to the best of her ability.[9] Lucy never forgot that vow. She deliberately practiced Christian principles even in the hardest of times, inviting herself into the lives of others to support and help sustain them. Her quarters, be they lean-to, campsite en route to a new location to escape the mobs, or a new cabin, were often filled with the sick and afflicted. Even while she was a heartbroken widow, her heart, arms, and larder knew no bounds. Hers were physically threatening times, and many people owed their very lives to her nursing skills, generosity, and compassion.[10]

This was the core of Lucy—she was totally consumed, passionate, practical, and undeviating in her relationship with God. She trusted him. She expected to be blessed and given witness, and to be sustained through all the experiences in her life. The marvelous point to reap is that Lucy applied eternal principles to life and she inevitably gave credit to God. She was an enlightened woman. Because she was privy to the glorious continuing revelations given through Joseph as well as the gospel truths from the Book of Mormon, Lucy Mack Smith grew into a fulfilled person who was herself a light.

In the beginning of marriage and family life, Lucy had led the way for the Smith family's search for religion, studying the Bible and discussing their findings. Many years later, when Father Smith lay dying, the tender family circle about him showed the literal pattern of their lifestyle according to the Word. Just before he died Father Smith followed the exemplary pattern of bestowing a father's blessing upon each child individually and having it recorded as did Jacob of old, and Alma, who "caused that his sons should be gathered together, that he might give unto them every one his charge, separately, concerning the things pertaining unto righteousness" (Alma 35:16).

Joseph Smith Sr., a father in Israel, had been Lucy's loved husband and tender companion. Many times he had been torn from her, even imprisoned, by the angry mob. Before he died he gave tribute to Lucy as "one of the most singular women in the world," cherishing her with a depth that assured an eternal relationship.[11] They both were strong personalities, vulnerable in turn but valiant spirits, intelligent and capable. That Lucy succeeded so stunningly as a wife and mother, as an independent leader, is part of what makes her fascinating to a student of character. She excelled in relationships and had rousing ovations in large congregations to prove it.

Lucy, a Dedicated Mother

It has been said that the Prophet Joseph had little formal schooling. True enough. However, he reaped the blessing of having a mother such as Lucy, whose intelligence is evidenced in her speeches and in her published history of her prophet-son. Lucy taught her children much, and she saw to it that Christian values were instilled in the normal day's routine. She was resourceful, and what she could not figure for herself, her relationship with the Lord would supply. The Bible was the family's favorite text, and the children learned its contents well.

As a young mother Lucy set her course of discipline. "I said in my heart that there was not then upon earth the religion which I sought. I therefore determined to examine my Bible and, taking Jesus and His disciples for my guide, to endeavor to obtain from God that which man could neither give nor take away."[12]

It was under the tutelage of Lucy and Joseph Sr. that young Joseph became comfortable with studying the Bible for answers to his own searching for religious affiliation. He had learned from scripture and put James 1:5 to the test. When he asked for God's help, the answer to his prayer was a vision that changed the world. And we have been forever blessed.

Joseph's experiences spread like the proverbial wildfire. As a result, the whole Smith family suffered through cruel misunderstandings and the keen interest of the adversary in their affairs. When continuing visions and revelations triggered hostility among their neighbors, Mother Smith stood valiant—even vocal in defense not only of her son but of the truth and beauty of what was being revealed through him. Lucy chose not to be bitter or resentful, but she was not one to remain silent when Joseph was persecuted for what he espoused. On one occasion Deacon George Beckwith counseled Lucy, "I wish, that if you do believe these things, you would not say anything more on the subject—I do wish you would not."

Lucy's reply was typical of her other choices and stance on such matters. She did not negotiate but rather stoutly replied, "Deacon Beckwith, if you should stick my flesh full of faggots, and even burn me at the stake, I would declare, as long as God should give me breath, that Joseph has got that Record, and that I know it to be true."[13]

Lucy the Activist

Immediately Lucy became an activist in the work of young Joseph. She knew her son. At each unfolding of his work for the Lord she was solace and service, never doubting him. She steadfastly followed him, always urging others to do the same. This is reminiscent of Mary, mother of Jesus, who said to the servants at the wedding in Cana, "Whatsoever he saith unto you, do it" (John 2:5).

When the Book of Mormon was published Lucy was tireless and self-sacrificing in working for the cause of the Restoration. She wrote numerous letters and actually took time to make personal visits proclaiming its validity. While in Michigan her niece's husband introduced her to his minister. The man of the cloth forgot, for the moment, his Christian calling to love all God's children. He took Lucy's hand limply as he sneered, "And you are the mother of that poor, foolish, silly boy, Joe Smith, who pretended to translate the Book of Mormon." Through the Holy Ghost, Lucy's testimony of the sacred work cloaked her in confidence. She simply said, "I am, sir, the mother of Joseph Smith; but why do you apply to him such epithets as those?" The minister answered that he knew Joseph thought he could overthrow other churches with that simple Mormon book. When Lucy asked if the minister had ever read the book the man mumbled that such a thing was not worth his time. Now Lucy was in her element. She quoted from Paul about an open-minded person proving all things. She bore her personal testimony that the Book of Mormon had been "written for the salvation of your soul, by the gift and power of the Holy Ghost." Still the man discounted the whole idea and declared that he was not afraid that any member of his intelligent congregation would be led away by such stuff.

Lucy shocked the minister with a prophetic declaration: "Now, Mr. Ruggles, mark my words—as true as God lives, before three years we will have more than one-third of your church; and, sir, whether you believe it or not, we will take the very deacon, too." This prophecy was fulfilled, a score for the unique intuitiveness and spirituality that often seems to come more easily to women.[14]

Lucy the Leader

This dainty-looking person had invincible drive. Hardship, stress, frustrations, inconveniences, difficult personalities, and mob violence notwithstanding, Lucy's position was in the thick of things, like a Joan of Arc, a Florence Nightingale selflessly serving others.

Lucy herself led a company of Saints leaving for Kirtland during the early part of 1831. When they had boarded their boat, Lucy asked an older gentleman to lead the company. He refused the assignment, saying that she should take charge, affirming that he would do whatever she said, and suggesting that others do the same. There was a unanimous vote of agreement.

Lucy's leadership style was a mix of practical tactics and spiritual nurturing. She conducted daily devotionals with plenty of hymn singing, knowing that a distracting round of hymns is good for the inner soul. She frequently pointed out that they all were traveling by commandment from God, and that they were to be solemn, lifting their hearts continually in prayer. All of this won the respect of the captain, whose wife, out of prejudice, had not wanted to board with the Mormons.

The journey was beset with challenges. Ice blocked their sailing. People had come ill-prepared and were hungry, uncomfortable, bored, full of complaints. Mother Smith attended to all their needs, using her own resources to get supplies from the ship's crew. But when the murmuring and grumbling and even mild flirtations got out of hand, Mother Smith went to the helm. She preached about their calling themselves Saints, removing themselves from the rest of the world for the purpose of their unique worship and strict way of life. She scolded, "Will you, at the very onset, subject the cause of Christ to ridicule by your own unwise and improper conduct? . . . You are even more unreasonable than the children of Israel were. . . . Where is your faith? Where is your confidence in God? Can you not realize that all things were made by him, and that he rules over the works of his own hands? And suppose that all the Saints here should lift their hearts in prayer to God, that the way might be opened before us, how easy it would be for him to cause the ice to break away, so that in a moment we could be on our journey!" Lucy invited all in her company to join in prayer about the ice. Immediately there was a deafening sound as the ice parted just enough for the passage of the boat.[15]

Lucy, a Woman of Courage

Salvation came at a high price for Lucy and her family, even though her faith bolstered her courage. One day Joseph was sitting in his parents' home when a large group of crazed mobbers pounded on the door. Undoubtedly it was Lucy's habit to utter a quick prayer for connection with God under such circumstances. When Lucy opened the door and inquired of their business, the wild men boisterously announced that they had come to kill Joseph the Mormon prophet. Joseph, hearing the commotion, stalked to the door in all his manly strength and handsome majesty. The mobbers quailed at his presence. Lucy formally introduced Joseph as the man they sought, and Joseph urged them to come into the house, where he talked earnestly with them for a time about persecuting the Saints. These would-be destroyers were so impressed by Joseph that they insisted on giving him a protective escort to his own home. As they left one of the men said to another, "Didn't you feel strange when Smith took you by the hand?" His companion replied, "I could not move. I would not harm a hair of that man's head for the whole world."[16]

Near his own 28th birthday Joseph said of Mother Smith: "And blessed . . . is my mother, for she is a mother in Israel, and shall be a partaker with my father in all his patriarchal blessings. . . . Blessed is my mother, for her soul is ever filled with benevolence and philanthropy; and notwithstanding her age, she shall yet receive strength and be comforted in the midst of her house: and thus said the Lord. She shall have eternal life."[17]

All of Joseph's life Lucy was seldom far from him. She had reared him and nurtured him to be stable, innocent, God-fearing (as she frequently explained—even proclaimed). Imagine the inimitable emotion for a mother to hear about the appearances of God, of angel visits, angel instructions; to learn the wonderful fulness of the gospel through the Book of Mormon; to marvel when Joseph allowed her to handle and examine the Urim and Thummim, which he used to translate the records from the metal plates! Thus joy filled her heart and repeated evil persecutions were overshadowed. These things were the answers to her early searching for truth that would bring a changed heart. After the manner of the strongest women, Lucy made a thoughtful, important choice and willingly suffered the consequences, though humanly she wrote that if she indulged her feelings on certain occasions, her strength might not support her.[18]

The Indomitable Lucy

Lucy had proven herself indomitable. Speaking out as she did at the October 1845 general conference may have seemed a daring thing to do, though surely Lucy was confident in the company of the presiding priesthood. The unusual request she made at that conference came after many other audacious outbursts in defense of the Restoration movement.

A frequently-referred-to incident took place in Far West, prefacing the Prophet's martyrdom by almost six years. During a scene of stark horror Joseph was taken captive by Missouri forces, who then terrified the Saints with their "horrid yellings" and vows to kill the Prophet. "Had the army been composed of so many bloodhounds, wolves, and panthers, they could not have made a sound more terrible," said Lucy. The following day Hyrum also was taken prisoner, and the two brothers were put into a canvas-covered wagon that would transport them to Independence. As the motley parade moved out of town they passed through throngs of rioters rimmed by stricken Mormons. Lucy, unable to press through the angry crowd, cried out, "I am the mother of the Prophet—is there not a gentleman here, who will assist me to that wagon, that I may take a last look at my children, and speak to them once more before I die?" One man helped her make her way to the wagon, where she grasped Joseph's hand which he had thrust between the canvas and wagon bed—that hand that she knew and loved so well, that hand that had been placed upon her head many times to bless her. "Joseph, do speak to your poor mother once more—I cannot bear to go till I hear your voice." There was a sob in Joseph's voice as he cried out, "God bless you, mother!" And the moving wagon wrenched their hands apart. Speaking later of the heart-breaking incident, Lucy testified that she was not left to suffer alone. "In the midst of my grief, I found consolation that surpassed all earthly comfort. I was filled with the Spirit of God."[19]

We have spoken of courageous choices. Sadly, there were those who made choices that brought death and carnage to the innocent. On the morning of 24 June 1844 Lucy's life changed drastically. Of the Martyrdom she wrote, "In the morning [the mob] rushed into Carthage, armed and painted black, red and yellow, and in ten minutes fled again, leaving my sons murdered and mangled corpses!"[20]

Lucy, Mother of Martyrs

Granted that while many women pass through life without even noticing the tiny perfect nails on a new baby's fingers or hunting shooting stars in a summer sky, Lucy dramatized even small situations. But her inimitable first-person account of the aftermath of the Martyrdom has been heartrending to millions of Latter-day Saints over succeeding generations. It is a sobering gift. What if an account of Mary's grief, written in her own words, were available to us?

Lucy had braced her every nerve to face the sight of her wounded sons. She had cried out to God for all the proper feelings at such a time, and for physical strength, and for the unwavering faith that restores peace in such a situation. The bodies were washed, dressed, and laid out for the mourners. Lucy said:

> When I entered the room and saw my murdered sons extended both at once before my eyes and heard the sobs and groans of my family and the cries of "Father! Husband! Brothers!" from the lips of their wives, children, brothers and sisters, it was too much; I sank back, crying to the Lord in the agony of my soul, "My God, my God, why hast thou forsaken this family!" A voice replied, "I have taken them to myself, that they might have rest. . . ." My mind flew through every scene of sorrow and distress which we had passed, together, in which they had shown the

innocence and sympathy which filled their guileless hearts. As I looked upon their peaceful, smiling countenances, I seemed almost to hear them say, "Mother, weep not for us, we have overcome the world by love; we carried to them the gospel, that their souls might be saved; they slew us for our testimony, and thus placed us beyond their power; their ascendancy is for a moment, ours is an eternal triumph."

I then thought upon the promise which I had received in Missouri, that in five years Joseph should have power over all his enemies. The time had elapsed and the promise was fulfilled.[21]

If only every mother's son could be beyond the power of his enemies, including Satan! Lucy's comfort came in her spiritual affirmation that, as Mother Smith, hers was a job well done. She was just as certain that the evil men would get their just punishment in the end.

When the Saints traveled west to the Salt Lake Valley, Lucy remained in Nauvoo. Discussions are still lively about why she did not make the journey. The suggested reasons range from her age, to the fact that the bones of so many of her family were buried in Nauvoo, to her pity for Emma. Lucy's choice resulted in her deeply missing the beloved brethren and their families. She was no longer in the center of things, though Lucy herself explained that, like Naomi, she would have the watch care of her daughter-in-law in Nauvoo. She remained active to her death and never used eyeglasses even for the smallest print. Lucy died on 14 May 1856.

Lucy Mack Smith lived two centuries ago, but her choices and actions—based on valid principles as fodder for endurance, happiness, and exaltation—are guidance for women today with families whose interests are like seeds in the wind. Lucy's very life—her example of turning hardship into growth experiences and choices into valued consequences, of keeping faith in God even when his answers to prayers were not what was hoped for—makes her worth careful study.

One looks at a portrait of Lucy Mack Smith painted by English artist Sutcliffe Maudsley about two years before the Martyrdom. After the manner of Whistler, a serene, puritanical Lucy is shown sitting in a carved and curved rocker beneath a framed image from the book of Abraham. Symbolically, Lucy holds a Book of Mormon on her knee. The resemblance to the Prophet is clear. What is not revealed in this hooded, dark profile figure is the vitality and unfailing acumen that was still evident in elderly Mother Smith, who spoke approximately three years later in general conference when the congregation declared her a mother in Israel.

NOTES

1. See *History of the Church* 7:470-72; Ronald W. Walker, "The Historians' Corner: Lucy Mack Smith Speaks to the Nauvoo Saints," *BYU Studies* 32 (Winter and Spring 1992): 276-84.

2. See Bruce R. McConkie, *Mormon Doctrine*, 2nd ed. (Salt Lake City: Bookcraft, 1966), p. 517.

3. LDS Bible Dictionary, s.v. "Israel."

4. See Lucy Mack Smith, *The History of Joseph Smith by His Mother*, ed. Preston Nibley (Salt Lake City: Bookcraft, 1954), p. 313.

5. Smith, *History*, pp. 36, 43-45.

6. Ibid., pp. 51-53.

7. Martha Jane Knowlton Coray's preliminary manuscript, as cited in *Encyclopedia of Mormonism* 3:1357.

8. See Richard S. Van Wagoner and Steven C. Walker, *A Book of Mormons* (Salt Lake City: Signature Books, 1982), p. 312.

9. Smith, *History*, pp. 33-35.

10. See Andrew Jenson, comp., *Latter-day Saint Biographical Encyclopedia*, 4 vols. (1901- 36; reprint, Salt Lake City: Western Epics, 1971), 1:691.

11. Smith, *History*, p. 313.

12. Ibid., p. 36.

13. Ibid., p. 161.

14. Ibid., pp. 215-17.

15. Ibid., pp. 195-205.

16. George Q. Cannon, *Life of Joseph Smith the Prophet* (Salt Lake City: Deseret Book Co., 1986), pp. 264-65.

17. Joseph Smith, *Teachings of the Prophet Joseph Smith* (Salt Lake City: Deseret Book Co., 1976), p. 39.

18. See Lucy Mack Smith, *History,* p. 208.
19. Ibid., pp. 273, 289-91.
20. Ibid., pp. 323-24.
21. Ibid., pp. 324-25.

❧

Elaine Cannon, a University of Utah graduate, has been an instructor for Brigham Young University's Continuing Education program, a daily columnist for the *Deseret News*, a freelance writer for national publications, and an associate editor of Church magazines. She was Young Women general president from 1978 to 1984. Elaine is married to D. James Cannon of Salt Lake City. They are the parents of six children and have numerous grandchildren and great-grandchildren. Elaine wrote about Lucy Mack Smith because she feels that Lucy exemplifies the ideal Latter-day Saint woman.

2

"A Deep Sorrow in Her Heart"
Emma Hale Smith
1804–1879

I first came face to face with the Emma Hale Smith "dilemma" in seminary during my senior year of high school. Our teacher gave us a two-page handout written by another seminary teacher, Brother Erwin Wirkus. He had written Emma's story in first person, as if she were pleading for understanding and consideration for all she had been through. Up until this time I had heard little about this woman who was a very present but somewhat mysterious figure in Church history. I had the general idea that she had left the Church after the Prophet's death and, as a result, was not held in high esteem. While I had never heard her openly castigated, I also had seldom heard her praised. Brother Wirkus's story (which he later developed into a booklet titled "Judge Me, Dear Reader") was the first hint I had that Emma Hale Smith was a remarkable woman—"an elect lady."

In the summer of 1977 I did some research on Emma for a special seminar on Joseph Smith that I took from Dr. Milton Backman at BYU. I thought that perhaps I could build upon Brother

Emma Hale Smith

Wirkus's thesis by adding insight from a woman's perspective. At that time in my life I was a wife and mother of two children. Emma's trials took on a new and deeply personal meaning for me. I was overwhelmed by the trials she faced and by her compassion. I felt sure that if I had been in Emma's place I would have failed long before plural marriage ever became my Abrahamic test. Moreover, I found that most historians who wrote about her were male and therefore could not fully understand her and empathize with her feelings and challenges as a woman, wife, and mother. It appeared also that historians were often tainted by the bitterness of the early Utah Saints who felt they had been betrayed and forsaken by the wife of their beloved Prophet. Because of this bias, much unkind and incorrect information became attached to her name through the years. (Unfortunately I still run into some of it even today.) In reading my paper Dr. Backman was so moved by this sympathetic view of this unfortunate heroine that he had me present the paper to the class.

It was still uncommon at that time to view Emma in such a compassionate light. However, other women and some men were also beginning to reexamine the traditional view of Emma Smith. Here and there positive articles appeared. Many lauded her courage and compassion but more or less overlooked the plural marriage problem and her eventual abandonment of the Church, as if they hadn't really happened. I began to feel an earnest desire to help members of the Church understand *all* of Emma Smith's life and judge her with increased understanding and greater compassion. I wanted others to be inspired by her singular fortitude and generosity, as I had been. I hoped to give them a glimpse of the steadfast love she possessed for her prophet husband, which was a driving force in her life. I sought not to excuse her failings but to help others empathize with them.

So when the opportunity arose, I developed a one-woman presentation in which I spoke as if I were Emma, telling her story and incorporating my own interpretation of how she may have felt and why she may have made some of the choices she did. Unbeknownst to me at the time, several other women in the Church felt moved upon to do similar creative projects favorable to Emma. There seemed to be a scattered but simultaneously inspired movement stirring within the membership of the Church to reclaim the reputation of Emma Smith. As people learned the true facts of her life and were able to put her struggles in proper perspective, they often were deeply moved by her profound contributions to the Church.

For several years I gave my presentation in wards and stakes and other settings. Audiences always received it with gratitude and deep emotion. One autumn I was asked to give my presentation to the Northeast Area Church Educational System administrators at their yearly before-school convention held that year in Palmyra, New York. My husband was the CES coordinator in northern Virginia at the time, and we were well acquainted with the men he served with and their wives. It should have been easy to perform among friends, but several of these men were institute directors at Ivy League universities and were very learned and scholarly. The night before I was to give the presentation I got into a spirited discussion with some of them about Emma Smith. Their view was that Emma had her chance and failed, and she would have to face her punishment—being cut off forever. They seemed to subscribe to Brigham Young's heated sentiments that Joseph would have to go to hell to find her.[1] They strongly hinted that any attempt to "rehabilitate" her would be purely sentimental.

I was devastated. I had never claimed to be a scholar. My presentation was as historically accurate as I could make it, but I began to feel that perhaps my interpretations of those facts were on shakier ground—clouded by my own imperfect inspiration and my love for Emma Smith. Were my views merely sentimental? Wishful thinking? Emotional distortions? I lay awake much of the night going through the presentation in my mind, praying to know if I were saying things that weren't true, or were unreasonable or sentimental inferences. For my 45-minute presentation I only felt the need to change one or two words. Nevertheless, I was scared to death to make a fool of myself in front of these distinguished scholars. I finally prayed that if the presentation was right and if the Lord was pleased with it, he would let me know. Then it wouldn't really matter what they thought.

The next evening I was nervous and stiff as I began my presentation. I was so anxious and intimidated that I couldn't seem to feel the Spirit with me as I usually had before. It seemed to me that my acting was unnatural and my tongue tangled at every turn. I rushed through it and then made my exit as quickly as possible, feeling that I had failed miserably. I stood out in the hallway, shaking my head and lamenting that I hadn't done well, despite reassurance from my husband, who always introduced and concluded my program. We waited for the meeting inside to resume so that I could make sure they were done with me and I could go collapse somewhere. Instead, an unusual silence filled the room. No one stood up to speak. The silence became more awkward, and I began to hear muffled sobs coming from the room. I glanced back inside and saw the man who had given me the most unbending argument the previous night unable to control his emotions and resume conducting the meeting. I suddenly realized that the Spirit in that room was so strong that no one could speak. After what seemed like several minutes, someone finally stood up and suggested that they all stand for a moment so that the group could regain its composure. At that moment I knew the Lord approved of my effort to bring Emma Smith the recognition and understanding she deserves. In spite of my stumbling, unemotional delivery, the Spirit still carried its message into the hearts of those present.

Indeed, it would now appear that Emma Smith's heroic sacrifices before her falling away will not go unrewarded or unheralded. An attractive, educated, much-admired young woman from a respected family, she gave up everything, including her family, to marry and follow a poor, uneducated farm boy who claimed to have visions. While others mocked Joseph and her father hated him, she humbly saw through his deep blue eyes into his soul and knew he was a man of integrity and spoke the truth. Thoughtful and well-bred, Emma would never marry any man on a foolish whim, let alone one whose reputation was so questionable in the community and objectionable to her parents. According to Lucy Mack Smith, Joseph "thought that no young woman that he ever was acquainted with was better calculated to render the man of her choice happy than Miss Emma Hale."[2]

Emma's contributions to the early Church were great. Her self-assurance and education must have been a great help to Joseph as he translated the Book of Mormon. She acted as a scribe for him when no one else was available. Once, as he translated a certain passage about the city walls of Jerusalem, he stopped, innocently asking her if there were walls around Jerusalem. Being well acquainted with the Bible, she was able to inform him that, indeed, there were.[3] Undoubtedly her education filled other needs and answered other questions as well. Her testimony of the Book of Mormon also remained strong till her death. Someone once asked her later in life if Joseph could have written the story privately, pretending to translate as he dictated. She replied that "Joseph Smith could neither write nor dictate a coherent and well-worded letter; let alone dictating a book like the Book of Mormon. . . . It is marvelous to me . . . as much as to any one." If such a deception had existed, lesser women might have fallen for it, but not Emma Smith. "I am satisfied," she continued, " that no man could have dictated the writing of the manuscripts unless he was inspired; for when [I was] acting as his scribe, [he] would dictate to me for hour after hour; and when returning after meals, or after interruptions, he would at once begin where he had left off, without having any portion of it read to him."[4] Emma is a credible, intelligent, and powerful witness of the authenticity of the Book of Mormon.

Yet Emma contributed far more than just her unwavering support for her young prophet husband. For instance, although pregnant with twins she worked tirelessly along with other women in weaving cloth and sewing clothing for the early missionaries of the Church. Lucy Smith commented on her daughter-in-law's remarkable devotion to the cause: "Emma's health at this time was quite delicate, yet she did not favor herself on this account, but whatever her hands found to do, she did with her might, until so far beyond her strength that she brought upon herself a heavy fit of sickness, which lasted four weeks. And, although her strength was exhausted, still her spirits were the same, which, in fact, was always the case with her, even under the most trying circumstances."[5]

She was also the only woman to have an official revelation directed to her and canonized as scripture. Because of that, the revelation warrants close examination. After Emma's baptism Joseph received in her behalf what is now the 25th section of the Doctrine and Covenants. Though Emma could not have fully comprehended it at the time, it lay her soul open before the world. Through it we see the many facets of Emma Smith—her strengths and weaknesses, as well as our own. Indeed, the Lord closed the revelation by declaring, "This is my voice unto all" (D&C 25:16). This makes a close reading of it even more imperative.

In verse 3 of this section Emma is called an "elect lady," important evidence of her previous greatness. Joseph later explained to her that when she became the first president of the Relief Society in 1842 it was in fulfillment of this designation. Because of her righteousness she had been "called and elected" to fill that position long before she was ever set apart for it.

After giving her this title the Lord then gently counseled her to "murmur not" because of things which she had not seen, "for they are withheld from thee and from the world, which is wisdom in me in a time to come" (verse 4). Some historians have pointed to this injunction as evidence that Emma was a whiner and complainer from the beginning—that she was nagging Joseph and making his life difficult even before plural marriage ever became an issue. Others have suggested that this means Emma was actually losing her faith. There is simply no evidence that Emma had been openly murmuring or complaining. However, if one considers how the faith of the elect lady must have been tested by not being able to view the plates when so many of those others who were assisting her husband were allowed to do so, perhaps we can understand the questioning that must have been in her mind if not on her lips. Though she handled the plates when they were covered by a linen cloth bag which she herself had made for them, moving them to dust under them, and they lay under the couple's bed for a long period of time, she "never felt at liberty to look at them."[6] What incredible trust Joseph must have had in her to leave them repeatedly exposed and unattended in her presence! However, the greatest question must have arisen when Mary Whitmer was shown the plates by a mysterious "old man" because of her tireless support of the men who were working on the translation.[7] Hadn't Emma given her all as well? Rather than chiding her, this counsel to "murmur not" must have reassured her that the Lord was mindful of her struggle and that there was divine purpose in her not seeing the plates.

Instead, she was given the office of being a comfort and blessing to her husband in his monumental responsibilities and frequent afflictions, of being his refuge and his earthly comforter at all times. While all married women are called to this office, few if any in history would need the strength, faith, and persistence to fill it as would Emma Smith. Being the wife of a prophet who must restore the gospel blessings of every previous dispensation of time would not be an ordinary job or for the faint of heart. The greatest powers of hell would be unleashed against her and her husband.

A letter Emma wrote to Joseph while he was in Liberty Jail after the Saints had been driven from Missouri gives us a small glimpse of Emma's painful struggle: "Was it not for . . . the direct interposition of divine mercy, I am very sure I never should have been able to have endured the scenes of suffering that I have passed through . . . but I still live and am yet willing to suffer more if it is the will of kind Heaven, that I should for your sake. . . . No one but God, knows the reflections of my mind and the feelings of my heart when I left our house and home, and almost all of everything that we possessed excepting our little children, and took my journey out of the State of Missouri, leaving you shut up in that lonesome prison."[8]

Another unusual aspect of the Lord's revelation to Emma was the commandment in verse 7 to "expound scriptures and to exhort the church, according as it shall be given thee by my Spirit." It would have been highly unusual in 1830 for any woman to expound and exhort in church, for women simply did not take visible or leadership roles in churches at that time. Presumably in preparation for this, the Lord also commanded her to spend her time in "writing" and "learning much." Intelligent and well versed in the Bible as she was, Emma was especially qualified among women to assume this role. The Lord entrusted her with much responsibility. Perhaps we Latter-day Saint women today have too easily overlooked this aspect of the revelation that was given to Emma but intended for all. In the true Church of Jesus Christ, women as well as men are expected to be well versed in the holy scriptures and able to teach others with testimony, confidence, and the guidance of the

Holy Spirit. Nowhere in Latter-day Saint doctrine is this right and responsibility reserved solely for the priesthood.

After further defining her role, the Lord then gave his elect daughter additional counsel that would have tremendous bearing on her life. "Thou shalt lay aside the things of this world, and seek for the things of a better," she was told (verse 10). Time after time as she moved away from her homes, left behind her belongings, and moved in with others, she must have reflected on this line from the revelation. Undoubtedly she endeavored to accept this as her lot in life, but like the rest of us she had her moments of weakness. One day when Joseph had been away for some time, Jesse W. Crosby dropped by to see if Emma needed anything. Letting down her guard and allowing a poignant glimpse into her heart, Emma unexpectedly burst into tears and told him that "if the persecution would cease they could live as well as any other family in the land. They could even have the luxuries of life."9 However, most of the time, until her disaffection from the Church, she accepted such inconveniences as the price of being the wife of Joseph Smith, and even when she had little, she willingly shared it with others.

It was also no accident that Emma was given further responsibility to make a collection of hymns for the Church. Emma, who had a beautiful singing voice, was raised in the Methodist Church, where she would often have participated in singing the great and inspiring hymns of the ages. Because of persecution, pregnancies, and other problems, it took her several years to complete this assignment, but in 1835, with the able help of W. W. Phelps, the Church's first hymnal was published. Even today we trace a number of hymns in our current hymnbook back to those included by Emma in the first compilation of hymns as she faithfully responded to this commandment.

Finally, in section 25 the Lord exhorted Emma to be faithful to her covenants—to "cleave" unto them (verse 13). His admonition that she "*continue* in the spirit of meekness" (verse 14) further implies that she was humble and unwavering and not complaining or faltering in her faith, as some have suggested. However, the Lord was aware that her greatest strengths—her independence, strength of will, and persistence—would also become her weaknesses and her stumbling blocks. Thus, he warned her to beware of pride and told her instead to let her soul delight in the glory which would eventually come to her husband, and, by implication, to her if she remained faithfully by his side (verse 14). I believe that this same strong spirit which helped Emma through untold persecution and suffering and kept her doggedly determined to stand by her husband also became the unbending will that would not obey the commandment that would have her share Joseph with others.

I'm not sure anyone could fully understand just what Emma did go through for her husband. As she was his wife and his comforter, surely her greatest anguish was during those moments—and they were many—when she did not know whether he was alive or dead, or worse. On one of the most harrowing nights of her life Emma waited in terror, clutching her children to her bosom to protect them from the piercing cold that invaded their bedroom after a crazed mob had broken in and dragged Joseph out into the black night. The loud, vile cursings of the mob against her helpless husband did not prevent the sound of Joseph pleading for his life from reaching her terrified ears. When the mob had done its dirty mischief and scattered, Emma waited helplessly in the dark silence, unsure of her husband's fate. Suddenly a tall black figure appeared like an apparition, silhouetted in the doorway. When Emma realized that it was Joseph, she fainted dead away. She did not know he had been tarred and feathered, but thought he had been crushed and was covered in his own blood.

It must have seemed at times that all the fiends of earth and hell were after her beloved husband. How often she must have had to summon up her undaunted faith to quell her fears! Her mother-in-law, Lucy Mack Smith, paid her a tribute of which few women are worthy: "I have never seen a woman in my life, who would endure every species of fatigue and hardship, from month to month, and from year to year, with that unflinching courage, zeal, and patience, which she has ever done," wrote Lucy: "for I know that which she has had to endure—she has been tossed upon the ocean of uncertainty—she has breasted the storms of persecution, and buffeted the rage of men and devils, which would have borne down almost any other woman. It may be, that many may yet have to encounter the same—I pray God, that this may not be the case; but, should it be, may they have grace given them according to their day, even as has been the case with her."[10]

In addition to suffering along with her husband, Emma lost six of her children, including one adopted child who had been sick with the measles and subsequently died from exposure to the cold after the tarring and feathering incident mentioned above. Perhaps as a mother she endured even more anguish than her husband in this trial. She had her own crosses to bear. She undoubtedly missed her dear parents and sorrowed over the fact that they were sorely disappointed in her, however unjustly. What's more, she worried over their salvation. In 1841, after the Lord had revealed to the Prophet Joseph the doctrine of salvation for the dead, Emma anxiously completed the ordinance of baptism for her father. A year later she did the same for her mother.[11] They had passed away shortly before that time and she had not seen them since the day she left Harmony, Pennsylvania, in 1830 with a man they considered a charlatan.

Above and beyond this, the most impressive thing about the elect lady to me is her consummate compassion. The list of her charitable works is not only lengthy but profoundly moving. For example, she once stayed dutifully by the bedside of her ailing mother-in-law, Lucy, for five nights straight and never left her side until she became quite ill herself. She took countless orphans, friends, strangers, travelers, and homeless people not only into her home but into her life. Lucy Mack Smith recalled, "How often I have parted every bed in the house for the accommodation of the brethren, and then laid a single blanket on the floor for my husband and myself, while Joseph and Emma slept upon the same floor, with nothing but their cloaks for both bed and bedding."[12] Emma and Elizabeth Ann Whitney once held a feast for the poor and needy of Kirtland. With the help of others in the community they provided simple but abundant fare, not only for the new Saints who were streaming into the city but also for the poor, disabled, aged, and infirm residents of Kirtland. When the Saints were draining the swamps of Commerce, Illinois, to build Nauvoo, many became ill with malaria. Joseph and Emma began taking in the sick to care for them and soon found their cabin full of the ailing while they slept in a tent in their own dooryard. Joseph Smith III recalled an autumn when Joseph was in Washington, D.C., that his mother took in and cared for 13 of the Saints by herself.[13] He also could scarcely remember a Sunday in ordinary weather when the house and yard were not crowded with callers.[14]

However, perhaps the most poignant and Christlike act of compassion occurred late in Emma's life. Ironically, after her rejection of plural marriage her second husband, Lewis Bidamon, fathered a son by a young woman while he was married to Emma. Without bitterness Emma took the child into her own home to raise him at the request of the child's mother. Later she gave the mother employment, which enabled her to be near her son. When Emma died the boy was only 12 years of age. Determined that he should grow up with proper parentage and a stable family situation, Emma had urged Bidamon to marry the boy's mother after her death.[15] Perhaps the whole thing was penitence of a sort, but above all it was the act of a great soul.

For these reasons I could not so easily dismiss Emma's ultimate exaltation. At the very least, I was in no position to judge her and doubted that many others would be either—perhaps not even her contemporary sisters who were struggling themselves with the covenant of plural marriage. They could not fully comprehend her feelings as the first wife of the Prophet, who was undoubtedly the most popular man in Nauvoo. Many women, young and old, wanted to be married to him and could now do so without paying anything approaching the price Emma had paid to be by his side. Indeed, she could give up everything else for him. He gave her strength to go through anything. She simply could not give up him or her place as the only one next to him. Perhaps she loved him too much.

Like countless other Latter-day Saint women I have had to ask myself what I would do if I were faced with living plural marriage. Many of us have wrestled mightily with that question. I still do not know what I would actually do if asked to share my husband, and that is why I cannot judge Emma. However, I know in theory and from past experience that, as the Prophet Joseph taught, "Whatever God requires is right, no matter what it is, although we may not see the reason thereof till long after the events transpire."[16] Commendable as Emma's great love for her husband was, the Lord requires that our whole souls be given to him at all costs and above all others—no exceptions, even for great prophets. Perhaps that was the real sifting and refining test of plural marriage. "He that loveth father or mother . . . [or] son or daughter [or husband or wife] more than me is not worthy of me" (Matthew 10:37).

Yet the elect lady did not reject the revelation on plural marriage in totality. Though at times she fought it doggedly, at other times she tried desperately to humble herself and accept the new revelation. She actually gave permission for Joseph to marry some of his wives, and even chose some of them for him. Some witnessed Emma's terrible struggle, perhaps made more visible or central because of her position as the wife of the Prophet. Allen J. Stout, who served as a bodyguard for Joseph, recounted a conversation he overheard in the Mansion House between Joseph and his tormented wife. A summary of his account states that "from moments of passionate denunciation [Emma] would subside into tearful repentance and acknowledge that her violent opposition to that principle was instigated by the power of darkness; that Satan was doing his utmost to destroy her, etc. And solemnly came the Prophet's inspired warning 'Yes, and he will accomplish your overthrow, if you do not heed my counsel.'"[17] Maria Jane Johnston, who lived with Emma as a servant girl, recalled the Prophet's wife looking very downcast one day and telling her that the principle of plural marriage was right and came from Heavenly Father. "What I said I have got [to] repent of," lamented Emma. "The principle is right but I am jealous hearted. Now never tell anybody that you heard me find fault with that principle[;] we have got to humble ourselves and repent of it."[18] Many of us struggle through life with one or two trials, challenges, or commandments that seem ready to overwhelm and swallow us whole. Perhaps if Joseph had lived longer the elect lady would have eventually conquered her pride and jealousy, especially with the mellowing of age.

Then again, maybe not. At the time of Joseph's martyrdom Emma seemed hardened and set against plural marriage. At her insistence he had moved all of his plural wives out of their home.

Some believe Emma thought she had actually talked Joseph into doing away with the practice. All we know is that after his death, whether to protect her children or because the acknowledgment of it was just too painful, her opposition to plural marriage crystallized into an unswerving denial that Joseph Smith had ever even lived the principle. Some have suggested that after her husband's death Emma suffered an emotional breakdown, which caused her subsequent rejection of the Church and its principle of plural marriage. Other than her understandable grief over the loss of her husband, there is really no evidence of an emotional illness in her behavior. At any rate, I don't feel it is necessary to make excuses for Emma. The Lord had warned her in a revelation found in D&C 132 (see verses 54-56) that she should support her husband in the new and everlasting covenant of plural marriage or she would be destroyed. Emma was about to be destroyed.

It is important to understand, however, what the Lord may have meant by the term "destroyed." Obviously she was not physically destroyed but lived a generously long life for her time, dying in 1879 at the age of 74. The Lord often uses figurative physical terms to represent graphic spiritual consequences—in other words, he may have been warning that Emma would be spiritually destroyed, or cut off from the Spirit of the Lord, left to face the buffetings of Satan without the guidance and comfort of the Holy Ghost. In the first section of the Doctrine and Covenants, those who will not heed the words of the prophets are designated to be "cut off from among the people" (D&C 1:14). Yet God does not literally come down and physically separate the disobedient from the flock and prevent them from mingling with the righteous. They tend to cut themselves off because they lose the Spirit and their testimony of the truth. They apostatize or drift away. I believe this is the spiritual destruction that befell Emma.

Because of her unwillingness to follow the Prophet—her own beloved husband—she lost the Spirit and her testimony of the importance of the institutional Church (though never of the Book of Mormon). Left to herself to the degree that she rejected the truth and turned her back on the authorized leaders of the Church, Emma nevertheless committed no egregious sins and remained compassionate and kind. Yet in leaving the Church she forfeited great blessings, honor, and spiritual safety that might have been hers. She struggled through many family problems that she might have been able to avoid had she stayed true to gospel principles and taught her children to do likewise. Besides the wrenching infidelity of her second husband already mentioned, her oldest, adopted daughter, Julia, suffered through an unhappy marriage to an alcoholic husband who eventually deserted her. Emma's youngest son, David Hyrum, who was born six months after his father's martyrdom, ended up in an insane asylum at the age of 32, in part tormented by the contradiction between the undeniable evidence of his father's plural marriages and his mother's unbending denials that Joseph had ever advocated or practiced such a doctrine.

Deep sadness pervaded Emma's life in later years. Her granddaughter Emma Belle Smith Kennedy remembered a melancholy grandmother: "Her eyes were brown and sad. She would smile with her lips but to me, as small as I was, I never saw the brown eyes smile. I asked my mother one day, why don't Grandma laugh with her eyes like you do and my mother said because she has a deep sorrow in her heart."[19] A maid of Emma's recalled that Emma would go upstairs to her room every evening after chores were done to sit in her rocking chair and gaze sadly out the window at the sun going down over the Mississippi River. No one dared approach her or attempt to dry the tears that would roll softly down her cheeks.[20] I can't help but wonder if the Lord's gentle admonition to "beware of pride" ever echoed through her weary mind.

Shortly before her death Emma reported a vision to her nurse in which she saw the Savior and her husband, the Prophet Joseph Smith. She told the nurse that Joseph came to her and said, "Emma, come with me, it is time for you to come with me." Emma explained, "I put on my bonnet and my shawl and went with him; I did not think that it was anything unusual. I went with him into a mansion, and he showed me through the different apartments of that beautiful mansion." One room was a nursery in which she found a baby in a cradle. "I knew my babe," Emma said, "my Don

Carlos that was taken from me." She swept the child up into her arms and cried for joy, but when recovered, stopped to ask, "Joseph, where are the rest of my children[?]" He assured her, "Emma, be patient and you shall have all of your children." Emma then related that she saw a personage of light standing by the side of her beloved husband—"even the Lord Jesus Christ."[21]

I consider myself more than just an apologist for Emma Hale Smith. She has become almost as much my sister and my friend as if she were my contemporary. Her personal tragedy is haunting and painful to me. Yet the possibility of her reward is joyous to me. Her saga is one of heroic proportions—her great deeds as well as her signal failings are legendary in the Church. I believe the profound lesson of the life of Emma Smith, however, is the manifestation of the triumph of God's far-reaching mercy and love over human failings. Unlike many heroines of the Restoration, she stumbled and was spiritually and physically left behind. Like Emma, I also grapple with sins and shortcomings that threaten to overcome me at times, and I am grateful to be able to hope that the Lord will do everything he can to find mercy for me, and for Emma as well. I have pleaded with members of the Church to refrain from judging her unfairly and condemning her, just as they should any other fellow Saint or human being.

Eliza Partridge, a plural wife whom Emma had given to Joseph, poignantly expressed similar sentiments in 1883: "After these many years I can truly say; poor Emma, she could not stand polygamy but she was a good woman and I never wish to stand in her way of happiness and exaltation. I hope the Lord will be merciful to her, and I believe he will. It is an awful thought to contemplate misery of a human being. If the Lord will my heart says let Emma come up and stand in her place. Perhaps she has done no worse than any of us would have done in her place. Let the Lord be the judge."[22]

Let us then remember Emma, our sister, as any of us would wish to be remembered by future generations—with gratitude for her sacrifices and contributions, empathy for her struggles and shortcomings, and a generous eye toward her eternal possibilities.

NOTES

1. See Brigham Young, in *Journal of Discourses* 17:159.

2. Lucy Mack Smith, *The Revised and Enhanced History of Joseph Smith by His Mother*, ed. Scot Facer Proctor and Maurine Jensen Proctor (Salt Lake City: Bookcraft, 1996), p. 126.

3. See *Saints Herald* 31 (21 June 1884): 396.

4. Joseph Smith III, ed., "Last Testimony of Sister Emma," *Saints Advocate* 4 (October 1879): 49–52.

5. Lucy Mack Smith, *History of Joseph Smith by His Mother*, ed. Preston Nibley (Salt Lake City: Bookcraft, 1954), p. 190.

6. Emma Smith Bidamon, interview by Nels Madson and Parley P. Pratt Jr., 1877, Archives Division, Church Historical Department, The Church of Jesus Christ of Latter-day Saints, Salt Lake City, Utah.

7. *Comprehensive History of the Church* 1:127.

8. Emma Smith to Joseph Smith, 7 March 1839, Joseph Smith Letterbook, as quoted in Valeen Tippetts Avery and Linda King Newell, "The Elect Lady: Emma Hale Smith," *Ensign* 9 (September 1979): 66.

9. Jesse W. Crosby, in Hyrum L. Andrus and Helen Mae Andrus, comps., *They Knew the Prophet* (Salt Lake City: Bookcraft, 1974), p. 143.

10. Smith, *History*, pp. 190–91.

11. See Linda King Newell and Valeen Tippetts Avery, *Mormon Enigma: Emma Hale Smith* (New York: Doubleday, 1984), p. 104.

12. Smith, *History*, pp. 231–32.

13. See Joseph Smith III, "The Memories of President Joseph Smith (1832–1914)," ed. Mary Audentia Smith Anderson, *Saints Herald* (6 November 1934): 1479.

14. See Joseph Smith III, *Joseph Smith III and the Restoration*, ed. Mary Audentia Smith Anderson (Missouri: Herald House, 1952), p. 73.

15. See Newell and Avery, *Mormon Enigma*, pp. 275–77, 303.

16. Joseph Smith, *Teachings of the Prophet Joseph Smith*, comp. Joseph Fielding Smith (Salt Lake City: Deseret Book Co., 1976), p. 256; emphasis added.

17. Allen J. Stout, "Allen J. Stout's Testimony," *Historical Record* 6 (May 1887): 230–31.

18. Emma Smith to Maria Jane Johnston, as quoted in Newell and Avery, *Mormon Enigma*, p. 161.

19. Emma Belle Smith Kennedy, journal, as quoted in Gracia N. Jones, "My Great-Great-Grandmother Emma Hale Smith," *Ensign* 22 (August 1992): 37.

20. As quoted in ibid.

21. Alexander Hale Smith, sermon given 1 July 1903, as quoted in ibid.

22. Eliza Partridge, in Emily D. P. Young, "Incidents of the Early Life of Emily Partridge," as quoted in Newell and Avery, *Mormon Enigma*, p. 309.

২৯

Wendy C. Top is the author of *Emma Hale Smith: A Woman's Perspective* and is the coauthor, with her husband, Brent L. Top, of *Beyond Death's Door* and *An Inward Stillness*. She has many interests but most of all loves being a wife, mother, grandmother, and home-maker. Currently residing in Pleasant Grove, Utah, Wendy and her husband have four children and one grandchild. Wendy derives courage from Emma's life and sees many of her own strengths and weaknesses in Emma's example.

3

"My Heart Is in God"
Patty Bartlett Sessions
1795–1892

*P*erceiving examples of heroism in the first 50 years of Patty Bartlett Sessions's life is like trying to find comfort in the vital statistics of a genealogy chart. From the sparse information recorded we learn that she was born on 4 February 1795 in the small township of Bethel, Maine. To support the family, her father, Enoch Bartlett, toiled as a cobbler, and her mother, Anna Hall Bartlett, worked as a weaver. At age 17 Patty was married to David Sessions in the Methodist church in Newry, Maine. Of the eight children born to their union, five died as infants during raging epidemics that swept through their small town, and only three lived to adulthood: Perrigrine, Sylvia, and David.

Though Patty's life was noteworthy, such a nondescript, skeletal biography lacks any of the detail needed for her to be recognized as a true heroine of the Restoration. In fact, Patty Sessions would most likely have remained an obscure figure, never to play a dramatic role in Latter-day Saint folklore or to become an inspiration for succeeding generations, had she not accepted a simple gift—a small notebook. The inscription on the notebook reads: "A

Patty Bartlett Sessions

34

Day Book, given to me, Patty Sessions, by Sylvia . . . this 10th day of
February, 1846. Patty Sessions, her book. I am now fifty-one years,
six days old. February 10, 1846, City of Joseph, Hancock County,
Illinois."[1]

As Patty made entries in her daybook she revealed her sorrows
and joys, her greatest desires, her unwavering faith, and her heroic
deeds. Although her diary entries pale in comparison with the literary eloquence of her friend, the poetess Eliza R. Snow, they led ac-
claimed Mormon historian Leonard J. Arrington to label her as "a
remarkable blend of things temporal and spiritual."[2] Her day-to-day
personal notations have made the heroic difference in her remembrance by posterity and admirers alike. These notations evidence
the Lord's promise that "by small means the Lord can bring about
great things" (1 Nephi 16:29).

In my failed quest to discover a journal, daybook, or letter written by one of my ancestors, I realize the significant contribution left
by Patty in her daybook. I echo the lament of Heber J. Grant, who
penned, "I would be willing to pay any reasonable amount of
money for a record of father's life; but he never recorded any of his
acts and there is today nothing worthy of mention on record regarding him."[3] Such could not be said of Patty. In her writing, although
she disregarded "proper" spelling, grammar, and punctuation, she
poignantly revealed the life of a pioneer midwife. Though her brief
entries leave the reader wanting to know more, they weave a fascinating tale of her courageous adventure as a Mormon pioneer traveling from the Mississippi River to the Rocky Mountains.

Perhaps her story is of special interest to me because I too am
51 years of age and am feeling some of the same frustrations and
joys she described. Believing that the wise can learn vicariously
from the experiences of others and that "history repeats itself," my
fancy turns to answers in her journal that, if applied to my own life,
can help make it more complete.

Patty made many sacrifices for her religious beliefs after joining
the beleaguered Mormons in 1834. By 1837 she and her husband
and three children left the quiet familiarity of their environs in
Maine to reside in Kirtland, Ohio, among the Saints of God. Within
a year they were brutally forced from their home by mobocrats. In

1838 they were residing in the Mormon community of Far West, Missouri, where again they were confronted with extreme hostility. An extermination order issued by Lilburn Boggs, governor of Missouri, against all Mormons living within the state's borders brought the horrors of war to Patty's doorstep. She and her family were forced to abandon all of their holdings—an estimated loss of $1,200 in land and $400 in livestock and corn—when they were driven from their home.

As exiles they suffered for want of shelter and food. For 14 days they had nothing to eat but parched corn. Their appetites were not satisfied until they crossed the Mississippi River and found Good Samaritans in Quincy, Illinois, anxious to minister to their needs. After a brief sojourn in Quincy the Sessions family settled in Nauvoo and once again enjoyed the society of the Saints. In beautiful Nauvoo they found a brief haven of peace, a refuge from the storms of hate and bigotry they had known in Ohio and Missouri.

However, as threats of extermination loomed again, Elder Orson Pratt advised, "Brethren awake! . . . Let every branch in the east, west, north, and south, be determined to flee out of Babylon, either by land or by sea."[4] The call to move on, this time to the Rocky Mountains, was familiar to many of the Saints. But for Patty it was most painful. It meant choosing between following her prophetic leader, Brigham Young, and staying behind in Nauvoo with her children, who refused to listen to the urgent counsel.

Throughout the terrors she had faced in Ohio and Missouri, Patty had been comforted by a solicitous husband and obedient children. Now the decision to journey with the Saints entailed an even greater sacrifice—saying good-bye to loved ones. Although the choice was difficult, she moved forward to follow her convictions: "I desire to do right and live my religion that I may enjoy the light to see as I am seen and know as I am known. O my Father, help me to live my religion, this is my greatest desire."[5]

Patty, like many modern Mormon mothers, made a most difficult choice. Being an absentee mother, or experiencing the pains of an empty nest, is not easy in any era for a loving mother. It becomes deeply poignant when a mother prayerfully makes the decision to abandon loved ones in order to follow the godly dictates of her heart. It is an Abrahamic test, with all of the emotional ramifications of refining fire and fuller's soap, for both mother and child. For Patty, though her youngest child was an adult, nearly 23 years of age, the decision to leave her children and follow Brigham Young across the Mississippi River, over 1,300 miles away from civilization, was not easy—as it would not have been for me.

As Patty traversed the wilderness of Iowa she wrote of her longing for news from Perrigrine, Sylvia, and David. One journal entry reveals her joy at receiving letters: "Brother Holman brought letters from my children in Nauvoo. I read them with joy and gratitude to God for the privilege of hearing from them. Have read Perrigrine's letter to Brigham. He says they will all get away soon."[6] Patty counted the days that passed before she could embrace her children again: "When I came home I find Perrigrine and family. . . . We were glad to see each other once more. It has been four months and ten days since I started and left my children."[7]

During those months of familial loneliness in the crowds of pioneering Saints, Patty expressed an optimism that is worthy of emulation. "I have been in the cold and in the mud. There is no food for our teams but browse," she wrote. "I never have felt so bad as now, but I am not discouraged yet." Even when she penned, "My health is poor, my mind weighed down," she concluded the entry, "but my heart is in God."[8] As I read the journal accounts written 150 years ago I marvel at the wisdom her simple words convey. The phrases "not discouraged yet" and "my heart is in God" reveal her hopeful attitude amid the hardships of the pioneer journey.

It appears that on the arduous trek Patty found the answer to the question philosophers and sages have pondered throughout the centuries: what is the secret to a happy life? For her a complete trust in the Lord, as conveyed in the hopeful refrain "All is well," brought a peaceful happiness. The campfire hymn "Come, Come, Ye Saints" did not just comprise pleasing words to Patty but expressed her chosen way of life. In one diary entry she shows how the equating of trust in God with peaceful happiness could also be recognized in the life of her prophet leader, Brigham Young. "Brother Brigham came up with his company driving his teams in the rain and mud to his knees," wrote Patty. "[He] was happy as a king."[9] A study of both lives makes apparent their belief in the message of that pioneer song:

> Come, come, ye Saints, no toil nor labor fear;
> But with joy wend your way.
> Though hard to you this journey may appear,
> Grace shall be as your day.
> 'Tis better far for us to strive
> Our useless cares from us to drive;
> Do this, and joy your hearts will swell—
> All is well! All is well![10]

Yet again and again their attitude of trusting optimism was tested. More than one faltering Saint believed, "If I didn't have bad luck, I wouldn't have any luck at all." But for Patty and Brigham Young and many of the heroines of yesteryear, the hardships on the journey westward and in the pioneer Mormon settlements in the intermountain west did not discourage or overwhelm them.

Patty never lost her dogged determination and hope. She drove oxen and journeyed on foot across the plains when necessary: "Travel 5 miles; March the first. Pitch our tents. Monday 2, travel on twelve miles. One of our horses has the thumps. I go afoot up and down the hills."[11] Even when illness took its toll, she moved onward: "I am quite sick again today. Saturday, 2. Fair weather this morning. It has rained for six days. My bed has been wet all the time and has not been made."[12] When her cow calved she stopped for only an hour and "after the rest moved on, then took the calf in our wagon and overtook the camp."[13] She penned of her journey, "I am happy all the time."[14] Her only lament in being among the first to follow Brigham across the Great Plains was the loss of the companionship of those who tarried: "We start for the mountains and leave Winter Quarters . . . ten years today since we left our home [in Maine] and friends. We now leave many good friends here, and I hope they will soon follow on to us."[15]

That hopeful attitude she consistently mentioned in her journal has become the legacy of an American pioneer heroine. The simple act of recording her forward movement elevated Patty Bartlett Sessions above the rank and file of those who traversed the nation in covered wagons to the status of a faithful Mormon pioneer who has become the epitome of courage, determination, and forbearance for women over more than a century. Patty Sessions is ranked among the great heroines who helped build a nation.

> They, the builders of the nation,
> Blazing trails along the way;
> Stepping-stones for generations
> Were their deeds of ev'ry day.
> Building new and firm foundations,
> Pushing on the wild frontier,
> Forging onward, ever onward,
> Blessed, honored Pioneer![16]

On the trek Patty discovered the joy that comes through selfless service. She learned from the sick and afflicted the powerful truth of the words spoken by King Benjamin centuries before: "When ye are in the service of your fellow beings ye are only in the service of your God" (Mosiah 2:17). Like the Saints of other dispensations, Patty learned that only when one lifts another's burden will God lift one's own cares. It is a holy paradox. The disciple who staggers and even falls because burdens are too heavy can lighten personal cares by carrying the weight of another's burden. In so doing, hearts become lighter, lives brighter, and souls greater.

The medical talents Patty shared with those who had forsaken the comforts of civilization for a box on wheels, with only a canvas for a covering, seemed heaven sent to her fellow travelers. Her 34 years as a practicing midwife made her one of the most important Saints in the Mormon encampments in Iowa and along the pioneer trail. Her skills were sought by men and women alike, whose complaints varied from a blistered foot to the ague, from muscle cramps to diarrhea. Although she had no formal medical training she was considered an expert in all matters of illness. Along with a handful of other Mormon heroines who possessed healing talents, she became widely known for her unselfish service.

Patty's brief journal entries evidence her willingness to be inconvenienced to minister aid: "About six o'clock in the morning I was called for to go back two miles. It then snowed. I rode behind the men through mud and water, some of the way belly deep to the horse. I found the sister that I was called to see in an old log cabin. Her child was born before I got there."[17] In a journal entry on 6 March 1846 she penned, "I go back ten miles this morning to see Sarah Ann. She is sick. Sent for me. I rode horseback. She was better when I got there. And I drove her carriage into the camp in the afternoon with her and her mother." Her last notation of the day: "I was sick last night."[18] Three days later she wrote, "Brother Ezra Benson came after me nine o'clock in the evening. I put his wife to bed with a daughter at ten o'clock in the tent. Came back and found Mr. Sessions [Patty's husband] in bed without his supper; no one to get it for him."[19] Even on the happy day in Winter Quarters when she was enjoying the company of all three of her children for the first time since leaving Nauvoo, she responded affirmatively to an urgent call to minister to the sick.[20]

Accounts of dues paid or owed to Patty Sessions for her medical assistance read like a "who's who" among Church leaders:

Mar. 9,	Ezra Benson 2.00
Mar. 11,	A.P. Rockwood . . . . . . .1.00/1.50, OX50 .25
Oct. 1,	Erastus Snow . . . . .paid 2.00
Dec. 8,	Wilford Woodruff . . . . .paid 2.00
Feb. 6,	Newel K. Whitney . . . .paid 2.00[21]

For those who lacked means she was just as accessible but did not ask for payment: "Was sent for to go back two miles to a sick woman, Sister Stewart. I asked her no pay."[22]

There is no hint of self-pity or resentment in her journal entries over hours lost in service to others. Missing also are any negative comments about those she served. Patty found joy in giving her time and talents to the Mormon pioneers. Her example of noble service must have been a beacon to those struggling pioneers of yesteryear.

Two days after her arrival in the Great Salt Lake Valley she assisted in the birth of a son to Harriet Page Young. Her care of mother and child was the fulfillment of a prophetic promise she was given in Nauvoo: "It was said to me more than five months ago that my hands should be the first to handle the first-born son in the place of rest for the Saints, even in the City of God. I have come more than one thousand miles to do it since it was spoken."[23]

Patty is credited with delivering 14 babies in the Salt Lake Fort that first winter. Near the end of the first year Church secretary Thomas Bullock reported, " 'Mother Sessions' has had a harvest of 248 little cherubs since living in the valley. Many cases of twins; in a row of seven houses joining each other, eight births in one week."[24] Most of her assisted deliveries were successful in saving both mother and child. However, a few instances of death were painful reminders to Patty of her limited medical knowledge. As she grieved over a young mother who lay dying, she heard the woman's consoling whisper: "I can meet you before the Lord, and hail you with joy."[25] Although death of a mother and child brought much sorrow to Patty, she mourned even more deeply over the passing in 1850 of her husband, whom she referred to in her entries as "Mr. Sessions." Although now very alone in the arid desert of the Rocky Mountains, she did not retrace her footsteps back to Winter Quarters. Instead she made the courageous choice to stay with the fledgling Mormon pioneer community in the Salt Lake Valley.

On 14 December 1851, after cutting her own firewood, she married John Parry, an immigrant from Wales who was more of a musician than a woodchopper or a pioneer. (John Parry became the first conductor of the now world famous Mormon Tabernacle Choir.) Biographer Susan Sessions Rugh writes that it was a marriage of convenience and that it "lacked romantic love, but Patty was content with her new husband."[26] However, after more than two years of marriage John entered the law of plural marriage with a younger woman. On one occasion Patty wrote, "I am here alone. Mr. Parry has gone down to the other house." Then, characteristic of her earlier optimistic writings, she concluded, "I feel well in body and mind."[27]

However, the attention her husband showered on the other woman brought sorrow to Patty: "I stay alone, my spirits cast down, I feel bad; yet my trust is in God. He is my all, and on His Holy name I call for His spirit to direct me through my life and for wisdom in all things." In her time of sorrow she wrote her prayer to God: "O Lord give me thy spirit that it may be a light to my path; give me knowledge that I may know Thy will and how to do it; give me wisdom that I judge between truth and error, for I desire to do good and not evil. Make the path of duty plain before me and give me grace to walk therein and give me patience to endure all that I may be called to pass through."[28] The prayer was answered as she reached beyond her own emotional stamina and found the strength and comfort in the Lord that she had known on the pioneer trek.

Patty Sessions became recognized by Church leaders for her unselfish giving of tithes and offerings and assistance to the poor: "Amount of Tithing paid by Patty Sessions for 1865, $86.25. Balance due her after settlement, $39.00. Geo. D. Keaton, clerk."[29] On 25 March 1862 she gave Brigham Young $175 cash "for him to use until I called for it."[30] The money was deposited in the Perpetual Emigrating Fund to help convey the poor to the Salt Lake Valley. In February 1864 she donated an additional "$110.00 to buy a yoke of oxen to draw up the poor to Zion."[31] And thus a recitation of her unselfish deeds is recorded for generations to view with admiration.

Patty did not remarry after the death of John Parry in 1868. She resided for four more years in Salt Lake City before moving to Bountiful to be near her son Perrigrine, who had followed her to Utah. In that northern Utah community she built a brick house and later a school called the Patty Sessions Academy. The academy benefited her grandchildren and the poor, who received an education without cost. She continued to assist in the delivery of babies, which number in total 3,977.

Although her medical work kept her busy in her later years, she found enjoyment and satisfaction in other activities. She was recognized in her neighborhood for her gardening skills, having developed the Sessions plum. The products of her talents as a seamstress—from the basics of carding, spinning, and weaving to the more sophisticated processes of creating clothes, rugs, and comforters—were enjoyed by friends and family. And it seems that one of Patty's favorite activities was quiet reading: "I take 3 papers: Deseret News, Juvenile Instructor and Woman's Exponent. I read them all."[32] Indeed, perhaps Patty could echo the sentiment expressed by Parley P. Pratt: "I [have] always loved a book. If I worked hard, a book was in my hand in the morning. . . . A book at evening, . . . a book at every leisure moment of my life."[33] Patty found inspiration in reading the scriptures: "I have been reading [the] book of Mormon and the spirit of the Lord rests upon me. Although alone by myself I am happy."[34] As she closed the scriptures she often pondered their messages: "My meditation is sweet and my prayer is that the Holy Ghost will be poured out upon the servants of God that they may ferret out evil until we become a just people."[35] She also found joy in reading her journal entries: "I am here alone. I have been reading my journal and I feel to thank the Lord that I have passed through what I have. I have gained an experience I could not have gained no other way."[36]

On 14 December 1892, at the age of 97, diarist Patty Sessions died. The *Deseret Evening News* announced her death: "She has gone to her grave ripe in years, loved and respected by all who knew her."[37]

The lessons taught by Utah's foremost midwife in a small pioneer daybook and subsequent journals are profound. Those short, seemingly insignificant notations documenting faith and courage changed an ordinary, too easily forgotten life into a heroic saga. Patty's writings teach us that trusting in God and following his anointed prophets will help us develop an eternal perspective and a joyous testimony that overshadows any momentary sorrow. Patty Bartlett Sessions truly was a heroine of the Restoration, a messenger equal to the message she wrote.

NOTES

1. Patty Bartlett Sessions, daybook, as quoted in Claire Augusta Wilcox Noall, *Guardians of the Hearth: Utah's Pioneer Midwives and Women Doctors* (Bountiful, Utah: Horizon Publishers, 1974), p. 22.

2. Leonard J. Arrington, "Persons for All Seasons: Women in Mormon History," *BYU Studies* 20 (Fall 1979): 44.

3. Heber J. Grant, as quoted in Francis M. Gibbons, *Heber J. Grant: Man of Steel, Prophet of God* (Salt Lake City: Deseret Book Co., 1979), p. viii.

4. *History of the Church* 7:516.

5. Sessions, as quoted in Elizabeth Willis, "Voice in the Wilderness: The Diaries of Patty Sessions," *Journal of American Folklore* (Boston: Houghton Mifflin, 1988), p. 45.

6. Sessions, as quoted in Noall, *Guardians,* p. 25.

7. Ibid., p. 29.

8. Ibid., p. 26.

9. Ibid., p. 25.

10. William Clayton, "Come, Come, Ye Saints," in *Hymns,* no. 30.

11. Sessions, as quoted in Noall, *Guardians,* p. 23.

12. Ibid., p. 27.

13. Ibid., p. 29.

14. Ibid., p. 37.

15. Ibid., pp. 36–37.

16. Ida R. Alldredge, "They, the Builders of the Nation," in *Hymns,* no. 36.

17. Sessions, as quoted in Noall, *Guardians,* p. 25.

18. Ibid., p. 23.

19. Ibid., p. 24.

20. Ibid., p. 34.

21. Ibid., pp. 35, 36.

22. Ibid., pp. 26–27.

23. Ibid., p. 40.

24. Ibid., p. 42.

25. Ibid., p. 49.

26. Susan Sessions Rugh, "Patty B. Sessions," in Vicky Burgess-Olson, ed., *Sister Saints* (Provo, Utah: Brigham Young University Press, 1978), p. 316.

27. Sessions, as quoted in Willis, "Voice in the Wilderness," p. 44.

28. Sessions, as quoted in Noall, p. *Guardians,* 45.

29. Ibid., p. 50

30. Ibid., p. 48.

31. Ibid., p. 50.

32. Ibid., p. 51.

33. Parley P. Pratt, *Autobiography of Parley P. Pratt,* ed. Parley P. Pratt Jr. (Salt Lake City: Deseret Book Co., 1985), p. 2.

34. Sessions, as quoted in Willis, "Voice in the Wilderness," p. 44.

35. Ibid., p. 45.

36. Ibid., p. 43.

37 *Deseret Evening News,* 22 December 1892.

Susan Easton Black is an associate dean of general education and honors and a professor of Church history and doctrine at Brigham Young University. She has written or edited 75 books and many articles, and her most recent book is *Who's Who in the Doctrine and Covenants*. She and her husband, Harvey B. Black, are the parents of eight children and live in Provo, Utah. Susan says that writing this chapter has rekindled her admiration for Patty Sessions, who was a key figure in bringing relief to those who suffered during the pioneer era.

4

"The Lord Will Support Us"
Mary Fielding Smith
1801–1852

*I*t's not that it's so hard to find a determined woman. We see them all around us: the older woman resolutely keeping up with youngsters who could be her grandchildren, finally working on her degree after years devoted to family; the young woman, tomato-splattered and flustered, intent on canning every single one of the tomatoes she grew and brooding over the zucchini surplus; the mother who has made up her mind that her offspring are going to have the musical advantages she missed, even if it means insisting on and supervising unenthusiastic practice sessions from now until the far side of forever. A lot of women are blessed with determination. A lot of men joke about it, looking nervously over their shoulders lest they find themselves over-taken by a resolute female person intent on her own business.

Mary Fielding Smith would have outdone them all. It's a matter of historical fact that she overtook a good many men in her day. Even in a field of determined women she would have stood out. Born in England, she was converted to the restored Church in Canada with her brother and sister, and with them came to Zion, which at that point was Kirtland, Ohio.

Mary Fielding Smith

She went on to become the wife of the second Patriarch of the Church, mother of the sixth president, and grandmother of the tenth, but it is not solely her relationship with the men of her family that makes her memorable. After her husband, Hyrum, was murdered by the mob with his brother, the Prophet Joseph Smith, Mary Fielding Smith—over the resistance of Smith family members who pressed her to remain in Nauvoo—gathered up herself and her possessions, her children, stepchildren, and several other miscellaneous dependents, and set off to travel west with the body of the Church.

The captain of her company, a man named Cornelius P. Lott, was so unenthusiastic about the idea of including her assortment of women, children, and half-broken wild steers and half-grown oxen in his company that he told her bluntly that she should go back to Winter Quarters and stay there until someone could take charge of her. If she persisted in her attempt to travel west, he said, she would never make it to their destination and would be a burden to everyone else in the company as far as she might manage to get.

Her son Joseph F. Smith, not yet 10 years old at the time, was standing with his mother as Captain Lott explained to her what he saw as the realities of the situation. There they stood, the young boy, the testy but powerful captain, and the indomitable woman. It was obvious to her son, if not to the captain, that Mary saw the realities rather differently. Joseph F. might not be very old, and she might be a widowed woman, but she had faith and determination, and Joseph Smith had promised her before his death that the Lord would take care of her.

When the captain finished, Mary said what she had to say. She told the captain that she would beat him to the Valley and would ask no help from him while she was doing it. Then, without further discussion on the subject, she went ahead and did exactly what she told him she would do. She got there a day before he did, and she got there without his help.

Mary was a Smith by marriage but a Fielding by birth, and the Fieldings had never been known for their wishy-washy stands on principle. When she, her brother, and her sister, with their Methodist minister, John Taylor, encountered a Mormon missionary in Toronto named Parley P. Pratt and recognized the truth of what he taught, the Fieldings' first hope was that they would be able to take that message and share it with their five brothers and sisters still living in the north of England. When her brother, Joseph Fielding, was later actually able to go to that very part of England as a missionary himself, he discovered to his and his sisters' disappointment that the English branch of the family wanted nothing to do with the Church and, consequently, nothing to do with him either. With true Fielding determination, the English Fieldings planted themselves as resolutely on the old faith as the American branch planted themselves on the new. Neither side would budge, and eventually they died as they lived from that time forward, estranged.

My family is descended from those Fieldings in a direct line from Joseph, and it's not only my mother who has remarked on the fact that the Fielding determination apparently rides on exceedingly dominant genes down to the present generation. We are three, four, and five generations away from Joseph and his resolute sisters now, and you can still see the shadow of their set chins in the set chins of my mother, my sisters, and my children when something they believe in is challenged or declared to be impossible.

Mary Fielding Smith's chin must have been set like that when, during her long march across the plains, one of her best oxen collapsed in the yoke, apparently dying. Captain Lott—not particularly grieved by the situation, one gathers—came to see what was going on and announced that the animal was obviously dead and they would just have to figure out some way to take the widow along, a burden on the company just as he had predicted.

Mary said nothing. (Unlike many of her collateral descendants, she appears to have been a woman of few words.) Instead, she went to her wagon and collected a bottle of consecrated oil, and then went to her brother Joseph, who was also part of the company, and told him he was needed to administer to the ox.

According to family legend, Joseph was somewhat taken aback by the request. Up until then he had apparently not seen administration to animals as one of his priesthood opportunities. His sister, however, was firmly determined that that was exactly what was going to happen, and Joseph took the oil from her and with another elder administered to the ox.

The ox, still in the yoke, got up and walked. The wagon jolted along after it, and so did Mary. What the captain said or thought is not recorded.

I think about the Fielding determination sometimes, and about how it led the English branch of the family to remain stubbornly close-minded to what the two sisters and brother in the New World recognized as revelation that opened all the promise and meaning of the dispensation of the fulness of times. I think about how that same Fielding determination worked to enable Mary to withstand the persecution she and her family endured in Ohio, in Missouri, and finally in Nauvoo, the determination that held her close to the strength of the gospel when the lifeless body of her husband was returned to her after the carnage of Carthage Jail. Would it have been easier to have thrown up her hands and taken her children and fled back to England, to sanity and safety? I don't know, but apparently the possibility never occurred to her. Mary Fielding Smith determined to live for the Church as her husband had died for it, and, alone among the Smith family, transferred her loyalty and her obedience to the new leaders and went west, as they did, to Deseret.

That determination had enormous consequences for herself and her descendants. Because she was prepared to do whatever was necessary to follow the direction of the new leaders, she managed to get her children and stepchildren across the plains to the Valley, where her family could grow up and prosper. Her son and grandsons matured into leadership positions within the Church, unlike their cousins who had stayed in Nauvoo and followed their own paths, rejecting the revelations directing the move west because they came to Brigham Young and not to the Prophet's own son. In a sense, the Smith family that stayed behind was determined too, but determined to follow their own course of action, without reference to the authority of leadership that rested in the Apostles. What made Mary Fielding Smith's determination remarkable was that it was determination tempered by obedience and humility. She was determined, all right, but ready to accept counsel on the direction in which that determination should be exercised.

I think about that distinction as I look around at the world I live in today, 150 years after the days when Mary Fielding Smith was fighting her battles with unfortunate oxen, skeptical men, and inex-orable geography. I think about myself and my sisters: we certainly seem to have no problem in making up our minds about things. But do we always remember, in small things as well as large, to ask for counsel on what we should do, and, having asked for the counsel, actually wait to find out what it is before charging off into action? I wonder. Sometimes it seems so much easier just to get going on whatever appears to be the most obvious thing to be done.

Oh, of course there are things we do that I know Mary Fielding Smith would understand and approve of fully. I think of one of my sisters, who lives, as I do, well out of the Valley and the heartland of the Church, and who has, over the course of four long school years now, bounded out of bed at some incredible hour so that she can be dressed and prepared—not at home, but over at the stake center—to teach seminary at six o'clock in the morning. Mary would have nodded approvingly and understood exactly why it was important to do that, even on the most uninviting wintry dawns. Mary knew about cold, and fighting fatigue, and instructing adolescents who might not fully appreciate the instruction at the time. She also knew it had to be done.

But then I think about some of the other examples of determi-nation in our time. I think of the stage mothers who are absolutely set on their young daughters finding fame and fortune, and who are not particularly concerned about the quality or moral principles or levels of violence in the productions within which they struggle to place their daughters. I think about some of the world-class women athletes who place every other consideration after their goal to achieve success in sports, and how marriages have been known to founder as a direct result. I think about women here at the tail end of the twentieth century who, whether their opportunities are in the commercial world or in charitable ventures or in political action, either postpone having their families until some vague future time when they might get around to it, or else, being encumbered with motherly or wifely responsibilities or both, work a patchwork of temporary arrangements and substitute child care and microwave dinners left with a hasty note of instruction or money on the kitchen counter for pizza. None of their achievements (and clearly they do achieve) are possible without determination, and none of them succeed in their chosen fields (and clearly they do succeed) without being determined in a way that is a shadowy reminder of Mary Fielding Smith.

But only a shadowy reminder. Viewed from the outside, the choices many women of today are making, however determined the women are, don't appear to be the choices that Mary would have made, given what we know of her and her character. Of course, it's true that as outsiders we are in no position to evaluate the choices of others or to pass judgment on whether they sought divine guidance and what that divine guidance might have been, or ought to be, according to our frame of reference. Still, perhaps I can learn from Mary's example something about my own choices and my reasons for making them.

First of all, there's that business of praying about choices and then paying attention to the answers, whether the answers seem wrongheaded and off base or not. I should learn from experience; I have a long history of apparently wrongheaded answers to prayer that worked out to be the best possible blessings that could have been given to me. Trusting that that will happen seems to be a lesson I need to learn over and over again.

Second, there's the point that I need to be very, very sure that I am really listening to the Spirit when it's necessary for other people to sacrifice something so that I can do what I believe I ought to do. That I myself should sacrifice for what I want is perfectly all right. But when I ask my children to get along on their own for a bit while I get whatever it is under control, or figure that my husband and I don't really need to spend all that much time together right now because we're both busy (at least I think he's busy—I haven't really had time to inquire), or decide my mother is doing just fine—she always seems to be pottering around comfortably when I get a minute to pay attention—and I'll just get these things done and *then* I'll spend some time with her—well, I guess when I think about Mary Fielding Smith and how busy she was and the choices she made, I think I'd better evaluate my choices very, very carefully.

True, her children had a rough time crossing the plains. It wasn't easy for anyone. But would staying in Nauvoo necessarily have been any easier? After all, it was from Nauvoo that her husband (and their father) went off to Carthage and his death. The choices Mary Fielding Smith made with such determination were for their better good in the long run, not primarily for hers.

True, she left her husband's mother behind, but at the time she left, Lucy Mack Smith had agreed to come west, if when she died her body could be brought back to Nauvoo for burial. That was promised to her, but she just never actually started the journey.

The person who sacrificed most for Mary Fielding Smith's determined fealty to the church and what she believed she was directed to do was Mary Fielding Smith herself. She was a woman in the prime of her life, in her forties when she crossed the plains. Not only did she make the journey but she had to make a home, quite literally, once she reached the Salt Lake Valley. She and her family built a two-room adobe house first, and cleared land for a farm. None of it was easy work. Mary had been a tall, attractive young woman; by the time she was working on the farm in the Salt Lake Valley she had become a strong but careworn old woman, her hair graying, shoulders stooped, hands rough and hardened by manual labor.

When she had done what she had to do—her children and stepchildren had a home among the Saints, safe in the West—her iron determination could support her no further. She had pushed her body relentlessly, month after month, year after year. In the end, her resistance crumbled. She caught what was described as a cold, and steadily worsened. In 1852, only four years after coming into the Valley, Mary Fielding Smith died. She was then 51 years old.

When I consider her accomplishments, there is only one possible verdict: she was one determined lady. More important, she seemed to know by instinct what the rest of us sometimes forget. Determination is a strong horse that needs to be harnessed by humility and obedience if it is to take us where we need to go. Mary Fielding Smith knew that. She organized her life around that truth, and she passed a rich heritage on to those of us who would come after, fighting different battles in different times but needing exactly the same principles that she lived by through good times and bad.

Mary Fielding Smith once wrote to her sister, "The Lord knows what our intentions are, and He will support us and give us grace and strength for the day, if we continue to put our trust in Him and devote ourselves unreservedly to His service."[1] Not only did she write it, she believed it and she lived it. She tamed the horse of determination simply by placing the reins in the hands of the Lord, as each of us can do.

And then she hung on tight, and rode.

<hr>

NOTES

1. Mary Fielding, letter to Mercy Rachel Thompson (no date), Canada, as quoted in Don C. Corbett, *Mary Fielding Smith: Daughter of Britain* (Salt Lake City: Deseret Book Co., 1966), p. 35.

๛

Beppie Harrison, who was born in California and raised in Hawaii, received her B.A. degree from the University of California at Berkeley. She is married to Geoffrey Harrison; they are the parents of four children and live in Birmingham, Michigan. She is the author of many books for both the LDS and the national market. Beppie chose to write about Mary Fielding Smith because of Mary's forthright, determined personality traits that can still be observed in her descendants today.

5

"To See the Game Thro', & Enjoy the Scenery"
Eliza Roxcy Snow
1804–1887

*E*liza Roxcy Snow is no stranger to Latter-day Saints. Her achievements and strengths, her leadership and fortitude, and her unshakable devotion to the principles of the restored gospel of Jesus Christ have been heralded for a century and a half. Her funeral, in fact, had all the earmarks of an affair of state. What she has meant to The Church of Jesus Christ of Latter-day Saints, and especially to its women, is well documented. Her writings fill several volumes, and recently Maureen Ursenbach Beecher collected and annotated, under one cover, Eliza's autobiography, "Sketch of My Life"; her Nauvoo journal and notebook; and her trail diary. Embedded in these documents are a number of previously unpublished poems and prose pieces, as well as many early versions of published poems.[1] Without question, Eliza R. Snow, the public person, merits our gratitude and admiration. And I do admire her for her splendid accomplishments, which include helping to reestablish the Relief Society in "Great Salt Lake City," institute the young

Eliza Roxcy Snow

women's and the children's organizations in the Church, and found Deseret Hospital. In all, she was the cement that held Mormon women close to their faith and close to each other in trying times. Nevertheless, the public resumé of Eliza Snow tells only part of the story, and even then not the part that I can get my heart around. It is not the "presidentess," as some called her, to whom I respond most keenly, or even "Aunt Eliza"; for both of those were public figures. Rather, it is the private person, the poet, the woman beneath the public countenance, who captures my imagination: the woman who loved language and wordplay; the woman who possessed a sly sense of humor; the woman who could laugh at herself; the woman who loved sisterhood; the woman who sculpted her intellectual and artistic endeavors into total compatibility with her devotion to the gospel and to priesthood authority; the woman who wore her own authority lightly; the woman who dearly loved Joseph Smith, her husband in plural marriage, and yet knew all the while that his heart belonged to Emma; the woman who spent her last dime for a bottle of writing ink.

Eliza Snow was not one to display her interior life. So in some sense, her public writings—including the larger part of her journals (she was clearly "company historian" as well as self-appointed chronicler of the Mormon exodus), her autobiography, and most of her poetry—mask more than they reveal of their circumspect creator. Still, Eliza dropped verbal pebbles along her path, whether intentionally or inadvertently, for the discerning reader to espy and follow. Leaving history and biography to scholars in those disciplines, I come to Eliza Snow through intuition as much as intellect, maybe more.[2]

Behind the ambitious, carefully constructed, highly polished texts, and also behind the jingles dashed off for any and every occasion (Eliza was the undisputed Hallmark greeting card of Zion), I have found a delightful woman. To trace my individual journey to Eliza, return with me to the title of this opus, which is quoted from her trail diary, 10 August 1846. The company is settled in a semi-permanent encampment where crops can be planted and preparations made for the major push west. Conditions are taxing at best. Eliza and the others have had a miserable week—in her words, "a growling, grumbling, devilish, sickly time" of it—and she hopes "never to see another week like" it. Her fate in other hands, and "a little at loss how to do," she "conclude[s] to see the game thro', & enjoy the scenery."[3]

This is Eliza: indomitable, courageous, enduring, yes, but also resilient, playful, sensitive to beauty, and optimistic. She was blessed by a sense of humor and a way with words. In these few lines from her diary I have discovered Eliza R. Snow, the woman and the poet, the woman of spirit and the woman who lived by the Spirit. Significantly, the poet inside the diarist is the revealer. She alliterates *growling* and *grumbling*, then presents the two aspects of the Eliza equation in a nicely balanced antithesis between "see[ing] the game thro'"; that is, grittily refusing to buckle; and happily "enjoy[ing] the scenery," finding beauty and reasons to rejoice along the way.

The question is, how does one accomplish such equipoise? How does one meet head on whatever physical and emotional trials present themselves, and at the same time decorate life with beauty and felicity? Eliza manages the balancing act; and her secret, I think, though inherent in all her writings, is put succinctly in this excerpt from a "greeting card" poem addressed "To Mrs.———."

> To me, it matters little now,
> To where I rise—to what I bow;
> Or toil or ease, I little care
> If Father's smiles I freely share;
> And when th' interior all is right,
> I have no outward foes to fight.
> I war for Zion—not for me:
> I've signed a gen'ral amnesty
> To all injustice, strife and hate,
> Which, to my single self, relate:
> Th' intenti'al [intentional] evil-doer will,
> Sooner or later, foot the bill.
> Then need we trouble? Surely, no;
> Nor stoop to fight an outward foe.[4]

This is not a great poem literarily, but it articulates an extraordinary life creed. The critical line is buried in the middle: "I war for Zion— not for me."

With her pen and her voice Eliza R. Snow took on plenty of "outward foes" of the Church: a "fallen" government (her term) that at the moment seemed to have abandoned the divinely inspired principles of its founding fathers, the mobocrats and their leaders who drove the Saints from their homes, the government agents who persecuted and prosecuted the Saints even in exile. These and others she blasted in poems and speeches, but the battles were Zion's wars, not Eliza Snow's. She also attacked, with action and with words, society's inner enemies—ignorance, disease, vice, and sloth. In her philosophy, however, personal wrongs are best not answered. A Zion society is no place for vindication of one's "single self." Everything Eliza did was for a larger cause than Eliza Snow; it was for Zion, for the Saints, collectively and individually. She might have said with her contemporary, Emily Dickinson (1830-1886), whom she could not have known,

> I had no time to Hate—
> Because
> The Grave would hinder Me—
> And life was not so
> Ample I
> Could finish—Enmity—[5]

Eliza found her life by losing it in a cause larger than herself.

Some have suggested that if Eliza had not embraced the gospel and joined the Church, she might have made her mark outside it, as a poet. Others, pointing to weaknesses in her poetry—sometimes faulty diction, doggerel rhythms, clichéd abstractions—have contended that she had no future as a writer. True, the Church gave Eliza a largely noncritical audience and ample subjects for her writing. And yes, I can count plenty of artistic blemishes in her verse, even after adjusting for the now odd-seeming poetic conventions of her day. But I can also see evidence of real talent. A number of her poems are very good, especially the hymns, and a few are superb.

Take, for example, some of the hymns we know well, not by her titles but by their first lines: "O My Father," "Though Deepening Trials," "Truth Reflects upon Our Senses," "How Great the Wisdom
and the Love," "Behold the Great Redeemer Die," and "Awake, Ye
Saints of God, Awake!"

This remarkable woman consecrated her gifts—all of them, literary and otherwise—to the building of her Father's kingdom. In
her words, when she "espous'd the cause of Truth, / The Holy Spirit
. . . / Promptly instructed" her "To lay my youthful prospects by." In
response, she "then did lay / My earthly all at Jesus' feet."[6] If the
breadth of her talents and service, and the depth of her commitment to the Church, meant her art could not be consistently fine-
tuned, so be it. But instead of dropping her artist-self when practical
demands became all-consuming, as many women and men of her
generation and later generations did, she managed to practice it
constantly. Not practice in the sense of "hone," but practice in the
sense of "employ." She used her poetry as sermon, as instruction, as
consolation, as encouragement, as political statement, as history, as
expression of affection, as celebration, as rallying cry. What Eliza
wished, with all her heart, was to be "useful" (again, her term) in the
kingdom. And she urged others to do the same, especially the
young.

It is perhaps inevitable that I would find some striking parallels
and contrasts between Eliza Snow and Emily Dickinson. Like Eliza,
Emily was born in Massachusetts, though a quarter of a century
later. Still, the durable Eliza outlived her by more than a year. Emily
spent her exterior life quietly and, the later part of it, reclusively, refining her extraordinary poetic gift in the microcosmic world of her
parents' home and garden. Her contribution to the world of literature is immeasurable, and we would be poorer without it. But in
Emily's lifetime she scarcely made a dent in lives other than those of
her family. If her gift had not been so immense, she would have remained after her death in the same obscurity in which she lived.

Eliza chose another course, but she was conscious that it ex-
acted a price. A poem that appears in several places, under the titles
"Yes, I Would Be a Saint," "Saturday Night Thoughts," and "Evening
Thoughts, or What It Is to Be a Saint," makes a glancing allusion in

its first stanza to her generally acknowledged potential for fame as a poet:

> 'Twas not for wealth—'twas not to gather heaps
> Of perishable things—'twas not to twine
> Around my brow, a transitory wreath—
> A garland deck'd with gems of mortal praise,
> That I forsook the home of childhood: that
> I left the lap of ease. . . .[7]

But even though Eliza elected a life of active faith and service while Emily's faith was uncertain and her activity largely mental, in some respects there is a fortuitous correspondence in outlook between the two women. Consider, for instance, these lines by Emily:

> This is my letter to the World
> That never wrote to Me—
> The simple News that Nature told—
> With tender Majesty
>
> Her Message is committed
> To Hands I cannot see—
> For love of Her—Sweet—countrymen—
> Judge tenderly—of Me[8]

Her poetry, Emily says, is a modest overture to a world that appears interested in neither her nor her message. Oddly enough, when I read among Eliza's countless rhymed notes to friends, family, and associates, produced for any and every occasion, almost from the beginning of her life in the Church, the lines "This is my letter to the World / That never wrote to Me" keep running through my head. So, too, does this two-stanza Dickinson poem:

> I'm Nobody! Who are you?
> Are you—Nobody—Too?
> Then there's a pair of us?
> Don't tell! they'd advertise—you know!

How dreary—to be—Somebody!
How public—like a Frog—
To tell one's name—the livelong June—
To an admiring Bog![9]

Furthermore, the closing lines of the previous Dickinson poem, and the spirit of both poems, seem echoed in the epitaph Eliza Snow composed for herself near the end of her life. Instead of being re-membered with tributes, tears, monuments, or flowers, Eliza asks only to remain in the memory of friends. These lines close her poem.

I feel the low responses roll,
    Like distant echoes of the night,
And whisper, softly through my soul,
    "I would not be forgotten quite."[10]

Perhaps even closer in tone to Emily's "I'm Nobody! Who are you?" is the poem below. It reveals that there was a reverse side to Eliza's seemingly interminable labor, both practical and spiritual, in establishing Zion, a side that took pleasure in being quietly alone with herself. Her words about "retirement" can almost be read as a gloss on the Dickinson poem, and "Eliza and I" almost construed as companions for Emily's "Nobody" and "you."

Retirement

O how sweet is retirement! how precious these hours
They are dearer to me than midsummer's gay flow'rs
Their soft stillness and silence awaken the Muse—
'Tis a time—'tis a place that the minstrel should choose
While so sweetly the moments in silence pass by
When there's nobody here but Eliza and I.

This is truly a moment peculiarly fraught
With unbound meditation and freedom of thought!
Such rich hallowed seasons are wont to inspire

With the breath of Parnassus, the languishing lyre
For sweet silence is dancing in Solitude's eye
When there's nobody here but Eliza and I.

O thou fav'rite retirement! palladium of joys
Remov'd from the bustle of nonsense and noise
Where mind strengthens its empire—enlarges its sphere
While it soars like the eagle or roams like the deer
O these still, sober moments, how swiftly they fly
While there's nobody here but Eliza and I.[11]

The poem just cited appears in Eliza's Nauvoo journal in late 1842. Another by the same title, but different entirely, appears in volume 2 of the *Poems*, and is likely a much later piece. In this poem, although Eliza continues to extoll the virtues of "retirement," that is, solitude, she also advocates a middle ground. There are, she implies, two equally vital, complementary sides to a person. The social being who functions in a gladsome community—which is quite different from the "empty" world of "fashion," "hollow" pleasures, and shallow "thought"—can be enriched by balancing sociability with periodic retirement into the soul's quietude. These are the final stanzas of the later poem:

Give me the happy medium between
The world's gay scenes, and dark, brown solitude:
Beneath the weight of which, the mind would lose
Its native elasticity, and would
Become absorb'd, and thus identify
With the dense mass of matter, lying round.

Pure social life, the holiest gem which heav'n
Confer'd upon this desert world—the bright
Oasis of our earthly pilgrimage—
The pearl that decorates the courts above;
Finds in retirement's treat, its richest zest.[12]

Not only do these last poems serve as windows to Eliza Snow's mind, but they introduce one of her most pervasive themes: opposition, or the duality of experience. In this as in other things, she is a child not only of Father Lehi but also of the 19th century (witness the oppositions, especially of dark and light, in Hawthorne, Poe, Melville, Emerson, and Whitman, for example). She is also a more complex, deep-thinking woman than many would suppose. Among the several qualities that draw me to Eliza Snow are the agility of her mind and the sureness of her intellect. When she playfully says, ". . . there's nobody here but Eliza and I," not only does she intentionally violate the grammatical principle that requires the objective case in that particular sentence, "Eliza and *me*," but she boldly reveals her sense that the world is not a simple, one-sided place and that she herself is not single, but compound.

Like Dickinson's "Nobody" and "you," and Whitman's "I" and "me, myself," Eliza Snow's two selves suggest a double perspective as well as a dual nature. We have already alluded to Eliza's practicality conjoined with her deep spirituality, her dynamic executive ability folded in with her artistry, her love of solitude matched by her delight in sweet society. We might also add, her capacity to guide and instruct mellowed by her immense compassion. In all, she was a woman of action and contemplation, garnished with a generous sense of humor.

The second "Retirement" poem cited above introduces a fine phrase that well describes its author: "native elasticity." We have seen that elasticity and understated humor in the poem about "Eliza and I." Those qualities also enliven the journals and the other poetry. For example, Eliza's trail diary entry for 11 October 1847 concludes with this note: "I made a cap for sis. J. Young for which she paid me in soap, 1 lb.& 15 oz. so much I call my own. I now begin once more to be a woman of property."[13] And note, too, rather than rounding the figure to two pounds, she cunningly specifies "1 lb. & 15 oz." On 4 January 1847, with the same finesse, Eliza makes this observation after a snow storm: ". . . the weather today will pass for winter."[14] In "Sketch of My Life" she tells of facing down a member of the militia in Missouri. He, unfortunate fellow, tried to browbeat her into denying her faith. At her firm rejoinder "his countenance dropped," she says, "and he responded, 'I must confess you are a better soldier than I am.' I passed on, thinking that, unless he was above the average of his fellows in that section, I was not complimented by his confession."[15]

One of my favorite passages in Eliza's autobiography, a resonant corollary to the dozens of buoyant, appreciative notations about scenery and weather recorded there, is the story of a night spent in a downpour, in a hut (shared with the temporarily absent Clara Decker Young) roofed only with mud and willows. The first winter in the Great Salt Lake Valley had been mild, and until now, mid-March, the roof had held. Eliza writes:

> Sally, an Indian girl who had been purchased from a tribe [to save her from execution] by which she was held captive, was with me. The roof of our dwelling was covered deeper with earth than the adjoining ones, consequently did not leak as soon, and some of my neighbors huddled in for shelter. One evening as several were sitting socially conversing in my room, the water commenced dropping in one place and then in another, and so on: they dodged it for a while, but it increased so rapidly, they concluded to return to their own wet houses. After they left, Sally wrapped herself in her buffalo robe on the floor, and I spread my umbrella over my head and shoulders as I ensconced myself in bed, the lower part being unshielded, was wet enough before morning. During the night, despite all discomfitures, I laughed involuntarily while alone in the darkness of the night I lay reflecting the ludicrous scene.[16]

Occasionally Eliza devotes an entire poem to humorous play with language and idea. Such a poem is "Mental Gas," which is composed as a dialogue between a student named Charles and his science teacher. Charles wants to know this:

> That space or vacuum, sir, explain—
> When solid sense forsakes the brain,
> Pray what supplies its place?

It is not air, as one might expect, the teacher explains, but something even less substantial, "lighter far than common air." When sense departs, "mental gas" ("Some Poets call it *pride*," the poet Eliza says) invades the head and "swell[s]" the "optics blind." If one wishes to acquire some of this gas, it can be "obtain'd / From sculls [skulls] whence sense is mostly drain'd, / or never had supplies."[17]

Eliza Snow is living proof that one's eye can be single to God's glory without being closed to humor or art, and without being constricted into tunnel vision. She grasped the whole of experience and understood that spirituality and temporality constitute the twin realities and necessities of human life. An immortal spirit resides in a mortal body. Her way of seeing and interpreting the world illustrates the broadness of her vision and the defining opposites in her nature.

Eliza penned this verse on the trail for Vilate Kimball, to bolster her spirits. The subject is duality, and the opposites are plainly overt.

> Thou much belov'd in Zion!
>   Remember life is made
> A double-sided picture,
>   Contrasting light and shade.
>
> Our Father means to prove us—
>   And here we're fully tried.
> He will reverse the drawing
>   And show the *better* side
>
> And then we'll be astonish'd
>   That ignorance could throw
> Such dismal shades of darkness,
>   Where light and beauty glow.
>
> The mists that hide the future
>   Are round our vision thrown;
> But when, as *seen, we're seeing,*
>   And *know as we are known,*

Whatever seems forbidding,
And tending to annoy;
Will, like dull shadows vanish,
Or *turn* to *crowns* of *joy*.[18]

Throughout her poetry and prose, and even her reported speeches, her subjects and her carefully balanced rhetoric declare that Eliza Snow saw life as a blend of opposites—dark and light, loss and compensation, works and faith—seasoned with a generous spoonful of humor. Some of her less formal writing demonstrates that same habit of mind. For example, in commenting on the departure of "Bishop W. & family" for the Valley, she writes in her trail diary, "It seems almost like the days of Peleg when the earth was divided but we hope to follow soon—may be the pleasure of meeting compensates for the parting."[19] Her very eyes seemed to take in the two sides of whatever lay before her. Camped one night "on an opposite hill" from the main group, she writes, "Here we have a fine view of the general Camp which presents a curious appearance of grandeur & rusticity."[20] I note that she does not say "rustic grandeur," as I might have, but instead sets up the balanced opposites and joins them with the conjunction *and*—"grandeur & rusticity." Her entry for 22 November 1846, which juxtaposes negative and positive observations without so much as a blink, is typical: "My health quite ill. The day very fine."[21]

Eliza is even more likely to juxtapose the spiritual and the practical, again without apology, as in this entry for 22 September 1847: "Mother Chase & I have a rich treat [lovely spiritual experience] in the carriage—with a promise of new int. [intelligence] if diligent & submissive.—Br. Love lost an ox—Capt. P. buys a pair & a cow & calf."[22] Her entry for 8 November 1847 reads, "A meeting of the young ladies at Ellens this eve. It was truly a time of the outpouring of the spirit of God." Immediately below that statement is the short entry for 9 November: "Br. P. brought us a mince pie."[23] The Spirit and livestock; the Spirit and mince pie.

It took a poet's eye to apprehend the phenomenon, but these kinds of opposites in tandem seemed to define the Saints' lives, as an entry two weeks later attests: ". . . for some days past the breth.

have been ploughing & dragging with the ground cover'd with snow. This day they commence baptizing."[24] Ploughing and baptizing, all in the same breath. It is really to be expected that enterprises of spirit and body would characterize lives in the community of Saints. They did then, and they do still. A recent Relief Society bulletin in my own ward advertised, without comment, that mini-classes for the next homemaking meeting included "Scripture Study" and "Portable Potties." Eliza would have chuckled approvingly. While most of us write and read such announcements without even noticing the incongruencies, Eliza catches and absorbs them with one glance of the eye and one sweep of the pen. She sees and makes apparent what most of us overlook.

Almost inseparable from the theme of opposition is that of mutability. In this world, Time (convention personified the word) cannot be stopped, and change is inevitable. The only permanence, Eliza knew, lies in the truths of the gospel of salvation, revealed and made possible through divine mercy and priesthood power. In her choice of themes, Eliza Snow may have looked in part to such accomplished mentors as John Milton and William Shakespeare. The latter wrote a good many sonnets in which he bewailed the ravages of "this bloody tyrant, Time" (sonnet XVI), "Devouring Time" (sonnet XIX), whose "cruel hand" (sonnet LX) "decays" even "gates of steel" (sonnet LXV) in its "thievish progress to eternity" (sonnet LXXVII). As the great bard saw it, his only weapon against Time was the survival of his art, and his only strategy, a humanistic one: "I will be true, despite thy scythe and thee" (sonnet CXXIII).

Milton, on the other hand, was a person of immense religious knowledge and faith, and his poem "On Time" may have suggested to the poet-saint of Zion not only a subject, but also a resolution in harmony with her own belief. Milton opens his poem with a scornful dismissal of Time: "Fly envious *Time*, till thou run out thy race."[25]

The artistry of Eliza's serious poetry must be viewed and assessed in light of the models available to her. She had not the genius of an Emily Dickinson, to burst the seams of old forms, nor the brash unorthodoxy of a Walt Whitman, to flout every respected convention. But she did have a gift, for both language and life. I

conclude this essay with excerpts from a most worthy poem, digni-
fied by the same blank verse (unrhymed iambic pentameter) that
Shakespeare chose for the noblest sections of his plays, and enlarged by heaven's grace. Her subject, again, is a consideration of
Time and opposition, life's inescapable change and duality. But this
particular poem is not her customary rhymed nod to the departing
year. The listed date of composition, in Eliza's Nauvoo journal and
notebook, is 1 January 1844. She revised the poem for inclusion in
volume 2 of the *Poems*, and the extracts below are from the later
rendering as she published it. This, I submit, is the work of a poet,
and I regret damaging her flawless rhythmic scheme by breaking
lines for omissions. The reader should note the unobtrusive integra-
tion of paralleled opposites and balanced compound structures.
Form and content work in nearly perfect conjunction.

The Past Year

. . . .

Where is the Year? Envelop'd in the past,
With all its scenes and all its sceneries
Upon its bosom laid. The Year has gone
To join in fellowship with all the years
Before and since the flood: leaving behind
A train of consequences—those effects,
Which, like a fond, paternal legacy
That firmly binds with int'rest, kin to kin;
United the future, present, and the past.

The Year is gone. None but Omnipotence
Can weigh it in the balance, and define
The good and evil mingled in its form.
None but an Omnipresent eye can view
The fountains and the springs of joy and grief—
Of pain and pleasure, which, within its course,
It open'd up and caus'd to flow thro'out
The broad variety of human life.
None else is able to explore the length
And breadth . . .

. . . .
Or count the seeds of bitterness . . .

. . . .
Or number the bright rays of happiness,
Whether in sunbeams written, or defin'd
By those soft, mellow pencilings of light,
Whose lack of dazzling brilliancy, is more
Than compensated by their constancy
In ev'ry-day attendance: little joys,
Which shed a soothing infl'ence on the heart. . . .

. . . .
            Ev'ry spirit is arous'd,
Both good and bad—each to its handy work;
Diffusing in the walks of social life,
Their honey and their gall. . . .

. . . .
A few more years of hurried scenery
Will tell the tale—the present drama close—
Decide the destiny of multitudes,
And bring this generation to the point
Where Time, extending to its utmost bound,
Will tread the threshhold of Eternity.[26]

My eyes and mind linger, with deep enjoyment, on that exquisite image of "mellow pencilings of light." It is a line I wish I had written myself, or were capable of writing.

For Zion's poet-testifier, there are no questions that God cannot answer, even if there are some that mortal understanding struggles merely to frame. She knew that ultimately all dualities, all time, and all change are subsumed in the magnificent unfolding of immortality. This is Eliza Snow's everlasting message, this is the affirmation of her trust, this is the force behind her art and behind the labor which her art was made to serve. Is it any wonder, then, that while many of Emily Dickinson's poems end with an introspective question, virtually all of Eliza Roxcy Snow's serious poems conclude with an expansive declaration of eternal promise? In a moment of despair,

British writer Matthew Arnold concluded in his poem "Dover Beach" that aside from human affection there is no certitude in this life, no help for pain; but Eliza Snow knew that there was. I love Emily Dickinson with my sometimes stumbling poet's soul, and at times I feel Matthew Arnold's anguish, but Eliza Snow is the enlightened hero of my faith.

NOTES

1. See Eliza R. Snow, *The Personal Writings of Eliza Roxcy Snow*, ed. Maureen Ursenbach Beecher (Salt Lake City: University of Utah Press, 1995).

2. For a dramatist's response to Eliza, see Elizabeth Hansen's play *A High and Glorious Place*, 1996.

3. Snow, *Personal Writings*, p.139.

4. Eliza R. Snow, "To Mrs.—," *Poems, Religious, Historical, and Political*, vol. 2 (Salt Lake City: Latter-day Saints' Printing and Publishing Establishment, 1877), pp. 195–96.

5. Emily Dickinson, *The Complete Poems of Emily Dickinson*, ed. Thomas H. Johnson (Boston: Little, Brown and Co., 1960), #478, p. 230.

6. Snow, "The Narrow Way," *Poems, Religious, Historical, and Political*, vol. 1 (Liverpool: F. D. Richards, 1856), pp. 221–22.

7. Snow, "Yes, I Would Be a Saint," *Personal Writings*, p. 42; see also *Poems*, vol. 1, p. 3.

8. Dickinson, *The Complete Poems*, #441, p. 211.

9. Ibid., p. 133.

10. Snow, "My Epitaph," *Poems*, vol. 2, p. 188. There are slight variations in the version published with Eliza's funeral proceedings; see *The Life and Labors of Eliza R. Snow Smith* (Salt Lake City, 1888), p. 37.

11. Snow, "Retirement," *Personal Writings*, p. 64.

12. Snow, "Retirement," *Poems*, vol. 2, pp. 183–84.

13. Snow, *Personal Writings*, p. 207.

14. Ibid., p. 151.

15. Ibid., p. 12.

16. Ibid., pp. 30–31.

17. Snow, "Mental Gas," *Poems*, vol. 1, pp. 49–50.

18. Snow, "To Mrs. V. Kimball," *Personal Writings*, pp. 130–31; see also *Poems*, vol. 1, p. 177.

19. Snow, *Personal Writings*, p. 133.

20. Ibid., p. 143.

21. Ibid., p. 146.

22. Ibid., p. 202.

23. Ibid., p. 211, 212.

24. Ibid., p. 212.

25. John Milton, "On Time," *Complete Poems and Major Prose,* ed. Merritt Y. Hughes (New York: Odyssey Press, 1957), p. 80.

26. "The Past Year," in *Poems,* vol. 2, pp. 11–12; see also Snow, *Personal Writings,* pp. 94–95.

Marilyn Arnold, who holds a Ph.D. in American literature from the University of Wisconsin, is an emeritus professor of English at Brigham Young University. She is the author of academic books and articles as well as articles for Church periodicals. Her most recent book is *Sweet Is the Word: Reflections on the Book of Mormon, Its Narrative, Teachings, and People.* She has also prepared lessons for Church curriculum and served on the Sunday School general board. With this essay Marilyn hopes to bring a new perspective to Latter-day Saints' appreciation of Eliza R. Snow.

6

"Wonderful, Unfailing Friend"
Jane Manning James
1821(?)–1908

*O*ctober 7, 1979—that was the day I was finally baptized and confirmed a member of The Church of Jesus Christ of Latter-day Saints. I was 18 years old. I say I was "finally" baptized, because I had been introduced to the principles of the gospel about two years before that time. Unfortunately my mother and my stepfather had not granted me their permission to enter into that covenant until I was 18. So, I waited.

During those two years I learned so many wonderful things that enhanced my life and helped to make it more ful-filling. For example, I learned about the pur-pose and need for the various auxiliaries of the Church. I began to understand certain doctrinal aspects and to appreciate the Church's history. I also began to realize that countless other Saints had endured the pains of having to wait for their long-promised day. Shortly after my baptism I realized that I had embarked upon a spir-itually guided journey to happiness, and that the journey would lead me safely into the eternities if I would but choose to travel its course to the end. I know that fact to be true now more than ever before.

Jane Manning James

71

Thus, my formal entrance into the Church was well worth the wait.

As a convert I learned of Latter-day Saint pioneers whose contributions were significant in the reestablishment of the Lord's church. From their stories I gained a great appreciation for the ongoing sacrifices they made, the trials they endured, and the capacity they exhibited to give of themselves continually for the Lord's cause. Now as a wife and mother, I have been touched many times by stories of pioneer women having to care for their sick children during the trek to the Great Salt Lake Valley. My heart has often been saddened to learn of the deaths of so many of those children who never saw the place where the kingdom of God would be established.

There is another population among our early pioneers that I have come to value highly: our early black pioneers. I feel as I do about that distinct group of people for several reasons, one of which being that I too am black. As a result of that commonality my heart and my soul have been touched by the stories of these pioneers in a manner that is very real and very personal. More important, I have come to value their experiences because they can be a strength not only to me and my family but to all members of the Church.

I was a senior at Brigham Young University and attending a class titled "Blacks in the Mormon Culture" when I first learned some of the histories of our black pioneers in greater depth. So few know the stories behind such names as Samuel and Amanda Chambers, Green Flake, the Grice family, or the Leggroan family, to name just a few, though all were black pioneers of The Church of Jesus Christ of Latter-day Saints, and all had stories worthy of being told, retold, and valued by Church members. But for now, this essay is about one particular black pioneer. It is about her character and her contribution to the Church and its members, past and present; about a woman who helped to pave the way for me. Her name is Jane.

Jane Elizabeth Manning was born in the small town of Wilton, Connecticut, to Isaac and Eliza Manning in the early 1800s. She and the members of her family were born free. They were fortunate enough to have escaped the unimaginable pains of slavery that their ancestors had suffered, but what they did not escape was the never-ending unpleasantness placed upon them because of the color of their skin.

After Jane and other family members joined the Church, they possessed a tremendous desire to gather with the Saints in Nauvoo. So in the fall of 1843, their journey began. There must have been excitement coupled with great anxiety as Jane and her family started on their way. But they soon encountered opposition, which made for a difficult trip. In her own words Jane tells of the experience: "We started from Wilton, Conn., and travelled by Canal to Buffalo, N.Y. We were to go to Columbus Ohio before our fares were to be collected, but they insisted on having the money at Buffalo and would not take us farther. So we left the boat, and started on foot to travel a distance of over eight hundred miles."[1]

I am humbled by Jane's determination and persistence to continue on her journey to a place where she had never been. I am strengthened by her faith to embark on that unforeseen quest to reach Nauvoo, with an assurance that God would protect her and her loved ones.

When I left for England as a full-time missionary I had no idea what experiences awaited me. I remember feeling prepared and anxious to do the Lord's will, but at the same time feeling nervous about what I would find once I arrived. As I look back I feel joy in knowing that the mission I served for the Lord was a successful one. But I will never forget the times of persecution I faced because I was a representative of the Church and because I was black.

In one of the areas in which my companion and I had been tracting, a group of young people threw rocks at us as we swiftly pedaled away. The obscenities and familiar yet hurtful racial slurs from my spirit brothers and sisters were ringing in my ears for days thereafter.

I try with all the energy I can muster to not let such experiences pain me too deeply. Nevertheless, there are times when the hurt seems to have more power than I do. When Jane had similar experiences she seemed to maintain a firm hold on the power that is greater than us all—the power of the Lord.

As I continue to push ahead on my own unforeseen journeys of life, I know that I will often be confronted with displeasing situations, whether they be due to race, religion, gender, or other factors. I pray that I will someday acquire the determination, persistence, and power that Jane possessed in order to carry on.

During the course of the Mannings' trek to Nauvoo, it became hard for them to continue because their feet were in so much pain. Jane shares the following: "We walked until our shoes were worn out, and our feet became sore and cracked open and bled until you could see the whole print of our feet with blood on the ground."[2]

It is difficult to lead a group of people when one is physically weak, and much more so when those being led are suffering as well. Jane had that role but witnessed to us all how difficult tasks can be tackled. She continues her account: "We stopped and united in prayer to the Lord, we asked God the Eternal Father to heal our feet and our prayers were answered and our feet were healed *forthwith*."[3] The 10th edition of Merriam-Webster's Collegiate Dictionary defines the word *forthwith* as meaning "immediately." That's powerful—to know that Jane and her family had such a fitting miracle occur to them because they offered a sincere prayer of faith to their Father in Heaven.

To successfully continue their journey, Jane and her family needed their feet to be healed, and that need was met. So often I look at the miracles or blessings others have received and I wish for similar, if not the same, miracles to come my way. I think many of us are guilty of this. But I am realizing that when my needs and the needs of my family are met, a fitting miracle has occurred, even if it is much more subtle than the miracle that the Manning family received. And if I show my gratitude by recognizing all of the blessings that Heavenly Father gives to me in my daily life, when my journey is through and I am blessed to behold him, that great moment will be even more wonderful as a result of my having acknowledged him in all things.

At last Jane and her family arrived in Nauvoo, where they could be among the Saints. O blessed day! Good fortune had it that the Prophet Joseph, along with his wife, Emma, were waiting for them, and they welcomed the Mannings into their home. It was they who greeted the Mannings in Nauvoo and extended the invitation to "come in, come in!"[4]

That was the beginning of what marked Jane's longstanding relationship with the Prophet Joseph and Emma Smith, with whom she stayed until shortly before the Martyrdom. The Prophet assured Jane that she was among friends and promised her that she would be protected. That promise was never broken.

In 1846 Jane, her husband, Isaac, and son Sylvester were among those who left Nauvoo, endured the perils of Winter Quarters, then made the move to the Rocky Mountains. Another son, Silas, was born along the way.

Once established in the Valley, Jane, like the other Saints, must have eagerly awaited the completion of the Salt Lake Temple. She made many inquiries of Church leaders regarding the temple of the Lord. Although she had not received much of a formal education, she did gain a spiritual education pertaining to the gospel of Jesus Christ after she was baptized, and because of her understanding and appreciation of the plan of salvation, one of her strongest desires was to enter the house of the Lord to receive her own endowment. Although she was able to participate in baptisms for the dead, her desire to receive her endowment was never granted because her skin was black.[5]

I can recall the day I went to the temple to receive my own endowments like it was only yesterday. It was 3 May 1986, one month before I was to enter the Missionary Training Center in Provo, Utah. I shall never forget that day. As a person of color it is difficult for me to feel accepted in many places, but in the house of the Lord I felt fully accepted for the first time in my life. I felt acceptance and love from my Heavenly Father and his son, Jesus Christ, and the eternal vision concerning my relationship to them finally began to unfold for me. Maybe Jane wanted to feel that too before she died. Still, her faith was unfailing, whereas my faith is sometimes weak.

In spite of Jane's disappointment in being denied the privilege of receiving her endowments, she remained strong, and continued to "press forward with a steadfastness in Christ, having a perfect brightness of hope, and a love of God and of all men" (2 Nephi 31:20).

Many of the Saints in the Valley were very needy and had little to subsist on individually, let alone enough to impart to others. Jane experienced prosperous years but more often her means were small; nevertheless, even during these difficult times she exhibited a generous spirit. Eliza Lyman relates a story in support of Jane's loving heart. At this particular time Eliza's husband, Elder Amasa M. Lyman, had gone with Porter Rockwell on a mission to California. She writes: "He left us without anything from which to make bread, it not being in his power to get it. Not long after Amasa had gone, Jane James, the colored woman, let me have two pounds of flour, it being half of what she had."[6] Jane was a woman who understood the meaning of charity. She understood what it means to love God with all of our hearts, and to love our neighbors as ourselves.

My family's means are small. We are always blessed to have enough to sustain us, and we are grateful for that. I must admit, though, that it has been a challenge for me to not have a great deal of substance to give to others. But, like Jane, I want to learn how to give what little we do have and to feel good about that. I know that it's not really *what* one gives but *how* one gives that matters. The Savior gave of his heart and of his soul. I believe Jane followed his example as closely as she knew how. I am seeking to do the same.

When Jane died in 1908 her funeral was attended by a large number of friends whose lives she had touched. In tribute to Jane, the *Deseret News* printed the following statements:

> Few persons were more noted for faith and faithfulness than was Jane Manning James, and though of the humble of the earth she numbered friends and acquaintances by the hundreds. Many persons will regret to learn that the kind and generous soul has passed from the earth.[7]

> The house was crowded, many in the congregation being of her own race. Flowers in profusion were contributed by friends who had learned to respect the deceased for her undaunted faith and goodness of heart.

> A sketch of her life, as dictated by Mrs. James, was read by Mrs. Elizabeth J. D. Roundy, and the speakers were President Joseph F. Smith and Bishop T. A. Clawson.[8]

Jane was buried in the Salt Lake City Cemetery.

Gospel music and hymns are an important part of my life and my heritage. They probably were important in Jane's life as well. During a trip to Southern California my family and I were able to visit my grandmother, who is a member of a Pentecostal church where gospel hymns are sung a great deal. While looking through her hymnbook I found a song that was suitable in describing Jane. She mentioned in her "Life Sketch" how she and her family sang hymns and praised

God for his goodness as they walked to Nauvoo. Perhaps a hymn titled "Wonderful, Unfailing Friend" was one that her family sang:

> There never was a truer Friend than Jesus,
> He hears me when my heart for mercy pleads;
> (for mercy pleads)
> And no one knows my burdens like my Jesus,
> For He alone can understand my needs.
> There never was a truer Friend than Jesus,
> My sorrows He will always with me share;
> (with me share)
> And since He bore His cross, my blessed Jesus,
> There is no cross He will not help me bear.
> Wonderful, Unfailing Friend is Jesus,
> He fills my soul with singing all the day;
> Wonderful, Eternal Friend is Jesus,
> And He'll go with me all the way.
> (all the way)
> There never was a truer Friend than Jesus,
> He is my life and strength, my all in all;
> (my all in all)
> Upon the strong and loving arms of Jesus
> My soul shall rest, and never, never fall.
> Wonderful, Unfailing Friend is Jesus,
> He fills my soul with singing all the day;
> Wonderful, Eternal Friend is Jesus,
> And He'll go with me all the way.
> (all the way)[9]

Jane Elizabeth Manning's life can inspire anyone who strives to be a follower of Christ. She is a woman to look to as one who bore her own cross and was worthy to be called Jesus' friend. How grateful I am that her life can teach me how I might be a better friend to my Savior.

Jane's life reminds us all that it's not the color of the skin that matters; it's the quality of the heart. She gives us hope in knowing that through the power of the Spirit, we may overcome. Her life was a testimony of that.

NOTES

1.   Jane Manning James, "Life Sketch of Jane Elizabeth Manning James," in Henry J. Wolfinger, "A Test of Faith: Jane Elizabeth James and the Origins of the Utah Black Community," Clark Knowlton, ed., *Social Accommodation in Utah* (Salt Lake City: University of Utah, 1975), p. 152.

2.   Ibid.

3.   Ibid.

4.   Ibid., p. 153.

5.   See ibid., pp. 148–51.

6.   Ibid., p. 131.

7.   *Deseret News,* 16 April 1908, as quoted in Kate B. Carter, *The Negro Pioneer* (Salt Lake City: Daughters of Utah Pioneers, 1965), p. 11.

8.   *Deseret News,* 21 April 1908, as quoted in Carter, *The Negro Pioneer,* p. 11.

9.   Albert Simpson Reitz, "Wonderful, Unfailing Friend Is Jesus," in Paul Rader, comp., *Tabernacle Hymns No. 2* (Chicago: Tabernacle Publishing Co., 1921), p. 197.

৵

Lita Little Giddins earned a bachelor's degree in sociocultural anthropology and a master's degree in social work from Brigham Young University, where she performed with the Young Ambassadors. She has made vocal recordings and performed on stage, on television, in commercials, and in Church videos. A native of Chicago, she now lives in Athens, Ohio, with her husband, Kevin Giddins, and their two daughters. Lita has been inspired by Jane Manning James and considers herself related to Jane as "a mutual sister in Zion."

7

"I Shall Know They Are True"
Susan Kent Greene
1816–1860

*W*hy don't you become great, like your great-grandmother?" questioned Edwin Kent Greene of his 15-year-old daughter, Shirley, who had just made this stirring declaration of her intent: "I want to make the world turn, and I want it to turn sharply!"

In a tone of surprise, not being aware of any evidence that might have classified her great-grandmother as one who made the world turn, Shirley asked her father, "What did she do?" After a moment of silent reflection, he responded to his daughter's earnest question.

"What did she do?" He repeated the question, and then, looking tenderly at this young woman who wanted to make a difference, leave a mark, break a record, simply said, "She loved the Lord, kept a good home, and raised a fine family."

Shirley turned away without comment, not satisfied with the answer but unable to let it go. Like a seed planted in fertile soil, hardly noticed at the time of planting, the thought took root and began to grow. Today, with years gone by, Shirley now stands where her great-grandmother stood,

Susan Kent Greene

79

and better comprehends. She loves the Lord, has a good home, and has raised a fine family of eleven children; and the married ones love the Lord, have good homes, and are raising fine families. The last lines of a poem written by her daughter Rebecca give evidence that the seed is still growing: "An inheritance supreme I gained from Mom—my great ambition: just to pass it on."

The Apostle Paul, wanting young Timothy to understand about the gifts of the Spirit, a legacy of faith passed from one generation to the next, spoke in these words: "I call to remembrance the un-feigned faith that is in thee, which dwelt first in thy grandmother Lois, and thy mother Eunice; and I am persuaded that in thee also" (2 Timothy 1:5).

My family also has a legacy of faith. In significant measure, this legacy has root in the life of a pioneer woman, Susan Kent Greene—great-grandmother to my sister Shirley and my two other sisters, my brother, and me.

There is a lineage, a continuity, an eternal fabric that is carefully woven over time into a dynamic tapestry that is passed from one generation to the next. The tapestry of our family has been woven from some of the same fabric as that of The Church of Jesus Christ of Latter-day Saints. The threads portray historic events ranging from the building of the Kirtland Temple in Ohio to the first break-ing of sod for the Cardston Temple in western Canada by Susan's son, Daniel Kent Greene, to my participation in the Utah statehood centennial celebrations in 1996.

On Memorial Day, 27 May 1996, I stood at the graveside of Daniel Kent, Susan's father, in Chester, Ohio, just a mile or two from Kirtland. The inscription on the broken headstone was hardly read-able: "Daniel Kent, born December the 31st, 1778; died July 23, 1853." Daniel Kent's wife and Susan's mother, Nancy Young Kent, was Brigham Young's sister. She was born 6 August 1786 in Ver-mont, and died 22 September 1860 in Salt Lake City, Utah. Susan was the sixth child and fifth daughter born to Daniel and Nancy, 3 April 1816, in Genoa, Cayuga County, New York.

To that hallowed ground in Kirtland, Ohio, where testimonies of faith were forged in the fire of adversity, Susan and her husband, Evan, a schoolteacher, had come soon after their marriage in 1835.

There, a temple of God was built by Latter-day Saints, led by a prophet of God, under extreme conditions of sacrifice and faith. Susan and Evan were acquainted with the Prophet Joseph. They were among the favored early members of the Church who helped with the building of the Kirtland Temple and received glorious manifestations, gifts, blessings, and promises in that holy edifice.

On that Memorial Day weekend as I stood at Daniel Kent's grave, it seemed that the clock stopped and the calendar rolled back for a brief moment, allowing a glimpse into the past. Within the walls of the Kirtland Temple, a marvelous choir united their voices in singing "The Spirit of God." I thought of the words of Zebedee Coltrin, who spoke of the wondrous events that occurred in the temple in 1836: "I have seen the power of God as it was on the day of Pentecost. . . . I saw the Lord high and lifted up. The angels of God rested upon the Temple and we heard their voices singing heavenly music."[1]

We sat in those historic pews where earlier Saints had sat for such a short time before being driven out. We saw the pulpit where Jesus Christ had appeared. We reviewed Heber C. Kimball's account of Sidney Rigdon's plea to the Almighty: "Looking at the sufferings and poverty of the Church, [Sidney] frequently used to go upon the walls of the building both by night and day and frequently wetting the walls with his tears, crying aloud to the Almighty to send means whereby we might accomplish the building."[2]

From the life sketch of Susan Kent Greene, written by her daughter Lula Greene Richards, we learn of her part and her faith in those early days of the Church:

"Susan was nearly sixteen years old when tidings of the religious works of the prophet Joseph Smith were brought to the notice of her near kindred and herself, who were strict Methodists. Her uncle Joseph (Brigham Young's brother), in the Young family, was a man of such saintlike characteristics and angelic life that when Susan heard that some of her uncles and aunts and their father, John Young Sr., were investigating the new religion, she said emphatically, 'If Uncle Joseph accepts those new teachings concerning religion, I shall know they are true.' That proof of the genuineness of the new religion was soon made manifest; but there were also other proofs which were readily accepted by this sincere young worshipper of God and seeker after his pure saving laws. Her father, Daniel Kent, like other real Methodists, believed in prayer; and morning and evening called his family together, and they all knelt and unitedly gave thanks for all blessings bestowed by our Heavenly Father and asked for continued help and guidance. After a careful reading and studying of the Book of Mormon, the following beautiful testimony of its truth was given to that honest worshipper and his devoted family: One morning while they were engaged in family prayer, the head of the household as usual voicing their united petitions, his speech was suddenly changed to another language, new and not understood by any of the family but the speaker himself. This remarkable and unexpected manifestation of an unseen power, before the petition was ended, simply changed again to the supplicant's usual manner of speech, giving a clear interpretation of the words which had been spoken in the unknown language. That interpretation was a strong and powerful declaration of the truth of the Book of Mormon and the divinity of the calling and the work of the prophet Joseph Smith.

"Susan's conviction of the truth of the Gospel restored to the earth in latter days was so strong that she could not reject it, although to join the hated and reviled Church of Jesus Christ of Latter-day Saints cost her so great a sacrifice that it came near taking her life. For two days and nights, friends and the family of which she was a favorite member all mourned her as dead. The sacrifice that she had to make [in becoming] one of the despised and persecuted Mormons was the giving up of a young man to whom she had given her maiden love with very high hopes of future happiness, but whose worldly pride would not let him have anything to do with one who favored the 'new religion' of whom he had heard so much evil spoken. When Susan became convinced of this fact concerning her lover, so deep was the wound occasioned to her sensitive heart that she could partake of no nourishment, and after some days she lapsed into a coma so profound it had the appearance of actual death, and was so considered and mourned over by those about her. But at five o'clock on the afternoon of the second day of her death-like sleep, as the clock was striking, Susan's eyes opened;

and she said to her mother, who was bending over her, 'Five o'-clock—how long have I slept?' On April 14th, 1832, Susan was baptized a member of the Church of Jesus Christ of Latter-day Saints."[3]

In her tender years Susan Kent covenanted in the waters of baptism to stand as a witness of God at all times and in all places, not knowing then where those places would be or what would be required in faith and endurance. Again from the writings of her daughter Lula:

"Two years after Susan's baptism, her cousin, Evan M. Greene, visited the town in which the Kents resided, and engaged employment there as a schoolteacher for a year. Soon after his arrival in the place he attended a testimony meeting of the Latter-day Saints, in which Susan bore a strong and interesting testimony in evidence of the truth of the Gospel as restored to the earth through the instrumentality of the prophet Joseph Smith. By listening to the young woman's talk, the feeling came to Evan that he would certainly be happy to become the husband of a girl who had so clear an understanding of and so great a love for the Gospel of Truth, as his cousin's remarks bore witness of, and that if he could win her affections he would certainly marry her and take her to Kirtland with him when he should return to his parents' home in that place. After gaining the consent of the parents, he asked Susan if she would accompany him as his bride to Kirtland, the then gathering place of the Saints. And Susan concluded that she loved her cousin Evan and the work of the Lord to which he was so ardently devoted sufficiently well to be true to them always, and so she accepted his proposal. At the time Susan's father said that she would not live a year as her health had always been so poor. She was very small, never weighed 100 pounds in her life. Two children were born to Evan and Susan while they remained with the Church in Kirtland, a daughter and a son. The daughter died when she was two years old and was buried in the Mormon graveyard there, which was the beginning of their real personal sorrows."[4]

Returning from Kirtland to my home, in full view of the Bountiful Temple, I wondered, *Is it possible to comprehend the blessings that come so easily to us today, available only through the endurance and faith of those who built up the kingdom in those early years? Their tests were constant, and their afflictions great. As we learn of the faith of those whose blood now courses through our veins, will we take their torch and hold it high as we learn from the past and face the future?*

Lula's narrative continues:

"They went with the body of the Church to Missouri and from there to Nauvoo, Illinois, where they again had the privilege of assisting to build a temple to the Lord and of receiving their blessings therein. They also witnessed the manifestation showing that the office and calling of the Prophet Joseph Smith had fallen upon Brigham Young. Their testimonies were strengthened even while their faith was tried. . . .

"Susan and Evan were among the first of those driven from Nauvoo to reach Mt. Pisgah, Iowa early in the summer of 1846. As soon as Evan had selected a spot of ground upon which to place their tent, for they were so fortunate as to possess one, he pitched it and there left with it his wife and their little ones while he went with his team and wagon to aid in bringing forward some of the Saints who were without means of their own and depended upon their brethren for assistance. Evan and Susan had, then, five living children. She, with her little ones, was left with no near neighbors. Almost as soon as her husband had gone, the baby, a lovely eleven-month-old girl, became very ill. Under those sad conditions she watched her little one grow weaker, until on the 16th of June, 1846, the gentle spirit was released. When Susan saw her baby grow cold and lifeless in her lap, she began to realize the utter loneliness of her situation more keenly than she had done before. To add still to the distress through which she was passing, it was a dark, rainy evening when the child died. She could only trust and pray earnestly that God would not forsake her and her children in that hour of extreme sorrow and helplessness. Her prayers were answered. About ten o'-clock a young man came to the door of the tent. The young man remained during the night and watched with the bereft mother over her dead, and the next day he made a little coffin for it. Susan had to prepare her dear dead child herself for its last long retreat. The young man dug the grave, and the babe was buried, which may have been the first Mormon burial on the noted Mt. Pisgah.

"Here at Mt. Pisgah, just a year after her baby had died, another baby was born, Melissa Greene Homer, in June of 1847.

"In the coming years, Susan would continue to carry her burdens dutifully, and lend strength to others not yet fully converted.

"At the time, President Brigham Young and his associate officers in the Church were making experimental efforts to have the United Order, or Order of Enoch, more fully established among their people. Susan and her family were among the converted ones, hence her favorite allusions to the subject.

"This letter was sent to her daughter, Lula Greene Richards, in Salt Lake City, when Lula was first editor of the *Woman's Exponent*, . . . and it was published in that paper.

> Smithfield, Cache County, Utah
> May 20, 1874

To My Dear Sisters, Women of the Latter-day Saint Church, . . .

. . . I can bear testimony that this uniting of the people together is of God for in his mercy and in his Holy Spirit he showed me the order more than twenty-seven years ago. The winter after we left Nauvoo when we were stopped at Council Bluffs and were destitute, often of even daily bread, when our men had to go to Missouri and work for a little corn and bacon to keep their families alive, while the women would stay at home and pray and fast—the latter they were sometimes obligated to do, I can speak for one at least—then we trusted in the Lord. We had nothing else to trust in. One day I got so faint and weak I had to lie down on the bed and my heart was drawn out in prayer and supplication to our Heavenly Father. I began to think how many good things there were in the world, how many people lived in pride and luxury while others were famishing for the commonest necessities of life, and a vision was opened to my mind. The Lord showed me the time when the Saints shall inherit the earth, when the spirit of the Lord shall be poured out upon them and the kingdom and the greatness of the kingdom shall be given to them and they shall possess it forever.

The contemplation of this has often been a great consolation to me since that time in days of poverty and distress and in the darkest hours I have never doubted that the Lord will yet do for his people what he then showed me he would do. But I will tell you further what he did for me at that time. How true it is he never forsakes them that trust in him. There was "A Good Samaritan" at hand. A sister who was living about three-quarters of a mile from me was impressed to come and see how I was getting along, knowing that I was alone with my little ones. In obedience to the impulse she came bringing with her a prairie chicken, one of several which they had caught in a trap. It was all dressed ready for cooking and she was not long in preparing me some broth, just what I needed in my weak and delicate state. And did I not thank Heavenly Father and that dear sister for their kindness to me. Can I doubt that God's care has been over his Saints or that he will cease to care for them?

Signed: Susan Kent Greene

". . . As soon as Evan was released from his mission they came on to Utah, arriving about the first of November, 1852. They had oxen and a wagon, but the oxen were poor and the wagon heavily loaded; and Susan had so much pity for the oxen that she could not ride and see them burdened so, so she walked most of the way and when there was an ear of corn to spare she would walk in front of the oxen and show them the corn once in a while, letting them take a little nip of it to encourage them on. They left about July 15, 1852, and arrived around the first of November, 1852.

"When they reached Salt Lake City they thought their journey was ended, but not so. Brigham Young requested Evan to go on to Provo and open a high school. Worn out as they were with their long journey across the plains, it seemed hard to travel on three or four more days longer; but on they went to Provo, and after reaching there Susan was very ill for a long time with a nervous fever from the effects of her travel.

"Later the Greenes were called to help pioneer other areas. In the late fall of 1863, Evan and Susan were called to move to Bear Lake, Idaho. Of the thirteen children Susan bore only seven were living after the Idaho storms had taken their toll."[5]

Susan inherited the faith of her mother, Nancy Young, who inherited the faith of *her* mother, Nabby Howe, who was also the mother of Brigham Young. The faith passed to Susan Kent Greene was reflected in the faith and dedication of her sons and daughters. Her eighth child, Lula Greene Richards, would play an important role among the women of the Church in those early years. In the May 1969 *Improvement Era*, historian Leonard J. Arrington writes of Louisa Lula Greene Richards:

> [Louisa] felt impressed that the young girls in the Church should have their own magazine. . . . Louisa wrote Eliza R. Snow, president of the Relief Society of the Church and a relative, asking for counsel. . . . [Sister Snow] wrote to Louisa that she would broach the matter to President Brigham Young, and suggested a plan of finance. President Young not only relayed his sanction, but, in Louisa's words, said "he would gladly appoint me the mission and bless me in it.". . .
>
> . . . The *Woman's Exponent* was the first publication owned and edited by Latter-day Saint women. It was also the first magazine (with one fly-by-night exception) published by and for women west of the Mississippi River.[6]

Lula was a great source of comfort and joy to her mother, Susan. It was from her mother's life journey, her courage and faith, that Lula was prepared to face her own frontier, to be guided by the Spirit, to respond to any request made of Church leaders, and to walk by faith.

Susan Kent Greene died on 17 April 1888, but her influence lives on. She has been a part of my strength and faith as I live my life and carry out the responsibilities placed upon me.

On 6 January 1981, just prior to my 50th birthday, I was reading and pondering Great-Grandmother Susan's journal. I thought of her life, her faith, her endurance, and I was drawn to read and reread an entry she had made at age 59 on the front page of her journal, dated 3 February 1875:

I make this covenant to do the very best I can, asking God for

wisdom to direct me in that I may walk with Him in all righteousness and truth. I much desire to be pure in heart that I may see God. Help me, Lord, to overcome all evil with good.
Signed: Susan Kent Greene

This covenant with the writings on this page is written with my blood and I have not broken my covenant and trust shall not.
Signed: Susan Kent Greene

On that day I wrote the words of Susan Kent Greene on the first page of *my* journal for 1981 and signed my name, with this additional thought:

I will look forward to one day seeing Great-Grandmother Susan Kent and trust I can tell her I have followed her path, kept the faith and all of the covenants.
Signed: Ardeth Greene Kapp

In April 1984, when I was sustained in general conference as the ninth Young Women general president, I felt an overwhelming sense of continuity from one generation to the next. I found myself reaching back in history for faith and confidence and courage from those who had gone before.

I remembered one afternoon after my father had passed away when I had contemplated whether those who have gone before are aware of what we do. I thought I heard my father's voice speak to my mind: *My dear, you have your privacy, but we know all of the important things.*

I thought on this occasion that surely those to whom I owed so much would be mindful of my thoughts, my needs, and my prayers. I did not need the strength required to cross the plains in an oxcart. Mine was a new and difficult frontier, but the "faith of our fathers"—and our mothers—would be needed.

As I spoke in the afternoon session of that general conference, I felt connected with loved ones on the other side of the veil. In my brief remarks I spoke of the heritage left us by those in years gone by, and of how, on the threshold of today, I felt my heart saying, "O

youth of the noble birthright, carry on, carry on, carry on!"[7]
    I quoted from the lines of a poem:

> If ye break faith with us who die
> We shall not sleep, though poppies grow
> In Flanders fields.[8]

I felt as though I were speaking to my mother, to my grand-mother, and to Great-Grandmother Susan Kent Greene. I felt the spirit of commitment as I spoke on that occasion:

> We'll not break faith, none of us. This is a generation of hope and faith and aspirations; and as leaders of young women throughout the world, our prayer is to live so that God's divine intervention will be felt in our hearts, in our actions, in our attitudes, and in our deeds, and that our receptivity to the priesthood power and direction will be sensitive and responsive. The forces of evil are so real today, and the subtleties of deceit would strive to divert us from the promises and blessings of the gospel of Jesus Christ. . . .
>   . . . We'll work to have every young woman throughout the Church stand in the valiant ranks of loyalty, commitment, and dedication. Mothers, stand firm; and fathers, have courage to be strong. Leaders, support those great parents. And together in unity we'll prepare a generation that will be prepared for the Lord's commendation, that he may have a house of worthy members when he returns.
>   To this solemn and sacred trust, I commit all of my energies and my efforts.[9]

There are many sunrises and sunsets before that glorious day when the veil will be taken from our eyes and we will see and know and love each other and express words of gratitude for the legacy of faith passed on from one generation to another—living water that quenches spiritual thirst.
    In 1996, citizens of Utah extended that legacy of faith as part of the centennial statehood celebration. A great groundswell and

awakening occurred for many while preparing for the rededication of the "This Is the Place" state park in Salt Lake City, Utah, on 28 June. President Gordon B. Hinckley would be directing and dedicating the park; the Mormon Tabernacle Choir would be singing. New buildings, replicas of the past, had been erected to commemorate Utah's history and values that can be lost in one generation's time if not preserved and passed on.

My direct participation in renewing the legacy began in January 1996 when I was asked to be responsible for producing the costumes to be worn by the volunteers at the park, using authentic patterns and materials from the period of 1847 to the year 1869, when the railroad came to Utah.

I was asked to produce "approximately 700 items of clothing," and more if possible. The fact that I know hardly anything about sewing was incidental to the major problem. It seemed like an overwhelming and impossible task. But I had been asked, and I had been taught in my youth from my mother, grandmother, and great-grandmother that the task is never too hard, the road never too long, the sun never too hot, and the request never too difficult if we turn to the Lord.

In quiet meditation I thought of my great-grandmother Susan Kent Greene and others, and the price they paid to get to the valley of the Great Salt Lake. *That's it,* I thought—or was it her thought that was whispering to me? *I can honor Great-Grandmother and other early pioneer women by having the costumes represent them. Then the volunteer women who wear the dresses in the park can develop a pioneer spirit.*

Yes, yes, I thought. I knew what to do, how to do it. I would have an authentic pioneer dress made both in pattern and fabric. Inside the dress there would be a label—an official centennial label with my great-grandmother's name attached inside the hem of the skirt. Accompanying this dress when it would be presented to the park would be a brief history of this great woman's life, her commitment, her dedication, her legacy of faith. Yes, Susan Kent Greene would be represented at the park, and so would hundreds, maybe thousands more if we could spread the word. "Make or donate a dress made in honor of your ancestor and give a brief history of her life to be filed in a register at the park," was the message. "On the inside of the hem of the dress will be an official centennial logo with your grandmother's or your great-grandmother's name as identification and your name as the donor." We called our project "Stitching History."

When I would speak about the dress made in honor of my great-grandmother Susan, it was as though the Spirit carried the message. We were not just sewing dresses; we were stitching history, preserving history, making history, celebrating history.

Over 1,700 articles of clothing, including dresses, bonnets, aprons, petticoats, trousers, and frock coats, were stitched and ready by 28 June. These articles of authentic clothing would help preserve, protect, and perpetuate the story of Utah and the faith of its people. One woman expressed with some emotion: "Every time I sat down to sew I felt my grandmother's presence, as though she were there with me and knew I was making the dress in her honor."

A brother who donated money to have a dress made in honor of his great-grandmother said: "After I researched a brief history initially motivated only by the desire to support 'your' project, I have become engrossed in reading my family history, which has now become 'my' project."

It has been 150 years now since Susan arrived in the Valley, but her legacy of faith remains. The life of Susan Kent Greene is perhaps best defined in the words of her grandson Edwin Kent Greene to his daughter Shirley: *"She loved the Lord, kept a good home, and raised a fine family."*

God bless you, Susan Kent Greene.

NOTES

1. Zebedee Coltrin, in minutes of the Salt Lake City School of the Prophets, 10–11 October 1883, as quoted in Karl Ricks Anderson, *Joseph Smith's Kirtland* (Salt Lake City: Deseret Book Co., 1989), p. 175.

2. Heber C. Kimball, *Times and Seasons* 6 (15 April 1845): 867.

3. Lula Greene Richards, "Life Sketch of Susan Kent Richards," typescript, in author's possession.

4. Ibid.

5. Ibid.

6. Leonard Arrington, "Louisa Lulu Greene Richards: Woman Journalist of the Early West," *Improvement Era*, May 1969, p. 30.

7. Ruth May Fox, "Carry On," in *Hymns*, no. 255.

8. John McCrae, "In Flanders Fields," in Hazel Felleman, comp., *Best Loved Poems of the American People* (New York: Doubleday, 1936), p. 429.

9. Ardeth Greene Kapp, "Youth of the Noble Birthright," *Ensign,* May 1984, p. 77.

୨ଈ

Ardeth Greene Kapp was Young Women general president from 1984 to 1992 and then served with her husband, Heber C. Kapp, who presided over the Canada Vancouver Mission from 1992 to 1995. She now teaches institute and is a temple ordinance worker and gospel doctrine teacher. She has had a long career in the field of education and has written 10 books, as well as educational guides and articles for Church magazines. Born in Cardston, Alberta, Canada, she now resides with her husband in Bountiful, Utah. Ardeth says she has been strengthened by the endurance and unwavering testimony of her pioneer descendant Susan Kent Greene.

8

"Sweep the Corners"
Maria Jackson Normington Parker
1820–1881

*I*t was the end of August 1969. The time for relocation had arrived. After 20-some years as a resident of Utah, I was leaving my home state for a graduate school experience in West Lafayette, Indiana. I felt like a pioneer in reverse: withdrawal from all that was familiar to travel from the mountains of Utah to the unknown territory of Indiana. I sorted, packed, shipped, and stored, finally confining my life's accumulations to a tiny U-Haul trailer. I was not traveling with my belongings—they went ahead with my husband while my two-year-old son, Greg, and I moved in with my parents to await the imminent arrival of a second child. My doctor would not allow me to travel the plains of Wyoming and Nebraska with delivery expected in two weeks. Neither would airline regulations permit me to fly to my new and distant home.

After the much-delayed arrival of a second son, Jeffrey, and a subsequent recuperation attended by my loving family members, I bundled my two babies, boarded a plane, and arrived at my new home in mid-November. The journey seemed impossible at the time: a newborn, a two-year-old, and four hours of flying time.

Maria Jackson Normington Parker

Somehow my weary body arrived in Chicago, then drove on to our student apartment in West Lafayette.

It was another summer: 1856. My great-great-grandmother packed her belongings into a few bulging bags and joined the Saints en route to Zion. Grandma Maria Jackson Normington left England on 22 May of that year, docking in Boston, then arriving in Iowa City on 8 July. She traveled in company with her husband, Thomas, four children, and what some records indicate was another child anticipated in the fall. Other records note that little Daniel, Maria's eighth child, was about a year old at the time of her immigration. She left three babies behind in England, each deceased at a young age. By the end of July, provisions were gathered and her little brood joined the Martin handcart company, departing for the Salt Lake Valley on 28 July.

I've often wondered if Maria was as apprehensive as I was about leaving her native countryside for an unknown world. Did she question the decision to travel with her tiny flock, especially after she'd laid three to rest? Were the meager savings she and Thomas accumulated after working together in a cotton mill enough to sustain the family on the journey? Did she imagine what a home in the desert could be after the lush green countryside of her homeland? What treasured possessions did she leave behind when packing required efficient use of space? Did following the prophet really mean following him across the ocean, across the prairies, and all the way to Zion? Did she ever doubt her fitness for the rugged journey? Did she ever dream that her beloved family members would not survive the expedition?

In my own experience, I asked some of those same questions: Would my sons and I find friends to replace our regular associations with family and loved ones at home? How could I leave my imposing mountain boundaries for the flat plains of the Midwest? Would our limited savings and student loans support our family through the graduate program? Could I manage my cozy household with so many of my cherished possessions in storage? Would I be able to serve with brothers and sisters in the "mission field" as the prophet directed? Was I truly fit for a major change in my environment? Did I ever imagine that my beloved family members would not survive the subsequent journeys?

Maria did not keep a journal. Her thoughts, feelings, and apprehensions went unvoiced to my generation. I cannot find answers to questions that push me to explore her experiences. I can only imagine her anguish and her joy as the facts of her existence rise from the notes and journals of others who traveled a similar path.

Maria was one member of the Martin handcart company. She was not the leader, the scribe, the heroine, nor a fatality. She was simply a 36-year-old mother following the command of a prophet to gather with the Saints to Zion.

The Lord instructed the Saints through Joseph Smith as early as 1830 that "ye are called to bring to pass the gathering of mine elect; for mine elect hear my voice and harden not their hearts; wherefore the decree hath gone forth from the Father that they shall be gathered in unto one place upon the face of this land, to prepare their hearts and be prepared in all things against the [last] day" (D&C 29:7-8).

In December 1847 the prophet Brigham Young advised the "Saints in England, Scotland, Ireland, Wales, and the adjacent islands and countries [to] emigrate as speedily as possible to this vicinity."[1]

Maria and Thomas Normington were baptized in November 1840, shortly after their 1839 marriage. More than 15 years passed before they were finally prepared to heed the prophet's words and travel to Zion. Under the stipulations of the Perpetual Emigrating Fund, Brigham Young directed President F. D. Richards of Liverpool that "in your elections of the Saints who shall be aided by the Fund, those who have proven themselves by long continuance in the Church shall be helped first, whether they can raise any means of their own or not."[2] Though no record exists to verify the distribution of funds, I assume that the Normingtons may have qualified for some assistance.

The prophet Brigham further suggested that a new means of transportation to Zion be attempted: the handcart. If immigrants traveled with the new method, he reasoned, "they will only need 90 days' rations from the time of their leaving the Missouri river, and as the settlements extend up the Platte, not that much. The carts can be made without a particle of iron, with wheels hooped, made strong and light, and one, or if the family be large, two of them will bring all that they will need upon the plains."[3]

With years of tireless labor and careful saving behind them, the Normingtons set out on their journey to Zion. Following the instructions of the prophet, they "perceive[d] the necessity of dispensing with all wooden chests, extra freight, luggage, etc., they should only bring a change of clothing."[4]

What valuable possessions remained in Iowa City as the handcart expedition commenced? Did Maria longingly leave treasures from her homeland on the edge of the prairie? In her determination to reach the mountains, Grandma undoubtedly deposited trunks filled with valued memories somewhere in the frontier town, then tucked a bundle of clothing for each family member into the wooden confines of the handcart.

The Martin company, under the leadership of former British missionary Edward Martin, "consisted of 576 souls, with 146 carts, 7 wagons, 30 oxen, and 50 cows and beef cattle."[5] Though a few members of the group dropped out before reaching Florence, Nebraska, most continued the hike to the West.

A report in the *Council Bluffs Bugle* described the faithful as they continued their journey: "It may seem to some that these people endure great hardships in traveling hundreds of miles on foot, drawing carts behind them. This is a mistake, for many informed me that after the first three days travel, it requires little effort for two or three men or women to draw the light handcart with its moderate load of cooking utensils and baggage."[6]

While the weather held, the handcart pioneers paced themselves day by day. Cyrus H. Wheelock wrote in his journal on 2 September 1856 that "all were in good spirits, and generally in good health, and full of confidence that they should reach the mountains in season to escape the severe storms. I have never seen more union among the Saints anywhere than is manifested in the handcart companies."[7]

Faith and dedication pushed Maria on after she laid her son Ephraim to rest on the plains. The five-year-old was among the early casualties of the expedition, dying on 10 August. Little Daniel became the second of Maria's family to succumb during the migration. On that sad day Maria was permitted to ride in a wagon half a day with her dead child until the company stopped and he could be buried.[8]

My own heart aches with Maria at the loss of her children: now five of her eight babies were gone. I, too, cradled a son for almost nine months before he was called home. Benjamin was born with undefined birth defects that ultimately shortened his turn on earth. In contrast to his pioneer cousins, Ben had the full benefits of medical research and pediatric specialists in a children's hospital to diagnose his needs. In the end, however, the loss was similar. The Lord called the youngsters home, young ones who had completed their earthly missions. Despite my testimony of that, my mind often fills with concern for Ben's everyday activities. I long to hold him once again, but even more I'm anxious to learn of his experiences on the other side of the veil. I'm certain that Maria also found lonely and longing moments as she mourned the passing of her children. Nevertheless she trudged on, mile after mile, as the company moved toward the Rocky Mountains.

Supplies diminished as the party neared the crossing of the North Platte River. Josiah Rogerson of the group noted in his journal that "more than a score or two of the young female members waded the stream that in places was waist deep. Blocks of mushy snow and ice had to be dodged."[9] Were my three surviving great-great-aunts, Maria's daughters, in that intrepid group?

Elizabeth Jackson, another Martin company chronicler, added, "Some of the men carried some of the women on their back or in their arms, but others of the women tied up their skirts and waded through, like the heroines that they were."[10]

Shortly after the crossing the company was buried with a "tremendous storm of snow, hail, sand, and fierce winds."[11] The intensity of the storm disabled the party and they were forced to make camp for nine days while the blizzards continued. Sister Jackson recorded her experiences, which parallel Maria's own tragedy. She wrote, "The weather was bitter. I listened to hear if my husband breathed, he lay so still. I could not hear him. I became alarmed. I put my hand on his body, when to my horror I discovered that my worst fears were confirmed. My husband was dead. I called for help to the other inmates of the tent. They could render me no aid; and there was no alternative but to remain alone by the side of the corpse till morning. . . . They wrapped him in a blanket and placed him in a pile with thirteen others who had died, and then covered him up with snow. The ground was frozen so hard that they could not dig a grave."[12]

Maria lost her husband, Thomas, to cholera on a night when 15 others also died. He was buried with the group, probably in a manner similar to Brother Jackson.

Sister Jackson continued her report: "I will not attempt to describe my feelings at finding myself thus left a widow with three children, under such excruciating circumstances. I cannot do it. But I believe the Recording Angel has inscribed in the archives above, and that my suffering for the Gospel's sake will be sanctified unto me for my good."[13]

In the absence of Maria's own words, I choose to assume her feelings were described by Sister Jackson. She, too, had lost her dear husband and was left with three surviving children as hope for a rescue of the stranded handcarters waned.

In another way I empathize with Maria. After 22 years of marriage I was left to raise my five children on my own. Though my loss was through the anguish of divorce, my feelings of loneliness and desperation must have paralleled Maria's. I wearied the Lord with questions over my circumstance, but just as he blessed Maria with strength to endure her challenges, he blessed me with little miracles that began to cement the pieces of my life back together.

In Maria's case, under the direction of Brigham Young a rescue party was dispatched to aid the struggling handcart companies. The Salt Lake wagon teams reached the Willie party on 21 October but found no sign of the Martin group. Half of the rescuers pushed on to Devil's Gate, where they expected to locate the missing pioneers. An express group of benefactors continued through the snow while the main body settled in the shelter of Devil's Gate. Finally the Martin party was located at Red Bluffs, more than 65 miles east of their predicted destination. Though the express men carried no provisions, they brought a message of hope to encourage the weary handcart group.

Maria later told her granddaughter that "her shoes were worn out, they had very little clothing and practically no food. Grandmother tried to eat dirt to satisfy the pangs of hunger. She walked until her feet were so terribly frozen and sore she could walk no more. Then she crawled, using her hands and knees, and when her hands were so frozen she could use them no more, she went on her knees and elbows until, even after many years there were great scars on her knees and elbows."[14]

Rescuer Daniel Jones observed the scene as he came upon the stranded Martin company. "A condition of distress here met my eyes that I never saw before or since. The train was strung out for three or four miles. There were old men pulling and tugging their carts, sometimes loaded with a sick wife or children—women pulling along sick husbands—little children six to eight years old struggling through the mud and snow. As night came on the mud would freeze on their clothes and feet."[15]

Another rescuer, Ephraim Hanks, concurred. "The sight that met my gaze as I entered their camp can never be erased from my memory. The starved forms and haggard countenances of the poor sufferers, as they moved about slowly, shivering with cold, to prepare their scanty evening meal was enough to touch the stoutest heart."[16]

Surely the weary travelers fervently thanked their God for the miraculous rescue efforts. Their earnest prayers had been answered and they were once again bound for Zion.

Maria, however, was "so overcome with the hardships, starvation and grief when the relief wagons came [that] she was unconscious, and almost out of her mind. She remembered nothing of the last part of her journey."[17]

Family records indicate that Maria and her daughters were rescued by William Parker, son of British immigrant John Parker. Though listings of the rescuers of the Willie and Martin handcart companies fail to include Parker,[18] other records note that the rescuers "ultimately amounted to 200 wagons and teams."[19] That fact leaves room for Parker to be an unidentified member of the rescue party and may verify the stories told in family histories.

Parker returned the weary handcart sisters to his father's home around the first of December. It was a full six weeks before Maria could finally walk,[20] though her daughters recovered more quickly. After several weeks of convalescence Maria assumed a share of the responsibility for the livestock, some farming chores, and then the maintenance of her own little log home on the Parker's Jordan River farm.

Could there have been a romance or was it simply a marriage of commandment when John Parker took Maria Normington as his third wife in November of 1857? Again, there is no record of Maria's feelings. I prefer to hope there was a love affair, but I do know that Maria never shirked her responsibilities to the Parkers nor questioned her commitment to the gospel of Jesus Christ.

I, too, was blessed with a second marriage, a union of love and laughter. It came about in a rather unlikely fashion as an elderly friend announced that she had the perfect man for me, and then proceeded to join us on the dinner date she arranged. She extolled the virtues of our union for almost two hours while we listened with embarrassment. Sister Durham was correct in her prediction; Russell and I married in the Salt Lake Temple 15 months later.

Maria bore John Parker two children, then traveled with his family as he was called to the Dixie Cotton Mission in 1863. Once again she struggled to eke out survival, first in a dugout and finally in a little log house. The barren landscape was blessed with rain 40 consecutive days after the Parker's arrival in Dixie, allowing them to collect water for ditches and irrigation. Slowly the new settlement blossomed, evidence to Maria's industry and thrift. "She washed and scoured the wool, then carded and spun it and dyed it with dock root or madder and wove it into cloth for their dresses and suits, which she also made. She was able to make the most of all she had, and soon was comfortable in her home."[21] Maria spent her remaining years in Virgin City, a bishop's wife and companion until her passing in 1881.

Since my original departure from Utah in 1969, I've moved eight different times. I've packed my belongings and watched as the moving company loaded trucks to transport my possessions. I've had help from the Relief Society and assistance from priesthood quorums to complete the transitions. Each time I struggled to settle into a new neighborhood, to relocate the children and the children's necessary services; yet I always felt sustained in those challenges.

Like Maria, my grandmother of the handcarts, I've been blessed with a testimony of the gospel of Jesus Christ, a testimony that's stretched without snapping into disbelief despite trials. Maria was well known for her "gift of faith and was a most unusual prayer. No one could pray like she did; she seemed to actually see and talk with her Father as she expressed her gratitude and asked for the blessings she needed."[22] Though my faith has wavered at times and I've questioned the Lord through challenges, I've learned, as I assume Maria did, that the Lord and his loving concern for his children always prevails.

Though many of my life's experiences seem similar in content to those of my great-great-grandmother, the circumstances markedly differ. Her struggles were often physical in a battle with the elements for survival. My challenges were emotionally based personal conflicts in the midst of physical plenty. Yet as I consider her as a heroine in her time, I understand how she lived by her daily philosophy, "Sweep the corners and the middle of the floor will sweep itself."[23] I've learned that if I take care of the things within the reach of my immediate responsibility, the Lord will take care of the remainder of my concerns. I often reassured the children during my single years that I wasn't certain how the Lord would help us resolve the current and perplexing problems, I only knew that he would. He did and continues to do so with a continuing series of little miracles meant only for me and mine, just as he did for Maria and her precious family more than a hundred years ago.

NOTES

1. *Millennial Star* 10 (15 March 1848): 84.

2. *Millennial Star* 17 (22 December 1855): 814.

3. Ibid., p. 813.

4. Ibid., p. 814.

5. LeRoy R. Hafen and Ann W. Hafen, *Handcarts to Zion* (Glendale, Calif.: The Arthur H. Clark Co., 1960), p. 93

6. *Council Bluffs Bugle*, 26 August 1856, as cited in ibid., p. 95.

7. L. Hafen and A. Hafen, *Handcarts,* p. 97.

8. See Annie Hilton Bishop, "Maria," in Kate B. Carter, comp., *Our Pioneer Heritage,* vol. 2 (Salt Lake City: Daughters of Utah Pioneers, 1959), p. 234.

9. L. Hafen and A. Hafen, *Handcarts,* p. 109

10. Ibid.

11. Ibid.

12. Elizabeth Jackson, *Leaves from the Life of Elizabeth Horrocks Kingford Jackson* (pamphlet), as cited in ibid., p. 111.

13. Ibid., pp. 111–12.

14. Annie Hilton Bishop, personal history, in author's possession.

15. Rebecca Cornwall and Leonard J. Arrington, *Rescue of the Handcart Companies* (Provo, Utah: Brigham Young University Press, 1981), p. 20.

16. Ephraim Hanks, interview by Andrew Jackson, as quoted in L. Hafen and A. Hafen, *Handcarts,* p. 135.

17. Bishop, personal history.

18. Cornwall and Arrington, *Rescue,* p. 20.

19. *Encyclopedia of Mormonism,* s.v. "handcart companies."

20. Bishop, "Maria," p. 235.

21. Bishop, personal history.

22. Ibid.

23. Bishop, "Maria," p. 236.

⁀❧

Ann Whiting Orton earned both her bachelor's and her master's degrees from Brigham Young University and is the former food editor of the *Deseret News.* She has written or compiled three booklets, *Friend to Friend, Eternally Yours,* and *Experiment upon the Word.* The mother of two daughters and four sons, one deceased, she is married to Russell B. Orton. Researching facts about her great-great-grandmother has expanded Ann's great admiration, respect, and gratitude for her.

9

"Sarah Has Got a Little the Advantage"
Sarah Melissa Granger Kimball
1818–1898

*M*y guess is it was a reluctant, melancholy heaven, me included, that released a scintillating, well-loved Sarah Melissa to take her turn on earth back in 1818. But with eternal perspective, knowing the twinkling-of-an-eye time frame and aware of the gifts she carried within her, heaven sent Sarah Melissa to Oliver and Lydia Granger as a belated Christmas gift, arriving 29 December at their Phelps, New York, home.

Was I really there, Sarah, wistfully saying good-bye to you because we were such confidantes and kindred spirits? It would certainly seem so. Did I wonder then why I wasn't sent along with you? Was I comforted—as I was held in reserve until this later time to come with my own gifts within—knowing we would renew our bond now in this fashion?

As a young girl, Sarah Melissa, born to a prominent local family, had "excellent opportunities for advancement and cultivation."[1] Reared as a "true Yankee type," coming from Puritan ancestors, she developed the " 'proper manners' and deportment of the

Sarah Melissa Granger Kimball

days in which she was born and reared," according to Emmeline B. Wells, and "was so thoroughly imbued with the prudish ideas of decorum of that early Puritanical period, that any departure from it was reprehensible from her point of view."[2]

I have no doubt, Sarah, that you would find me a major departure from Puritan decorum! Born into this less well-bred era the century after yours to bright but impoverished parents, any childhood refinement of me was meager. With time, education, and circumstance, however, perhaps I now have sufficient polish that you might find me refreshingly genuine and delightful!

In 1830, when Sarah Melissa was almost 12 years old, her father acquired a Book of Mormon just a few months after it was published. Apparently having read the book, "about which his mind was exercised," Oliver Granger had a "heavenly vision" regarding it, as Sarah later wrote. "A personage who said his name was Moroni" told Oliver the book was true and that Oliver would "be ordained to preach the everlasting Gospel to the children of men." Oliver was also given assurance that he was "approved of God," a comfort that "remained with him until his dying hour."[3] This experience no doubt had a lasting effect upon Sarah Melissa and the rest of the family as well, all of whom, I assume, were baptized into the Church during that time.

When presented with the gospel at 15, Sarah, my spirit was immediately receptive; everything I learned I felt I already knew, only couldn't quite remember without rehearsal, like knowing someone well yet being unable to remember the name. I studied, prayed, and gained my own witness of Christ as my Savior and of the divinity of his gospel, and my commitment is sure.

Three years later Oliver moved the family to Kirtland, Ohio, where the Prophet Joseph and the Saints were gathering. Astute, inquisitive Sarah Melissa, still in her teens, was one of the few feminine faces present among the priesthood elders, her father included, who attended the School of the Prophets there.[4]

Sarah, unlike you, when I was young I lacked discipline and was withdrawn from the junior high gifted program for lackluster perfor-

mance, although later in graduate school I did achieve according to my intellect. From my first exposure to the gospel, however, I continuously gained spiritual knowledge precept by precept, although the hardest-won, farthest-reaching scholarship of my life was learning that possessing the gospel is not at all sufficient. I learned that I needed to apply the gospel with consistent accuracy in order to make the power of its principles mine.

Due to mounting pressure against the Mormons in Kirtland, the Granger family moved to Commerce, Illinois (later renamed Nauvoo) a few years later. Hiram S. Kimball, at 34 an affluent non-Mormon Commerce merchant, was drawn to the beauty, grace, and intellect of 21-year-old Sarah Melissa, and courted and then married her in 1840. Their home soon became the setting for many social and religious functions for Church leaders and their wives.[5] Because of Sarah's own refinement and elegant taste, along with her adeptness at gardening and painting, the small but lovely home was remembered long after the Saints had left Nauvoo and, in fact, was fully restored in the early 1980s during general Relief Society president Barbara B. Smith's administration.[6]

I live single, Sarah, with my early eclectic garage sale furnishings, multitudinous cats, and raccoons that come for dinner! I have a black thumb and not a gene's worth of artistic skill. The chasm between your refinement and my lack of it would seem to stretch in magnitude. But my gifts and circumstances differ from yours, Sarah. Blessed with a writer's heart, I refine thought into prose and poetry, speeches and publications. An educator now in administration, I honed my skills daily as a designated master teacher in the classroom for nearly 20 years; I continue that process monthly now in the Relief Society room. I was blessed with an enduring love of music and not one melodic note in me; nevertheless, my piano and drums will one day sound with rhythm and chords that my practiced hands and ears will eventually master!

Sarah and Hiram's first child was born in 1841, during the time the Nauvoo Temple was under very slow construction. At the time, the walls of the temple were only about three feet high. The Church needed time, money, and supplies from the Saints to complete it. Sarah had a keen desire to assist the effort, but since Hiram wasn't a member, she didn't feel right about asking him to make a contribution. When Hiram came to her bedside one day and admired their three-day-old son, Sarah initiated the following conversation, as recorded in her own words, by asking, "What is the boy worth?"

Hiram: "O, I don't know, he is worth a great deal."
Sarah: "Is he worth a thousand dollars?"
Hiram: "Yes, more than that if he lives and does well."
Sarah: "Half of him is mine, is it not?"
Hiram: "Yes, I suppose so."
Sarah: "Then I have something to help on the Temple."
Hiram: "You have?"
Sarah: "Yes, and I think of turning my share right in as tithing."
Hiram: "Well, I'll see about that."[7]

Soon after, Hiram recounted the interchange to the Prophet Joseph, saying, "Sarah has got a little the advantage of me this time, she proposes to turn out the boy as Church property."

The Prophet "seemed pleased with the joke" and replied, "I accept all such donations, and from this day the boy shall stand recorded, *Church property*." Joseph then gave Hiram the option of paying $500 and keeping the boy or collecting $500 and forfeiting possession. Hiram offered an alternative: property just north of the temple. Joseph agreed, saying, "It is just what we want," and the deed was soon transferred.[8]

When the Prophet saw Sarah, he told her: "You have consecrated your first born son, for this you are blessed of the Lord. . . . Your name shall be handed down in honorable remembrance from generation to generation. . . . You shall be a blessing to your companion, and the honored mother of a noble posterity. You shall stand as a savior to your father's house, and receive an everlasting salvation."[9] That and other promises made by the Prophet were "very sacred and very comforting" to Sarah the rest of her life.[10]

While I have no son to consecrate, Sarah, I do have my own life, and as I offer it in service, testimony, and virtue, consecrating my time, talents, and energies in covenant, I garner rich blessings and abiding peace, which are no small part of what daily sustains me.

In 1842—the year before Hiram was baptized—the Saints were still laboring to finish the Nauvoo Temple. Sarah learned that her seamstress, a Miss Cook, wanted to help the cause but had no resources. Sarah offered to buy the material if Miss Cook would make shirts for the workmen. Then they thought other women might be interested in pooling their efforts, possibly even forming a "Ladies' Society" for future service projects.[11]

This, in essence, was the beginning of the Relief Society. Sarah invited about a dozen Mormon sisters over; they decided to form an official organization and ask Eliza R. Snow to draft a constitution and bylaws. Eliza "cheerfully and efficiently" responded, and when completed per the group's request, the documents were given to Joseph Smith for approval.[12]

The Prophet thought the charter clearly superior; nevertheless he said, "This is not what you want. Tell the sisters their offering is accepted of the Lord, and He has something better for them than a written constitution." He then invited all the sisters to meet with him and a few brethren the next week to "organize the sisters under the priesthood after the pattern of the priesthood."[13]

Accordingly, Sarah and 17 other women met on 17 March 1842 as Joseph officially organized the Female Relief Society of Nauvoo. Until that time, he said, the Church "was never perfectly organized."[14] The Nauvoo Relief Society thrived, garnering 1,341 members by 1844.[15]

For me, Sarah, since my first days of college, Relief Society has been catalyst to leadership, scholarship, inspiration, sisterhood, service, and instruction. No organization, except the Church as a whole, has blessed my life and my spirit more abundantly. Immeasurable gratitude I offer you for being the Esther of the Restoration, having come "for such a time as this" to inaugurate the reality of Relief Society (see Esther 4:14).

As the Saints began their exodus to the Salt Lake Valley, Hiram's business concerns in the East obligated the Kimballs to remain in Nauvoo until 1851. Even then, because Hiram was detained in New York City, Sarah had to come west alone with the children and her widowed mother. By the time Hiram finally joined them a year later, he was basically bankrupt in both money and health.[16] This was apparently not the first or worst hardship Sarah endured, since she was also victim to the persecutions borne by the early Saints, although she records but one sweeping mention of the adversity and affliction she had suffered before leaving Nauvoo: "In the wanderings and persecutions of the Church I have participated, and in the blessings, endowments and holy annointings and precious promises I have also received. To sorrow I have not been a stranger; but I only write this short sketch to instruct and happify, so I will skip to Salt Lake City."[17]

In my early years, Sarah, tribulation and I were nearly inseparable companions. But that is past, and I am the wiser for it, kinder of heart, more compassionate in nature, and now bless lives for my knowing. Mine also are endowments, holy anointings, blessings, and precious promises, and now I, too, write to "instruct and happify."

Arriving in the Salt Lake Valley, Sarah exchanged all her oxen and outfit for a small, comfortable home in Salt Lake City, a transaction she "always considered providential." During this time an Indian agent gave her a "nine-year-old wild Indian girl" to raise, who died 10 years later.[18]

Because of their financial slump, Sarah utilized her sound childhood education to teach school for eight years until Hiram regained his health and prosperity. She spent most of those eight years teaching school privately in her home or the schoolroom she had her husband and sons build for her.[19]

Sarah, for 19 years I taught school, reveling in the light that shone in a student's eyes as a new concept was finally understood, or as youthful ears delighted in the sound of poetic alliteration, or as adolescent hearts resonated to splendid literature. Now in administration, I miss the classroom but appreciate the boost in salary that permitted the purchase of my first home (for $10 down!) and now my second and new home. Providence was clearly apparent in both purchases, as it has been in innumerable particulars throughout my life.

As an initial force in the formation of the Relief Society organization, Sarah must have found it gratifying and invigorating to be named president of Salt Lake City's 15th Ward Relief Society in

1857, a position she held for nearly 42 years until her death. For the first 10 years, however, most of the organization's activities were greatly curtailed because of the Utah War and other factors. Relief Society was not fully revived until 1867.[20]

Maybe it was just as well as far as Sarah was concerned. Those intervening 10 years had been arduous for her—first, her mother, who had lived with the family for 20 years, had died. Then her missionary husband, Hiram, had drowned in a steamship explosion on his way to the Sandwich Islands. Later Sarah had adopted another little girl, and her two oldest sons had married. Now 49 years old and a widow, Sarah was ready to get involved with the ward as Relief Society president. Actually, from that point on hers became a public life and she became a major influence on Utah's social, religious, and political scenes.[21]

Forty-nine? Exactly where I am now, Sarah. Not widowed, just single, but like you I now find myself involved in writing, teaching, and leadership in my neighborhood, work, Church, and professional affiliations. While leadership is often my lot, in the Church it is more often as Relief Society teacher, with nearly 25 years commended to that effort. Given time, I may reach your 40-year mark! And, perhaps like you, I find that one of the reasons I can offer my time and heart in this fashion is that I am single. I have made a conscious choice to trust in the Lord's timetable for me and to exercise my faith in that trust to the benefit of others. Marriage, children, and exaltation will be mine in his due time as I remain faithful.

My last 10 years, less arduous than yours, have been ones of service, personally and professionally, civically and religiously. I realize that the skills and expertise I've developed in that service may be continually sought as I serve in my own day and way. Your years that followed those difficult 10 are now known—and so awe-inspiring! My next years are just beginning, and while I endeavor to "be not weary in well-doing" (D&C 64:33), even now I am so exhausted sometimes—how did you accomplish so much for so long, Sarah?

Although Sarah became involved as soon as she settled in the Salt Lake Valley, "gathering and distributing charitable funds, [and] holding sewing meetings varied by personal testimonies,"[22] it was as ward Relief Society president that her administrative skills, business acumen, compassionate service, doctrinal and academic scholarship, public speaking, and civic leadership all acquired such luster and acclaim.

In her first year as ward Relief Society president, Sarah "drew up a description of the duties of Relief Society officers, a listing [only] slightly revised by Eliza R. Snow and used by her as she carried out her assignment from Brigham Young to organize Relief Societies throughout the territory."[23] In 1872 Sarah organized a "physiological and nursing class" that met twice a week.[24] By 1880 her administrative skills were expanded as she concurrently served as general Relief Society secretary. Twelve years later she became a counselor in the general Relief Society presidency. At the time of her death, Sarah was both ward Relief Society president and general Relief Society counselor.

Sarah played major roles in "raising and distributing funds to support immigration, the Deseret Hospital, teacher training, temple building, [and] the furnishing of chapels."[25] "Sister Kimball had largely developed executive ability to accumulate property and to take care of it to the best advantage."[26] For example, having established successful procedures within her ward Relief Society to collect funds from the sisters and from the sale of their handiwork, by 1868 the first "Relief Society hall" was built, with Sarah laying the cornerstone.[27] At that time the project attracted some attention—"the novelty consists in its being a female enterprise."[28]

From that same source, sufficient monies were accrued to build the first Relief Society wheat granary and to stock it with grain, in compliance with President Brigham Young's 1876 admonition to then general Relief Society president Emmeline B. Wells to store wheat against times of need.[29] Over time, storing wheat became such a significant part of the general Relief Society program that wheat sheaves became a part of the organization's insignia.

In the welfare session of general conference in September 1978, general Relief Society president Barbara B. Smith, with President Spencer W. Kimball's affirmation, gave all 266,291 bushels of Relief Society wheat to the Churchwide grain storage program, along with the sizable wheat fund. The wheat fund was set aside for the exclusive purchase of more grain.[30] That program continues to this day.

Sarah was active and vocal in the political and social issues of the day. In 1870 she presided at a Salt Lake Tabernacle mass meeting held to protest federal legislation against Mormons.[31] In 1882 she was a member of the Utah Constitutional Convention. She was on the territorial committee of the People's Party.[32] For a time Sarah was even "quite an advocate for dress reform,"[33] declaring that "tight lacing was a sin against humanity"![34]

By 1890 Sarah was president of the Utah Woman's Suffrage Association, and the next year she served as Utah's delegate to the National American Woman's Suffrage Association in Washington, D.C.[35] She worked in close association with Susan B. Anthony in that cause and was considered of like stature in the women's movement. She was the voice of Utah women in successfully lobbying the constitutional convention delegates to include women's suffrage in the Utah state constitution of 1895.[36] Never failing to give a word "in due season and to sound the rising note," her voice again sounded in the Relief Society general conference held in the Assembly Hall in 1896: "Sarah M. Kimball confined her remarks to the subject of a house for the Society. She felt it a humiliation to be without a place of our own; we had contributed to all public places and at all times. Now we want to have a house and we want land to build it on, and it should be in the shadow of the temple. It should be a place to receive strangers in when they come, a place where letters can be written from and information given. . . . 'Now,' said Sister Kimball, 'I want to ask you sisters if you want such a building as I have described.' The motion was put and the vote was unanimous."[37] After at least three different buildings and many years later, this initial petition finally resulted in a central Relief Society building.

Sarah, those are incredible achievements for a lifetime, let alone your last 40 years! Mine is a day when the family as a traditional unit is in peril, when youth are bombarded by evil influences, when neighborhoods are ravaged by crime and murder, much of government is corrupt, and society and the nation hang in the balance. Would that within my own sphere of influence I might prove to have come "for such a time as this," like you, addressing the exigencies of my time.

Writing in Sarah's autograph book in 1892, George Q. Cannon of the First Presidency summarized her accomplishments in this manner: "What an amount of interesting history you have helped to make. . . . Now you stand . . . as a representative woman among your sex."[38]

Sarah Melissa Granger Kimball, now venerated, was well loved by all who knew her. She stood Victorian straight, with a "tall, commanding figure, [and] a face of remarkable dignity and sincerity in expression."[39] Her "presence was always inspiring"[40] and her name was "synonymous with charity."[41] Her bishop described her heart as "full to overflowing with love and kindness to [her] fellow creatures."[42] It was said that nothing about her was commonplace.[43] Although her health had failed rapidly during her last year, Sarah was active and involved until the day she died. A historian has written, "Her contributions to the Church and her work in behalf of women place her among the most influential of early Mormon women."[44]

Heaven having done without you long enough, Sarah, finally insisted on calling you home. In your honor a grand reunion was surely held on 1 December 1898. After nearly 80 years of most remarkable mortality, I imagine you, as well as heaven, were ecstatic at your homecoming.

We must part company again for a season, Sarah, and it is I who feel the loss anew. But how I look forward to that eternal reunion—I've so many questions, so much to tell! Did I tell you how I love that you were "Sarah M." throughout time and history, forgoing your maiden name, but never your middle name? You're the only one I know who used the middle initial instead of the maiden initial. When I learned that, I instantly identified with you. For me, my whole name is who I am—always the middle name, too—Blythe Darlyn Thatcher. Now, that looks right, feels right. It must have felt that way for you, too, Sarah Melissa.

In so many ways I relate to you, and although the chasm between who you've become and who I am yet to be is canyon-wide for now, I have days and years before me, and with life expectancy what it is these days, I may live even past your long years, Sarah. However long I live, I hope it's enough that my refinement of manner, intellect, leadership, and spirit will elevate to yours, for I desire to be confidantes and kindred spirits again. But for now, Sarah, you indeed have got "a little the advantage."

Notes

1. Emmeline B. Wells, "President Sarah M. Kimball," *Woman's Exponent* 27 (15 December 1898): 77.

2. Emmeline B. Wells, "R. S. Women of the Past: Personal Impressions," *Woman's Exponent* 37 (June 1908): 1.

3. Sarah M. Kimball, "Sarah M. Kimball: Secretary of the L.D.S. Women's Organizations," in Augusta Joyce Crocheron, ed., *Representative Women of Deseret: A Book of Biographical Sketches* (Salt Lake City: J. C. Graham and Co., 1884), p. 24.

4. See *Sarah Melissa Granger Kimball: Woman of Charity* (Salt Lake City: The Church of Jesus Christ of Later-day Saints, 1982).

5. See Jill Mulvay Derr, "Sarah M. Kimball," in Vicky Burgess-Olson, ed., *Sister Saints* (Provo: Brigham Young University Press, 1978), p. 27.

6. See Barbara B. Smith, *A Fruitful Season* (Salt Lake City: Bookcraft, 1988), pp. 195–96.

7. Kimball, "Sarah M. Kimball," p. 25.

8. Ibid., pp. 25–26.

9. Ibid., p. 26.

10. Wells, "President Sarah M. Kimball," p. 77.

11. See Kimball, "Sarah M. Kimball," pp. 26–27; Kimball, "Reminiscence of Sarah Melissa Granger Kimball," in Carol Cornwall Madsen, ed., *In Their Own Words: Women and the Story of Nauvoo* (Salt Lake City: Deseret Book Co., 1994), p. 191.

12. See Kimball, "Reminiscence," p. 191.

13. Kimball, "Sarah M. Kimball," p. 27.

14. Ibid.

15. See *Encyclopedia of Mormonism*, 4 vols. (New York: Macmillan, 1992), 3:1200.

16. See Kimball, "Sarah M. Kimball," p. 27.

17. Ibid.

18. Ibid., p. 28.

19. See Derr, "Sarah M. Kimball," p. 29.

20. See ibid.

21. See ibid.

22. *Sarah Melissa Granger Kimball: Woman of Charity.*

23. Derr, "Sarah M. Kimball," p. 30.

24. See *Centenary,* p. 45.

25. Madsen, *In Their Own Words,* p. 190.

26. Wells, "R. S. Women," p. 1.

27. See Derr, "Sarah M. Kimball," p. 30.

28. *Woman's Exponent,* 15 June 1885, as quoted in *A Centenary of Relief Society: 1842–1942* (Salt Lake City: General Board of Relief Society, 1942), p. 67.

29. See Jill Mulvay Derr, Janath Russell Cannon, and Maureen Ursenbach Beecher, *Women of Covenant: The Story of Relief Society* (Salt Lake City: Deseret Book Co., 1992), p. 103.

30. See Smith, *A Fruitful Season,* pp. 149–50.

31. See *Sarah Melissa Granger Kimball: Woman of Charity.*

32. See Wells, "President Sarah M. Kimball," p. 77.

33. Wells, "R. S. Women," p. 2.

34. *Woman's Exponent,* 1 March 1873.

35. See ibid.

36. See Madsen, *In Their Own Words,* p. 190.

37. *Centenary,* p. 26.

38. George Q. Cannon to Sarah M. Kimball, 21 September 1892, *Sarah M. Kimball Autograph Book,* 1850–98; as quoted in *Sarah Melissa Granger Kimball: Women of Charity.*

39. Crocheron, *Representative Women,* p. 28.

40. Wells, "Sarah M. Kimball," p. 77.

41. Jill Mulvay, "The Liberal Shall Be Blessed: Sarah M. Kimball," *Utah Historical Quarterly,* summer 1976, pp. 219–21; as quoted in *Sarah Melissa Granger Kimball: Woman of Charity.*

42. Derr, "Sarah M. Kimball," p. 35.

43. See Wells, "R. S. Women," p. 2.

44. Madsen, *In Their Own Words,* p. 190.

Blythe Darlyn Thatcher, a high school administrator, holds M.Ed. and Ed.S. degrees from Brigham Young University and is active in leadership positions in professional and civic organizations. She has written Church curriculum, edited two professional newsletters and a national magazine, and coauthored or coedited several books, including *The Legacy Remembered* and *A Singular Life.* Sarah M. Kimball's "vibrant personality, precision with words, ingenious leadership, and lively longevity" made her Blythe's heroine of choice.

10

"This Is the Truth, Truth, Truth!"

Zina D. H. Young

1821–1901

*I*t was with my call to serve on the Relief Society general board that Zina D. H. Young came into my life. I remember the uneasiness I felt in taking my place as a new member of this group. I had long loved Relief Society, and I looked forward to a new opportunity, but walking into the board meeting for the first time and introducing myself to those women seated around the room was a little daunting. Soon these sisters became my friends, but one could not be in that board room long without recognizing another circle of women present there. Portraits of the past general presidents of Relief Society hung on the wall just behind those seated at the table. Beginning with Emma Smith, nearest the door, followed by Eliza R. Snow, then Zina D. H. Young, they continued in turn around the room to Belle S. Spafford. While they were not often spoken of as a group, individually their influence was felt. Or so it was for me. Though I observed them all (and surely Sister Spafford, then president, served as a mentor to each of us), it was Zina D. H. Young who became much more than a painting on the wall to me.

Zina D. H. Young

Her picture was exactly across the room from where I sat, and each time I looked in her direction my eyes met hers. Until other board members were called and we all moved on around the table, I continually felt a curious awareness of her. The agendas for the meetings changed and assignments varied, but Sister Young remained. Lace trimmed the front of her dress, and though it was feminine and pretty, it did not soften the intensity of her gaze. Except for Louise Y. Robison's merest turn of the lip, not one of the presidents smiled in her picture—that being the style of portraits in their day. So while Sister Zina, as she was often called, did not smile, neither was her look stern but rather steadfast and purposeful. Her eyes always seemed to be looking into mine as though projecting a message to me—something like, "This work matters. It must be done with excellence, and nothing less than this will do."

As board members, each week we reported to the presidency and board our visits to stakes and regions, and I felt as if I were reporting to Zina as well. In other assignments, too, I often thought about her and wondered if what I was doing measured up to her scrutiny. Her look was so compelling that it seemed to require a response. I can remember wanting to say to her, "I really am trying very hard. Is it good enough?"

While I may have read more into a picture on the wall than I needed to, it was good to have the feeling I did about Sister Young. That sense of needing to answer to the past became a measure for the immediate.

Recently I have been happy to find that much has been written about Zina Huntington Young, and even written by her in diaries and journals. Reading has taken me beyond the search of her eyes to learn something of her heart. In fact, many who knew her have said she was all heart. While I am not sorry to have had my earlier experience with Sister Young—for it is often those who see us through stressful times that remain our closest friends—still I am pleased to have become better acquainted with the lovable Aunt Zina whom so many have revered.

She was a part of the Church and of Relief Society from their beginnings. As the Church moved West and grew, so also grew the Relief Society, and Zina D. H. Young was ardent in helping to establish it throughout the settlements of the Saints. She served for many years as a counselor to Eliza R. Snow, and it was sometimes said that whereas Sister Snow was the head of the Relief Society—not only as the general president, but also in temperament and talent—Sister Young was its heart. "Sister Snow was keenly intellectual, and she led by force of that intelligence," wrote Susa Young Gates. "Sister Zina was all love and sympathy, and drew people after her by reason of that tenderness."[1] These two sisters presided in succession but were often spoken of together, for although Zina was 17 years younger than Eliza, they were close friends. Along with both having been sealed to the Prophet Joseph and married for time to Brigham Young, they served side by side in the organized work of women in the Church. In my reading to learn more about Sister Young, I quickly learned that she was warm, loving, and compassionate. Still, I wondered what made her so, and how the lovable Zina related to the person in the boardroom I thought I knew.

Zina Diantha Huntington's family converted to the Church in upstate New York, then gathered to Kirtland, Ohio, in 1836. Here Zina, still in her teens, heard the Prophet Joseph Smith speak for the first time. She described him as "truly affecting," saying, "Anyone that ever heard [him], I should think, could never forget."[2] And throughout her lifetime, she never did. The Huntingtons' faith in the restored gospel was confirmed in Kirtland, through associating with the Saints and through being "in the temple on the Sabbath," as Zina stated, "Whare we received many sacred testimonies from God that he accepted the labours of the Saints and visited them."[3]

From Kirtland the family moved with the body of the Church to Missouri. While perhaps nothing could have prepared them for what happened there, it was good to have had the spiritually rich 19 months in Kirtland. They suffered severely in Missouri, along with so many others, but finally made their way to Illinois, arriving in May 1839—survivors, but struggling. Biographer Mary Firmage Woodward wrote: For one whole year they had . . . barely subsist[ed]. Because of malnutrition and fatigue the entire family fell victim to the sickness which beset Nauvoo the first week of July, 1839. The Prophet Joseph sent his daughter Julie (one of the Murdock twins adopted by Emma and Joseph) to care for them. The Prophet was the only doctor available for all of the brethren and their families and went the circuit every day."[4]

Zina's mother succumbed to the illness and was considered a martyr to the truth because her death was attributed to the effect of the persecutions. Zina's brother Oliver recorded that sad scene in his diary: "In only a few days all our pleasant prospects seemed blighted for our mother died, ourselves all sick and none to follow her remains to the hastily prepared grave. . . . There was scarce anyone well & strong enough to dig a grave. . . . Indeed, we were a pitiful sight & none to pity us but God and his prophet."[5]

We can try to comprehend what the people endured in the Missouri difficulties, but it may have been more than we can know. Zina, who saw the violence at close range, later wrote, "I will here state that the mobings & final expulsion from Missouri I witnessed. The history of these days are partially written, but the sufferings cannot be told."[6]

After a time Zina's father, William, married the widow of the late Bishop Edward Partridge. This was an agreeable step, as the children of William attested, for she was a good mother to them. On 7 March 1841 Zina married Henry Bailey Jacobs, a friend of her older brother. She later married Joseph Smith and, after Joseph's death, Brigham Young. She had two sons, Zebulon William and Henry Chariton Jacobs, and, later, one daughter, Zina Presendia Young.

The Nauvoo days for Zina were alive with home duties, church responsibilities, and visits with friends and relations. And although she was busy with her own small family, frightened parents frequently brought a sick child to her for help because she had a gift for caring for and healing the sick. Wherever Zina was known, her kindness was known too, even beyond those near her. A Lamanite girl, Nancy, was touched by it. On 11 September 1845 Zina wrote: "Lewes Damp, a Lamanite, gave me a money purse that his step Daughter Nancy sent to me from the Mo Territory. She has been here and was baptized some years ago. When she left me or this plac[e] for the far west, I took a ring from my finger and gave it to her. . . . The purse is velvet, beautifully ornamented with beads or her own hands work."[7]

This account provides the facts of what happened. But the

purse, with the hours the intricate beading must have taken, is witness to what Zina's giving her ring meant to Nancy. That small incident assumes heightened interest through a picture. Many years and several moves after receiving the purse, Zina sat for a portrait with her three children. In the picture can be seen a beaded purse suspended by a cord from Zina's waist. It looks as if it could be that beaded bag.[8]

The mood in Nauvoo was tragically changed with the martyrdom of Joseph and Hyrum Smith on what Zina called "the ever to be r[em]embered awful day of the 27 of June 1844."[9] Her diary entry three days later reflects the gloom hanging over them: "It is Sunday, a lonely h[e]art sorrowful day. Also it rains."[10]

Zina shared her vivid memory of another important day. The succession of Brigham Young to the presidency of the Church became conclusive with the meeting held 8 August 1845. Zina wrote, "As for Brigham Young's being the true leader of this Church I saw him the 8 of August . . . when he was transfigured. Before the assembled saints the voice of Joseph perfectly, looks, jestures, the same spiret was there, he wore the mantle."[11]

As eyewitness to the Saints' last days in Nauvoo, Zina saw fearful evidence of tensions mounting: "When I cast mine eyes out, what do I behold, every brother armed, his gun uppon his shoulder to protect his family and Bretheren from the violence of the furious Mob who are now burning all that falls into their way round about the Country."[12]

Then, on 7 February 1846: "Clear and cold. . . . Shall I ever forget standing on Major Russells porch and seeing Tomas Grovers wagon had sunk on a sand bar, the Brethren taking the little ones from the wagon cover, the bows just peeped above the water. At the same time the bells were ringing, the Temple was on fire, and we leaving our homes for the wilderness, trusting God like Abriham."[13]

With each document and biographical account I have read of Zina Huntington's life, an image of her emerges more clearly. The challenges she faced, so unlike our own, sometimes seem overwhelming to me, and nearly always were hard for her to bear. But she endured them, and I salute her courage and fortitude. While her trials were not all physical, many were. These excerpts from her diary let us see some of the hardships she experienced: "Saturday 12, 1849. I washed scrubed Coloured & Ironed. Weary weary am I this night. O Father wilt thou be merciful and mindeful of me. I humbly Pray & let not hard labour shorten my days. I truly feel thankful for all past blessings. Saturday 26. It is Dimick B Huntington's birthday [Zina's brother]. He is 32. I washed and scrubed. The Sun set this night uppon a weary mortal traveler, a Pilgrim & A sojourner."[14]

When we think of Brigham Young's family, we usually think of that prosperous and happy group living in the Lion House and the Beehive House. And when a general board member thinks of the Lion House, it is often of having lunch in the Pantry, or of the occasional party in fully decorated upstairs rooms. Those two homes are lovely, and there were parties there in Zina's day. But when she arrived in the Valley in September 1848, there were not yet enough homes to house the many pioneers. In the beginning some stayed in the fort, some in tents, others in wagon boxes. Zina seems to have stayed mostly in the fort, spent a while in her wagon, then moved into "Log Row." This was a series of rooms constructed of logs, as the name implies, and covered with dirt roofs. She and her children lived in two rooms there for three years, some of that time sharing with another family, until the Lion House was finished. The log rooms were an improvement over a wagon, but the dirt roof did not always keep out the rain: "June Tuesday 5. [Cared for a sick sister before teaching school.] After school cleaned the house as the rane last night come through and covered the house with clay. The sun [set] uppon a weary traveler. After milking I retired to rest. O Hevenly Father give me strength I humbly pray."[15]

Zina frequently closed her diary entries with a prayer. She felt the Lord with her continuously and included him in her diary as she would any other person she might have encountered that day. Heavenly Father was Zina's strength, and she knew it. This was the power that enabled her to endure hardship, storm, and privation. I relate little to the kinds of things she endured, but I can identify with "the strength of our Father in Heaven." I pray to that same Father and for the same thing: "O Heavenly Father give me strength I humbly pray." It is through reading her frequent prayers that I am beginning to feel a spiritual kinship with Zina.

In another way I feel a kindred spirit in Zina—with her musings. Although as a young girl I sometimes gazed at cumulus clouds while wondering, whereas she watched the dying embers of a fire, both are expressions of a reflective mood partaking of the same pensive turn of mind. She included some of her contemplative thoughts in the account of her life: "In my earliest reading of history, confuscious, Columbus and Wm. Wallace I used to muse while watching the consuming back log in our old fireplaces why I could not have been born in a day when something was going on in the nations of the Earth, not that I wished to see distress, but some enterprise."[16]

Had she been able to see in a brighter light, Zina might have known not only that she had been born in a day when something was going on in this nation, but that she had been born unto a calling to help establish a work, the word of which would be taken to every nation, kindred, tongue, and people (see D&C 42:58). She might have foreseen that she was to be a significant player in an enterprise that would raise an ensign to the nations and build an empire in the tops of the mountains, to the amazement of other peoples and to the glory of God.

For Zina, as for most people, her life's work was cumulative; she wasn't having "mountain top" experiences or achievements that she could perceive each day. When the Lion House was completed she moved into her rooms on the third floor and there found contentment with her children. Then when Ziney, the youngest child, was eight years old, Brigham Young asked Zina if she would accept into her family four of his other children, whose mother had died. There is no suggestion of her weighing the matter; she, of course, did it. But that night she had a serious talk with Ziney. Mary Firmage Woodward writes: "[Zina] exacted a promise from Ziney that she would never by word or deed indicate that the new family were any other than her mother's very own. And eight-year-old Zina kept her promise with pride and thanksgiving for her brother and sisters. Mary was eleven, Maria, nine, Willard, six and little Phoebe only four."[17]

Thus Zina's family was increased twofold, and, because her loving and expansive heart made it so, these four motherless children always considered Mother Zina to be their own.

Once her children were grown Zina Young began giving more time to service outside her home. It was actually during these next years until her death that she accomplished the work for which she is most remembered. Health care was always a need, and she was willing to help. As early as 1848 she had attended classes in herbal medicine, midwifery, diseases of children, and home nursing. This training was valuable, but Zina's unusual effectiveness in caring for the sick lay more in the certain sense she had of how to help. Participating in health care was a natural expression of her compassion and the gift of healing she seemed to possess. Emmeline B. Wells said, "In the true charity that hopeth all things . . . she so distinguished herself among the sick and the sorrowing, that she . . . gained with many the appellation of 'Zina, the comforter.' "[18] "In the sick-room, she was a ministering angel, having always something to suggest that would be soothing and restful. . . . No other woman knew better what to do when death came into a home."[19] Later, when Deseret Hospital was founded, Zina served as the vice president; her interest in health care also extended to the training of nurses.

Another activity Zina pursued was sericulture. In anticipation of silk production in Deseret, Brigham Young requested immigrants from Europe to bring with them silkworm eggs and seeds from the mulberry trees upon which the worms fed. As the needed components began to arrive with the immigrants, some of the more adventuresome settlers attempted the production of silk, but with only sporadic success. Then President Young established the Deseret Silk Association, coordinating all separate projects by wards into one effort, and appointed Zina D. H. Young as its president.

Zina organized a board to promote the project, she traveled the territory to encourage and teach the procedure, and she even managed a cocoonery herself to increase the production; but in spite of her efforts the undertaking was never a financial success. Its accomplishment and greatest worth lay in what it did for the people of this far west outpost. In coming there the Saints often had to leave behind many of the refinements of life, but the production of silk made it possible again to have some of the nice things they enjoyed. Through their own efforts women could wear silk dresses and lovely shawls and have beautiful objects to enhance their homes. They received some recognition for their achievements in silk production from people outside the territory, but the lasting benefit came in the lives and homes of the participants themselves.

At the death of Sister Eliza R. Snow in 1887, Zina D. H. Young was called to be general president of the Relief Society and matron of the Salt Lake Temple. During her 13 years as president, the Relief Society became affiliated with the National Council of Women and the International Council of Women. Utah became a state during these years, and participation in national programs necessarily meant interaction with people of other beliefs. At the same time, the Church was growing, bringing a need to strengthen the bonds of sisterhood in Relief Society. Zina Young, with her outgoing, friendly mien and her genuinely loving heart, was well suited to these requirements. Susa Young Gates said that "she was eloquent, and had a personal magnetism that attracted the nearest stranger instantly to her side."[20] How better to represent the women of the Church in national councils than with the personable Mrs. Young, or who better to reach out and bring together the sisters of Relief Society than beloved Aunt Zina?

Zina Huntington Young lived in a way to call forth admiration. She was known for her loving kindness in spite of circumstances that could have taught her to be otherwise; she often served with a capability beyond her own in the strength of the Lord. For Zina that strength is best characterized in her unwavering faith in the truth of the gospel and in the power of love, the pure love of Christ. With her, love was a corollary to truth—one did not exist without the other.

In recounting her own days she tells of her faith. An autobiographical sketch she wrote later in her life contains one line that at first reading seems incidental and only a part of something else; but upon looking more closely, one finds that within these words lies the defining belief of Zina D. H. Young. She explains the failure of the Church's bank in Kirtland due to the dealings of a dishonest man, and then she makes this significant statement: *"Those that had embraced the gospel for some other reason than the love of the truth left the church."*[21] She was not among the number who left the Church then, nor did she waver in any other test of faith, though many had come and gone since she was first convinced of the truth.

When she was 15 years old, missionaries had brought a Book of Mormon to her home. She recalled, "I saw the Book of Mormon . . . on the window sill of our sitting-room. I went up to the window, picked it up, and the sweet influence of the Holy Spirit accompanied it to such an extent that I pressed it to my bosom in a rapture of delight, murmuring as I did so, 'This is the truth, truth, truth!' "22

It has been said that to be educated is to understand the implications of one's beliefs. For Zina Huntington Young, we might expand that idea: to be a faithful Latter-day Saint is not only to understand the implications of one's belief but also to love it. Zina found the truth, accepted it—recognizing the implications of such a commitment—and never forsook it. She built a life around her love for it, a life that embraced love and truth, the two as one. This became evident in her every relationship and calling. It was the love of the truth that sustained Zina Huntington Young to the end of her life.

Although our times and circumstances have put a distance between us that does not allow a mutual association, I have found in Zina D. H. Young a special kind of friend. I think of her as someone coming from the past, bringing into my life a new richness of understanding, and for whom I feel a warm affection in return. Reading of her trials has made me weep for her; learning of her triumphs has brought me joy. While there is much more to her life than can be written here, even these few excerpts and episodes have opened to me a time and a season in the life of a noble woman I am only now learning to know well enough to fully appreciate.

When I read of Zina and Eliza R. Snow traveling to many small settlements in southern Utah organizing Relief Societies and teaching the women, it sounded not unlike the board assignments we were given—only they traveled by horse and buggy, often camping out at night and sometimes being required to repair a broken harness or buggy wheel. I thought for a brief moment of how it might have been were Zina in the circle around the table rather than in her place on the wall. We might have been assigned to travel to Parowan or Pine Valley together, or to Boise or maybe Berlin.

But no, Zina is now bigger than life. She has taken on truly heroic proportions. She belongs in a gold frame just where she is, so that she can be read about and revered—and loved. Then others will know how she tried to establish a silk industry in a desert wilderness and to begin a school before a schoolhouse was built; they will hear how she nursed and cared for the sick and dying and helped to establish a hospital and a school of nursing when there was little but will with which to do it. Others will be told of how she crossed the plains with a wagon train, giving birth to a baby along the way, and later burying her father. And what is more than all of these events, and motive to them all, is to know that she had the courage to accept a new faith, an unpopular belief that required the full commitment of one's heart, might, mind, and strength. Of that price Zina wrote about Joseph "laying down his life for the truth's sake" and then, suggesting some of what she paid, said, "If we loved our good names & homes . . . more than salvation then the world would love us as its own."[23] Zina willingly laid "aside the things of this world [to] seek for the things of a better" (see D&C 25:10).

The poet T. S. Eliot may not have understood eternal truth nearly as well as Zina Young did, but he penned some words that describe very well its cost. He speaks of searching for the understanding of all things—the truth—and believes that when we do succeed in that search, we will find "a condition of complete simplicity / (Costing not less than everything.)"[24]

Zina Huntington Young paid dearly for the truth. And in the end it matters little if the "world loved her as their own," for those who love the truth—the truth she loved and helped to establish—love her. Susa Young Gates concluded, "There have been many noble women, some great women and a multitude of good women associated, past and present, with the Latter-Day work. But of them all none was so lovely, so lovable, and so passionately beloved as was 'Aunt Zina.'"[25]

When I was a new board member I tried hard to please Zina Huntington Young, to give her my best effort. It seemed she expected it of me. I may never know why I felt the way I did about her and her picture; I had always tried to give my best to Church assignments. But I believe the insistent expectation I thought was hers is appropriate to the loving, caring Zina Young I have come to know.

To help another succeed in an assignment, or to earn salvation in the celestial kingdom, is an act of love—love for the truth and love for another of our Father's children. Giving one's finest effort to fulfill an assignment is to express one's love for it and for the truth it represents. This echoes the Savior's injunction "If ye love me, keep my commandments" (John 14:15).

To learn about Zina Huntington Young's life is to learn about love and truth and what giving all can mean. Though she is not on the wall before me now, she continues to prompt. I'll think endearingly of her as I give my best to the truth we both love.

NOTES

1. Susa Young Gates, *History of the Young Ladies' Mutual Improvement Association, November 1869 to June 1910* (Salt Lake City: Deseret News, 1911), p. 21.

2. Zina Diantha Huntington, autobiographical sketch, holograph, p. 2, Zina Card Brown Collection, Historical Department, The Church of Jesus Christ of Latter-day Saints, Salt Lake City, Utah.

Zina Diantha Huntington Young has given eloquent voice to an era in the history of the Church. Her expression is often vivid and articulate. We are indebted to her for both the quality and the extent of her writings. In including excerpts from her works, little has been done that changes her original material, only the occasional editorial mark to make it more readable. Her spelling is sometimes irregular, and if that could be called a "weakness" in her, surely the Lord has made "weak things strong" (see Ether 12:21) when we consider the value of her writings.

3. Ibid.

4. Mary Firmage Woodward, "Zina," unpublished draft, typescript, p. 11, courtesy Maureen Ursenbach Beecher.

Mary Brown Firmage Woodward is a direct descendant of Zina D. H. Young; her mother, Zina Card Brown, was the daughter of "Ziney," Zina Diantha's only daughter. She is preparing an extensive work on Zina Huntington Young and graciously allowed use of these materials.

5. Ibid.

6. Huntington, holograph, p. 5.

7. Zina D. H. Young, "'All Things Move in Order in the City': The Nauvoo Diary of Zina Diantha Huntington Jacobs," ed. Maureen Ursenbach Beecher *Brigham Young University Studies* 19 (Spring 1979), p. 319. Maureen Beecher

generously provided many of the valuable materials about Zina D. H. Young used in this chapter—the much appreciated kind of help that was not available through library sources.

8. See photograph in *Encyclopedia of Mormonism*, ed. Daniel H. Ludlow, 4 vols. (New York: Macmillan, 1992), 4:1612.

9. Young, "All Things Move in Order," p. 292.

10. Ibid., p. 293.

11. Huntington, holograph, p. 9.

12. Young, "All Things Move in Order," pp. 319-20.

13. Woodward, "Zina," p. 15.

14. Marilyn Higbee, "'A Weary Traveler:' The 1848-50 Diary of Zina D. H. Young," pp. 26, 27, University Scholar Project, Brigham Young University, 1992.

15. Ibid., p. 29.

16. Huntington, holograph, p. 1.

17. Woodward, "Zina," p. 25.

18. Emmeline B. Wells, "A Distinguished Woman," *Woman's Exponent*, 15 November 1881, pp. 90-1.

19. Emmeline B. Wells, "Zina D. H. Young—A Character Sketch," *The Improvement Era*, November 1901, p. 44.

20. Gates, *History of M.I.A.*, p. 25.

21. Huntington, holograph, p. 3, emphasis added.

22. Zina D. H. Young, "How I Gained My Testimony," *Young Woman's Journal*, 4 April 1893, p. 318.

23. Huntington, holograph, p. 8.

24. T. S. Eliot, "Little Gidding," *Four Quartets* (New York, Harcourt, Brace and Co., 1943), p. 39.

25. Gates, *History of M.I.A.*, p. 21.

২

Shirley W. Thomas lives in Provo, Utah, with her husband, Robert K. Thomas. They have three married children and 11 grandchildren. Shirley served as second counselor to Barbara B. Smith in the Relief Society general presidency. A graduate of Brigham Young University, she coedited *Where Feelings Flower* and coauthored *Words for Women: Promises of Prophets*. Writing about Zina D. H. Young has helped Shirley realize how closely her life is associated with others who have served the women of the Church.

11

"I Gently Closed the Door"
Bathsheba W. Smith
1822–1910

When I was a little girl, I used to take naps on the gold damask couch in the living room. Right above it hung an imposing portrait of a stately woman with refined demeanor, elegant clothes, and commanding stature. An ornate mantilla draped her white hair; an exquisite handmade lace collar ringed her dark silk, fitted dress. Her eyes followed me. Every time I walked into the room she looked at me. When I was dusting the furniture, when I was racing through in a chase with my brother, when I was practicing the piano, there was Bathsheba W. Smith.

She scared me.

In later years I became much better acquainted with my great-great-great-grandmother Bathsheba. My image of her matured and her picture took on new meaning. Framed as she was in an ornate leaf pattern of antique gold, Bathsheba Wilson Bigler Smith looked like a queen whose portrait should hang in the hall of a castle suggesting a life of privilege, polish, and ease. But not so. In her lifetime she faced the persecutions of the early Church, the sorrow of losing hosts of loved ones,

Bathsheba W. Smith

the harshness of the pioneer trail, the settling of a desert Zion, and the complexities of helping "grow a Church." Put simply, her life was hard.

The wife of George A. Smith, the youngest Apostle called in this dispensation and cousin of the Prophet Joseph Smith, she was at the heart of early Church activity in Nauvoo. She was a charter member of the Relief Society, the youngest married woman. In the years that followed she was mother and grandmother not only to her own two children, George A. and Bathsheba, but to those of her sister-wives and close friends as well. She was on the board of directors of Deseret Hospital, was in the presidency of the Retrenchment Association, and served as treasurer, counselor, and then president of her ward's Relief Society. For 17 years she served in the Endowment House in Salt Lake City. She was matron of the Salt Lake Temple and fourth president of the general Relief Society for the Church, serving from 1901 to 1910. When she died her obituary ran on the front page of the *Deseret News*, and her funeral was held in the Salt Lake Tabernacle. Said Apostle Anthon H. Lund at the service, "She was a woman of God."[1]

I could discuss in detail all of these significant contributions, but I am leaving that to history. Her influence on me is more personal, for in many ways I grew up with Bathsheba Smith. Once I got past the portrait to the person, I found many parts of her life that have profoundly impacted mine.

What strikes me most is her repeated ability to "Come" when the Lord called, to put her life in his hands. Each time it meant leaving part of her life behind, yet it proved the making of a latter-day heroine. A line from poet Robert Frost speaks volumes when applied to the life of Bathsheba Smith: "I took the [road] less traveled by, and that has made all the difference."[2]

Like Bathsheba, I, too, have had to turn and walk away from hopes and dreams. Most of us have been there. We have had to bury the children we wanted to raise, drive cars without hubcaps, and give up so many other desires. We have had to stand in the rain at soccer games, put an arm around a third baseman who missed too many balls, walk grocery aisles with a child in leg braces that bumped the bottom rows of cereal boxes. We have had to find comfort in disaster, friendship in a new ward, strength when a friend is fighting cancer, and hope when there seems to be none at all.

Bathsheba may have lived in a different time, but the way she addressed life's trials speaks wisdom to my soul. She took to heart the Lord's counsel in 1830 to "lay aside the things of this world, and seek for the things of a better" (D&C 25:10). She lived by it. For her, the gospel came first, and she closed the door on everything else, one door at a time. Her incredible faith and testimony gave her strength sufficient to face relentless hardships and find peace in the process.

I talk about closing doors because my favorite story from her life involves just that—walking out of her home in Nauvoo, closing the front door, getting in the wagon, and going west. Bathsheba left her home in the bitter cold of February 1846. She and her husband crossed the Mississippi in the first exodus that left Nauvoo. They, and hundreds like them, left behind their temple, their fields and orchards, their gardens and their homes. Every time I think of her experience I am impressed that I, too, can do what has been asked of me.

Bathsheba's autobiography tells how she sacrificed her earthly treasures for what she knew to be true. She fervently believed in the Lord's work and in his promised glory, and her exodus from Nauvoo bore witness to that testimony. She wrote:

> We left a comfortable home, the accumulations of four years of labor and thrift and took away with us only a few much needed articles such as clothing, bedding and provisions. We left everything else behind us for our enemies.
>
> My last act in that precious spot was to tidy the rooms, sweep up the floor, and set the broom in its accustomed place behind the door. Then with emotions in my heart which I could not now pen and which I then strove with success to conceal, I gently closed the door and faced an unknown future, faced a new life, a greater destiny as I well knew, but I faced it with faith in God.[3]

That resolve—to face it "with faith in God"—reaches right into my heart. Bathsheba recognized what was being asked. I have pondered how she must have felt sweeping the floor for the last time, straightening the cushions that she had so carefully made, setting out of the draft the plants that she had nurtured from cuttings, then closing the door on that life she had worked so hard to sustain, on that house which had given her dignity and security when persecution had stripped so much away.

She completed her entry with this powerful summation: "Now I was going into the wilderness, but I was going with the man I loved dearer than my life. I had my little children. I had heard a voice, so I stepped into the wagon with a certain degree of serenity."[4]

I believe that the voice she heard was the voice of the Lord and that he had said, "Come, Bathsheba." She did. She knew that voice. The words of Paul to the Corinthians were being repeated to her and all the beleaguered Saints: "Come out from among them, and be ye separate, saith the Lord . . . and I will receive you" (2 Corinthians 6:17).

All of us at some point are asked to close the door and then walk into the wilderness. That Bathsheba did this with a "certain degree of serenity," in a fulness of faith, took the edge off the fierce forces all around her. What a lesson!

I have closed a door like that, though my house was never even built. My husband and I had lived for five years in an apartment in the center of Salt Lake City. I longed to share a street with neighbors, not fire trucks, buses, and commuters. We purchased a lot on a hill with a view of the city and hired an architect to design our house, complete with gabled windows and doors with beveled glass. Then we moved, renting a home in our new area while we built our dream. Except we never broke ground.

Although we had already moved out of our ward, our stake president called and invited us in for a visit. While it appeared the appointment was only a formality in releasing my husband as a counselor in our bishopric, I had a feeling it was something else. The stake president's request was bold. "Come back," he said. "The Lord needs you here. He wants you in this area; we need you on the high council."

Come.

I was shocked by his request, but when my husband accepted, I was stunned. We moved back but not until I did some serious soul-searching. The scripture "As for me and my house, we will serve the Lord" (Joshua 24:15) suddenly took on new meaning. Four days after the call from the stake president, I walked into the backyard of our rented home, lit a match, and burned our house plans. Now I was in the wagon with Bathsheba. I didn't know then that my husband would be called to serve in a succession of leadership positions there. I only knew the Lord had said, "Come."

Bathsheba's example of closing her front door takes on additional significance when we follow her from home to home leading up to that time in Nauvoo. Bathsheba was born in 1822 and had been raised on her father's Virginia estate in a spacious and beautifully appointed home. She was educated, skilled as an equestrian, and interested in religion. Her family moved to Missouri shortly after joining the Church in 1837, and her surroundings changed dramatically. Persecution forced them to abandon their newly purchased farm, and for many months the struggle was simply to survive. The stress and exposure took the lives of many Saints. Her father, Mark Bigler, died in Quincy, Illinois, in 1839.

Bathsheba married George A. Smith 25 July 1841. He was one of the elders who had been a frequent visitor to her home in Virginia, and she had agreed "to keep his cabin" in three years when he completed his missionary service. The two first moved in with his parents. Within a month they started housekeeping in a small log cabin that was highly unsuitable. According to Bathsheba, "The house leaked and the chimney smoked."[5] When George A. was asked to move to Nauvoo, they did, renting a log house "that was open and that chimney, too, smoked."[6]

They tried renting a room, which was much more comfortable, but then Brother Joseph gave them a lot with a small log house. "My husband fixed up the place as best he could," wrote Bathsheba, "but, after all, it was the worst looking house we had yet lived in. I was ashamed to have my acquaintances see me in such a looking place. It, however, had the desirable qualities of neither leaking nor smoking."[7]

They decided to build a home there in Nauvoo. George A. went to work and soon had constructed a story-and-a-half frame house with four rooms, two up and two down. He fenced and drained the lot, and the young couple planted a garden, with "fruit trees, flowers, vegetables and corn." Called on another mission, George left it to Bathsheba to get the house finished. Bathsheba "spared no pains or effort to make this home a place good to look upon."[8] She struggled to afford workers to plaster the rooms, finish the roof, and hang the glass windows. Trained by her mother in many forms of needlework, she made curtains, lace cloths, pillows, and special pillow covers to give the home her touch. She repeatedly got up in the middle of the night to take her turn watering the orchard.

In the short years before the exodus, Bathsheba opened her doors to refugee Saints who had been burned out of their homes and then fled to Nauvoo for safety. Right before she abandoned Nauvoo, her parlor was used as a workshop for painting wagons in preparation for the exodus. It was the door of this house, which had so much of her labor and heart, that Bathsheba gently closed, leaving the house to her enemies.

Though Bathsheba's experience in leaving her home was only a footnote in the unfolding drama of the flight from Nauvoo, it was a defining moment for her. Her significant Church responsibilities later in life were perhaps the showpiece experiences of Bathsheba Smith, the headlines, but it was there in Nauvoo that she fully committed her course to Christ.

That was not the first, or last, of her trials of faith. In Nauvoo the Lord asked only for her home; before, due to the persecutions in Missouri, Bathsheba had determined that she might have to give up her life for the Church. She had felt that way with good reason.

When Bathsheba's family, the Biglers, had been traveling to Far West, they had joined with a company of Saints from the eastern states, held a service, and worshipped together. In the morning, to make better time, the two groups separated, crossing the river on different ferries. While Bathsheba's family arrived safely, the other company was overtaken by an armed mob at Haun's Mill and 17 were killed, with many others wounded and maimed for life.

The Biglers had purchased a farm in the area of Far West, and they "were well received by the Saints among whom [they] had cast [their] lot."9 But things were already out of control. Within days mob activity escalated; Bathsheba was in the room when David W. Patten, the first martyr among the Twelve Apostles, died following a vicious attack.

"I witnessed much," she wrote in her journal, "very much suffering which was brought upon our people by these lawless men. In these distressing times the Spirit of the Lord comforted and sustained me. I had an abiding testimony that we were being persecuted for the Gospel's sake and . . . that though many of us might be called to lay down our lives, the Gospel must survive."10

Years later, having left Nauvoo, Bathsheba found the trail west through Iowa in the middle of winter to be grueling. She wrote, "We traveled through snow, wind and rain . . . how we suffered in poverty and sickness, and many died of the hardships and privation, and were buried by the wayside, as we journeyed along."11

At this point many of us may have been inclined to shake our heads, already bent down from the strain and the miseries, and say, "No more." What Bathsheba said was, "But the Lord was with us and His power was daily made manifest."12

Bathsheba had heard the Lord say "Come," and she went to Missouri. He had said "Come," and she left her home in Nauvoo. In Winter Quarters he said "Come" again, but this sacrificial call perhaps tested her strength and resolve to the limit.

People died crossing Iowa; they died at Winter Quarters, too. In March of 1847 Bathsheba lost her mother, Susannah Ogden Bigler, herself a woman of faith and refinement. In April, a month later, Bathsheba's second son, John, was born. Her record of that time is brief and telling: "He was my last child, and lived only four hours."13

Anyone who has lost a child at birth or in their youth knows that this brings extraordinary pain. I think the closing of this door was when Bathsheba turned to the Lord and pleaded for peace. Her testimony of Joseph Smith and the Savior had sustained her through many trials. This one required that she feel the Spirit with her in great abundance.

In the same cemetery where Bathsheba rests, I stood by the grave as we buried my oldest son, Christian, one of my twins, who died 22 hours after he was born. The grief was enormous, the peace greater still. Into my mind came the scripture in John, "Peace I leave with you, my peace I give unto you: not as the world giveth, give I unto you. Let not your heart be troubled, neither let it be afraid." (John 14:27.)

I was closing the door on my earthly hopes and dreams for this child. Bathsheba had already been there. I learned, as she must have, that when the Lord says to one of our most precious, "Come home," he also fulfills his promise to us, "I will be on your right hand and on your left, and my Spirit shall be in your hearts, and my angels round about you, to bear you up" (D&C 84:88).

Bathsheba faced this anguish again in 1860 when her other son, George Albert, was murdered by Navajo Indians. He was only 18. On a special mission with pioneer leader Jacob Hamblin to the Moqui (Hopi) Indians in what is now Arizona, he was shot by a band of young warriors retaliating for an attack by white soldiers on their settlement. They were evening the score by killing this young elder who had left the safety of his party to retrieve his horse, which had bolted. His father, George A. Smith, who was very involved in the settlement of southern Utah and for whom St. George is named, had to tell Bathsheba of their loss. It was agonizing for them both.

Bathsheba had learned to find peace. Over the years she became known for saying as she walked out of the door of a home she had visited, "Peace be with you." That message was grounded in her testimony that the gospel of Jesus Christ was true, the Book of Mormon was the word of God, and Joseph Smith was a prophet. That understanding was fully framed in Nauvoo, where, because of George A.'s assignment as an Apostle, the two had numerous opportunities to hear Joseph Smith preach the doctrines of the kingdom of God.

Bathsheba's testimony of priesthood authority was grounded in personal experience as well. In an official statement to the United States Congress, she stated: "It was my privilege to attend a regular prayer meeting in the lodge room over the Prophet's store. There were present at this meeting most of the Twelve Apostles, their wives and a number of prominent brethren and their wives. On that occasion the Prophet arose and spoke at great length and during his remarks I heard him say that he had conferred on the heads of the Twelve Apostles all the keys and powers pertaining to the Priesthood, and that upon the heads of the Twelve Apostles the burden of the kingdom rested, and that they would have to carry it."[14]

Bathsheba was sealed to George A. on 12 July 1843 in what she described as "the holy order of the Celestial Marriage which order is for time and eternity."[15] In December of that same year she wrote: "I received my endowment in the upper room over the Prophet Joseph Smith's store. The endowments were given under the direction of the Prophet Joseph Smith who afterwards gave us a lecture or instructions in regard to the endowment ceremonies."[16]

When the Prophet Joseph taught the principles of celestial marriage, Bathsheba heard again the call to "Come," this time opening the doors of her heart to sister-wives. She wrote: "Being thoroughly convinced as well as my husband that the doctrine of plurality of wives was from God, and having a fixed determination to attain to Celestial glory, I felt to embrace the whole gospel. Accordingly like Sarah of Old, I have given to my husband five wives, good, virtuous, honorable young women, this gave them all homes, with us."[17] These sister-wives were Lucy Meserve, Nancy Clement, Zilpha Stark, Sarah Ann Libby, and Sarah's sister, Hannah Maria Libby. Later George A. also married Susan Elizabeth West.

In my own marriage I have Bathsheba to thank for my husband. We both descend from George A. Smith. Jeffrey's great-great-grandmother is Hannah Maria Libby, George A.'s sixth wife.

Bathsheba fully embraced her husband's large family. In 1849, when the Lord said "Come" to the Valley, George A. was in charge of the company in which they would travel, but he lacked the resources to obtain the necessary outfits. Said Bathsheba, "It would have been impossible for any of us to go had it not been for the money and property left by my mother when she succumbed to the hardships of Winter Quarters. This I readily gave to my husband to satisfy the needs of his large family so that he was able to purchase equipment for this journey."[18]

In 1875 another door closed in Bathsheba's life. George A. Smith, then a counselor to President Brigham Young, died of a lung ailment, and Bathsheba was left a widow for 35 years. "I believe but few in this wide world have been as happy as we have been," Bathsheba wrote of their union. Her description of his death says it all: "I could not think of myself. I loved him more. He was now through. All was quiet and his head lay against my bosom, good angels had come to receive his precious spirit, perhaps our sons, prophets, patriarchs, saints beloved were there, but he was gone. My light, my sun, my life, my joy, my Lord. Yea almost my God. But I must not mourn but prepare myself to meet him but my heart sinks with in my bosom nearly."[19]

Bathsheba was so much a part of the early era of the restored Church—when the cornerstone was laid for the foundation of the Nauvoo Temple, when the Relief Society was organized, when the Prophet and his brother Hyrum were killed. According to Bathsheba, those days following the Martyrdom were ones "of anguish and horror and mourning." But then she witnessed the resiliency of testimony and faith. "The people emerged more hopeful and more determined that Truth would triumph."[20]

The Church did not collapse, as its opponents had hoped. The members carried on the work. Bathsheba assisted day and night in the Nauvoo Temple as every effort was made to endow the Saints while they raced against the clock of persecution. Years later she was called to "officiate as a priestess"[21] in the Endowment House in the Logan, St. George, and Manti Temples. When the Salt Lake Temple opened, she was called as the assistant matron and later as the matron.

Bathsheba Wilson Bigler Smith's portrait hangs in the hall of the women's area of the Salt Lake Temple; it draws me to it each time I am there. It has added another dimension to my temple experience because I know she loved the work more than anything else the Lord had called her to do. When he said "Come" to the temple, he knew Bathsheba would embrace the experience with all her heart. This is where Bathsheba made her signature contribution. She knew the power of the temple and the significance of the temple ordinances, and felt the power of the Lord's promises when she was there. Bathsheba found peace all around her in the temple; I do too. Perhaps it's because in the temple the doors are open to eternity. We reach beyond temporal time to the promises of eternal life.

Bathsheba faced challenges that would daunt even the most resilient. Yet she carried on with dignity and determination, always resounding one particular theme: "I know Joseph Smith for what he professed to be, a true prophet of God, and the Lord through him restored the everlasting gospel and every ordinance and endowment that will lead us into the celestial kingdom."[22] Her second counselor in the general Relief Society presidency, Ida Smoot Dusenberry, said at her funeral, "If the book of Life were written there would be something beautiful on each page."[23]

President Joseph F. Smith, in tribute to Bathsheba, said in a written note to her, "Your life has been one of constant energy, fraught with toil and sacrifice of personal comfort and mixed with plentiful sorrow. And yet, your life has been full of good works, and true womanly deeds with real Christian patience, and with love divine, the crowning virtues of a well spent, virtuous, generous life. You have the surest promise of most glorious rewards."[24]

That's the woman that now looks out of that painting at me. Her eyes still follow me, but the message is now more clear. She speaks to my heart of healing with the peace of the Lord. She speaks of listening for his voice. She exemplifies the blessings that come to those who hear his call. When I think of Alma's call to works of righteousness—"Have ye been spiritually born of God? Have ye received his image in your countenances?" (Alma 5:14)—I think of Bathsheba in her portrait framed in all her nobility and holiness.

From Bathsheba I have learned that life is all about opening and closing doors. Bathsheba's door closed on this life when she died on 20 September 1910 at age 88. My door to this life opened when I was born on that same day 38 years later.

NOTES

1. *Deseret Evening News,* 26 September 1910, p. 5.

2. Robert Frost, "The Road Not Taken," *The Poetry of Robert Frost,* ed. Edward Connery Lathem (New York: Holt, Rinehart and Winston, 1969), p. 105.

3. Bathsheba W. Smith, autobiography, ed. Alice Merrill Horne, typescript, pp. 14–15, in author's possession.

4. Ibid., p. 15.

5. Ibid., p. 9.

6. Ibid.

7. Ibid., p. 10.

8. Ibid.

9. Ibid., p. 7.

10. Smith, pp. 6–7.

11. Ibid., pp. 15–16.

12. Ibid., p. 16.

13. Ibid., p. 18.

14. Affidavit notarized by Martin S. Lindsay, 19 November 1903, Bathsheba W. Smith Collection, Archives Division, Church Historical Department, The Church of Jesus Christ of Latter-day Saints, Salt Lake City, Utah.

15. Smith, p. 7.

16. Ibid.

17. Ibid., p. 13.

18. Ibid., p. 22

19. Ibid., p. 42.

20. Ibid., p. 12.

21. Ibid., p. 42.

22. Smith, p. 19.

23. *Deseret Evening News,* 26 September 1910, p. 5.

24. Joseph F. Smith, as quoted in "Sister Bathsheba Smith Sees Her Seventy-Fifth Birthday," *Deseret News,* 3 May 1897.

꙾

Heidi Swinton graduated from the University of Utah, where she majored in English and journalism and was the editor of the *Daily Utah Chronicle.* She also attended Northwestern Medill School of Journalism. A professional writer, compiler, and editor, Heidi has written seven books, her latest being *The Pioneer Spirit.* She is a Gospel Doctrine teacher and has served on general Church writing committees. She is married to Jeffrey C. Swinton and they are the parents of four sons. Of this essay on Bathsheba W. Smith, Heidi says, "My heart is on each page."

12

A Life Story Patchwork Quilt
Elizabeth Stowe Higgs
1824–1913

The summer of 1978 was never to be forgotten. My husband, Richard, and I were thrilled to find out we were having our first child. Before I had a chance to share our news with my only living grandparent, he died. He was my only link to the past—at least, that is what I believed at the time. Passing beyond the veil, he left me with a heavy heart and something else I had not known before—I felt a great desire to seek out the personal history of my kindred dead and to discover the stories of their lives.

My husband is intensely interested in the past, especially the history of the Latter-day Saints. While in California for my grandfather's funeral, he began asking questions about my progenitors. I soon became consumed with the desire to find answers to his and my own questions about my family history, and so began my adventure.

In October 1979, with an eight-month-old baby in arms, Richard and I drove to Manti, Sanpete County, Utah, to visit a 91-year-old Saint, Alice Johnson Nielsen. The timing was providential because she died on 20 November, just a few weeks after our afternoon meeting. For me, the visit

Elizabeth Stowe Higgs

was important since Sister Nielsen knew my great-great-grandmother, Elizabeth Stowe Higgs.

"Little Sister Higgs," as Sister Nielsen called her, was born in England in 1824 and died in Utah in 1913, long before I was born. My desire to find living bridges to Elizabeth brought me into contact with several aged Saints, including her last living grandchild, George Henry Higgs, my mother's uncle. Within a short time these people were gone, and I was grateful for the opportunities to record their thoughts and remembrances of my great-great-grandmother before their voices became silent.

Elizabeth Stowe Higgs lived during an exciting time of world history and was an active participant in the Restoration drama that unfolded during the 19th and early 20th centuries. Just a year before my visit with Sister Nielsen in 1979, I had begun to piece together her life story as if making a quilt. The first patch of this quilt was a photograph of Elizabeth that I saw in the home of a distant relative during a visit in Salt Lake City. Since my husband and I had been attending school in Utah, we had begun looking up information about my family in libraries and historical repositories in the state, particularly in Salt Lake City. One discovery led to another, and soon I was on the phone with Roberta Slater Barker, Elizabeth's great-granddaughter, whom I had never had the pleasure of meeting before.

I had found Roberta's name on a genealogical sheet she submitted on our common family line. Although she had never met Elizabeth in person, Roberta had shown enough interest in family history that she had managed to collect a wealth of photographs and other information from Elizabeth's children and grandchildren. Later, she and her husband served a mission at the London Temple, which allowed them to continue their search for names in Elizabeth's line and to visit her birthplace. I made an appointment to visit Roberta and soon thereafter drove to her home in Salt Lake City. As Richard and I stood on her porch, I knew that a whole new world awaited me inside. We were greeted by the friendly retired couple—Roberta and her husband, Elwood—as though we had known each other for years.

Soon, envelopes, folders and small boxes of material were

brought into their living room to be opened. My anticipation at Christmas or birthdays as a child could not have been greater than at that moment. Each envelope, folder, or box contained a family heirloom or document revealing something about Elizabeth and her family.

Just after we began, Roberta opened a folder and said, "Here is a picture of your great-great-grandmother Elizabeth." Before that day Elizabeth had been just a faceless name in my genealogy pedigree line.

I examined the photograph carefully, searching every part for clues of this person and her world. The image had been taken by the famous Utah photographer George Edward Anderson when Elizabeth lived in Manti sometime in the 1880s. She was shown standing near a table on which a photograph of the Manti Temple was carefully displayed. This image of Elizabeth and the temple was symbolic of her service in the Church, as I would eventually discover.

My efforts to piece together the patchwork quilt of her life story brought into my life wonderful blessings, such as meeting people like Roberta and Elwood Baker, George Henry Higgs, and Alice Johnson Nielsen. However, the most important blessing for me personally was the recovery of an intensely interesting story of an individual Saint who loved the gospel she had embraced with her whole heart. The same fire that burned in her bosom—dedication to family history research and temple worship—had sparked in mine and drew me into her world. I sought photographs and word pictures of Elizabeth Stowe Higgs, along with other information about her life, and I began a personal mission to find out everything I could about her. Pieces of the quilt I was making were found in cemeteries, in attics and basements of old homes, in the vaults and storage areas of modern archives, and in the closets and libraries of churches and courthouses in England and the United States.

Some of the best preserved patches of Elizabeth Higgs's life were found in the LDS Church Archives in Salt Lake City. I spent long hours at a stretch in the quiet search room on the second floor of the Church Office Building where the archives are located. With only a scratch pad and the obligatory pencil to transcribe by hand her voice as found in ward, Relief Society, and temple meeting minutes, I began to grow closer to her with each word and sentence. Whether I was able to see the original records or a microfilm copy of them, I began to feel a connection with Elizabeth as I read her words, often recorded by a secretary, during a meeting where she took the time to not only bear testimony but also reveal the threads of her life. Though she originally spoke to those present, she also spoke to me through these records. Sometimes I marveled that they had been preserved—precious books containing the sweet words of my great-great-grandmother. What I discovered about her in this manner changed my life forever.

Elizabeth's father and mother were landless laborers in Warwickshire, England. They lived in several homes, mostly on the property of the West family—the landed aristocratic family in the area. Elizabeth was born on 22 June 1824 in the small community of Aldeminster. Apparently her father died as the result of an accident sometime thereafter, leaving her mother to raise the young family by herself. They eventually immigrated to America and made their home in Utica, New York.

Elizabeth married Thomas Higgs in Utica on 21 May 1844, just over one month before the martyrdom of Joseph and Hyrum Smith. Elizabeth's older brother William had married Thomas's sister Mary Susannah a few years before. During Elizabeth and Thomas's first years of marriage they found themselves in a secure circle of family and friends. They needed that support, as their first two children, William Wallace and Sara Ann, died on the same day in May 1848. During the next year Elizabeth bore a baby girl, Mary Susannah, who lived a long life. The next child, Sophia, died in 1853, however, at three years of age. A fifth child born in New York, Annie, lived a long life.

Elizabeth's brother Daniel joined the Restoration movement in 1834, just a few years after the organization of the Church in Fayette, New York, in 1830. Later, Elizabeth's mother, Anne Kite Stowe, was baptized a member of the Church in Utica in 1841. What conversations took place between Elizabeth and these family members are unknown. Daniel, for some unknown reason, discontinued his association with the Church within a short time, however.

Sometime in 1854 Elizabeth and her husband left their family, friends, and three buried children in Utica and moved west to eastern Iowa to begin a new life. Some of Elizabeth's family, including her brother Daniel, had settled in Davenport earlier and welcomed Elizabeth, Thomas and the two daughters.

Within two years John Van Cott, on his way home to Utah after serving as president of the Scandinavian Mission, visited their home. Elder Van Cott notes in his journal: "In the evening I baptised Elisabeth Higgs wife of Brother Higgs. Returned to the house and confirmed her. During my stay I was treated very kindly they rejoiced in the privilege of having an Elder with them."[1]

Swept up in the spirit of the gathering, Elizabeth and Thomas left loved ones in Davenport along with another buried child, Thomas Young Higgs, who died in 1856 shortly after Elizabeth's baptism, to join the Saints in Utah. The small family took Elizabeth's mother with them as they made their way to the Mormon staging ground near Iowa City. Assigned to the Hodgett wagon train, they accompanied the Martin handcart company to Zion.

The story of the struggle of these companies of emigrating Saints is well known. The family finally arrived in their new home on 15 December 1856 after experiencing bitter cold, heavy snowstorms, and meager food rations.

With a letter of introduction, the Higgs family finally found refuge from the cold in the home of Hiram B. Clawson. The Higgses spent their first winter in Zion in a room furnished with a stove that gave them an opportunity to forget to some extent their suffering on the plains. Such hospitality was not forgotten. In 1860, with a full house, Elizabeth and Thomas enabled German convert Karl G. Maeser and his family to live with them for one year until the Maesers could establish their own home. Elizabeth and Thomas's actions helped reveal how the Church titles "Brother" and "Sister" were more than forms of address—they represented community unity.

In 1858 Elizabeth delivered her seventh child, Brigham Thomas Higgs, named in honor of Brigham Young and Thomas Higgs. Shortly after his birth the family was on the move again as they followed the Saints to Utah County during the "move south." Their stay there was brief, and they returned with many of the northern Utah Saints to their homes following the peaceful conclusion of the Utah War.

A year later Elizabeth began another important step that ultimately bound her to the temple. She entered the Endowment House on the Temple Block in Salt Lake City on 20 August 1859. There she received special promises through the ordinances revealed by the Prophet Joseph Smith in Nauvoo, including the privilege of being sealed to her beloved husband for time and all eternity.

Three years later Elizabeth received her patriarchal blessing. Patriarch C. W. Hyde told her: "Thou art of Jacob, a lawful heir to the fullness of the priesthood with your companion and numerous posterity. You shall be a Queen and your companion, a King and Priest. . . . You shall go into the temple of the Lord . . . and redeem the living and the dead."[2] If she remained faithful, the patriarch promised, her life would be bound up in temple worship and family history research, and through this she would be a blessing to her progenitors and posterity. The blessing also implied that she would help the living by serving as a temple ordinance worker. Of course, no temple stood in Utah in 1862—the Endowment House was a preparatory structure limited to work for the living only, except baptisms for the dead, which were performed there briefly. Work on the Salt Lake Temple began in 1853, but it had not risen above the ground and was not completed until 1893—40 years later. The St. George Temple (1877), Logan Temple (1884), and Manti Temple (1888) were yet to be completed. Nevertheless, Elizabeth was being prepared for temple service. Endowment House records indicate that she later was busily engaged in identifying her kindred dead and performing baptisms in their behalf.[3]

As Elizabeth grew older she confronted the inevitable tide of mortality—cherished friends and family continued to die. She lost a daughter, Harriet Eliza, on 7 April 1865. Her mother died on 7 February 1868.

In 1870, after the arrival of the first trains to Utah, Elizabeth's husband was called on a mission to the East. The principal purpose was to contact family and friends and invite them to be baptized and come to Zion. Family ties were important to Elizabeth and her husband so that they could be strengthened and family history information could be collected for temple work.

Later, when the St. George Temple was completed in southern Utah, Elizabeth made the journey south to participate in the same ordinances now confined to this structure—the only fully functioning temple on the earth where the blessings of the holy house were extended to the dead. From 19 April through 22 April, Elizabeth stood proxy in baptisms, confirmations, and endowments for many of her loved ones who had died without the blessings of the everlasting gospel.[4]

In 1879 Elizabeth's husband was called to serve as the engineer for the temple being built by the Saints in Manti, Utah. On 1 May 1884, four years before this beautiful building was completed, Elizabeth expressed her desire to "live near to God that we might be worthy to go into the temple of the Most high and be worthy to do work for our dead." She helped in her own way to see the temple completed. The Manti Historical Record and the Manti North Ward records mention her donations to the temple fund. At different times her donations included five pounds of dried apples, a pair of knitted socks, five pounds of flour, a chicken, and a few eggs.

In 1888 the promises given to her through the inspired patriarch in Salt Lake City in 1862 were fulfilled. President Wilford Woodruff called Elizabeth to be among the first ordinance workers of the newly completed temple on 18 May 1888. She served faithfully for 24 years and was finally released in 1912, just one year before her death.

The Higgs family "Temple Book," the Manti Temple Historical Record, diaries of other temple workers, and letters addressed to Elizabeth demonstrate her personal concern to do the work. Much hard work and expense allowed her to provide hundreds of names so that temple ordinances could be performed. The Lord must have been pleased with her efforts, because on occasion he sent an extra witness of his concern about this important responsibility. J. Hatten Carpenter described one of Elizabeth's experiences: "Sister Smoot was here [in Manti] doing Temple work. One night a personage of spirit came into her bedroom and told her that her name was Collins and they had passed over her name in the Temple. The next day she told Sis. Smoot of the vision and they examined the books and found it was so and the work was done for Mrs. Collins."[5]

Elizabeth led a quiet life committed to Jesus Christ and the restored gospel. If she had been alive now, or if I had been alive then, I rather think I would have liked and admired her. My life has been blessed because she took the bold step to begin a new life with a new religion in Utah, far away from so many people whom she dearly loved. Her dedication to temple worship and family history work has welded me to her, not only by the sealing promises of the temple but also by a special spirit that accompanies temple worship and family history work.

While many view family history work as simply identifying individuals and their vital statistics so that their names can be submitted for temple ordinances, I have come to believe that it also includes filling in the contours of ancestors' lives with photographs (when possible) and word pictures gathered from written records and from the landscapes and buildings they knew. The Lord has said, "Behold, I will send you Elijah the prophet before the coming of the great and dreadful day of the Lord: and he shall turn the heart of the fathers to the children, and the heart of the children to their fathers, lest I come and smite the earth with a curse" (Malachi 4:5–6). The Spirit "turns our hearts" to our progenitors. Just as we come to love those we associate with because we know more than simply their birth, marriage, and death dates, so comes a special relationship with our own progenitors when we move beyond vital statistics.

Certainly Elizabeth is interested in what I do as I continue her efforts in collecting the names of her and my progenitors for temple work. She collected and recorded the names in a "Temple Book," and I have utilized the modern conveniences of a Pentium processor and the Church's Personal Ancestral File program. We both have helped fulfill the Prophet Joseph Smith's dream he expressed when he said, "Let us, therefore, as a church and a people, and as Latter-day Saints, offer unto the Lord an offering in righteousness; and let us present in his holy temple . . . a book containing the records of our dead, which shall be worthy of all acceptation" (D&C 128:24). In this effort we join together in bringing souls unto Christ and binding together our family through the ordinances of the holy priesthood. Through her family history work Elizabeth has left me a legacy of faith and commitment that I can leave to my children, grandchildren, and great-great-grandchildren.

The intimate and personal side of my efforts has given me the greatest blessings as I have striven to build bridges to the past, turning my heart to my great-great-grandmother. One of the special moments in my life was 11 January 1980, when Richard and I went to the Provo Temple with Roberta and Elwood Barker. I had discovered while making my patchwork quilt that one of Elizabeth's sons, Wallace James Higgs, had not had the opportunity to receive the ordinances of the temple or to be sealed to his wife, though he had been baptized a member of the Church. Wallace and his wife, Matilda, had died childless and apparently had been forgotten. I prepared the necessary documents and eventually received permission to have the temple ordinances performed for Elizabeth's son and to have him and his wife sealed together. As we entered the temple that day in January, I could not help but think of my great-great-grandmother, who had spent so many years serving in the Manti Temple to help "bring to pass the immortality and eternal life" of so many others (see Moses 1:39). Now, decades after her death, we were about to complete her immediate family circle by performing the sacred ordinances of the house of the Lord for her son and his wife.

Richard stood proxy for Wallace for the washing and anointing, the priesthood ordination, and the endowment ordinances. Following the endowment ceremony we gathered in one of the sealing rooms of that beautiful edifice. Again, my husband stood in Wallace's place and Roberta stood proxy for Matilda, Wallace's wife. By the authority of the holy priesthood, the welding link was completed for Elizabeth's family. We left the temple rejoicing in the privilege to perform such an important work—especially for people I was coming to know beyond their simple vital statistics. Following the special temple experience, we gathered at our small apartment in Provo for lunch. It was a time of refreshing as we joined together in the bonds of the gospel covenant.

As we traced the life of Elizabeth, my husband and I ventured to the places where she had lived. In England I stood in the cool, damp Anglican Church in Aldeminster just a few kilometers south of Stratford-upon-Avon, looking at the baptismal font and trying to imagine the poor family coming to have their little daughter christened. I thought about her family making the decision to leave their native land for a new life in America, where Elizabeth would meet and marry another English immigrant and then settle in eastern Iowa.

At another time I gazed along the Mississippi River shoreline in Davenport, Iowa, with a copy of pages from the missionary diary of the elder who had baptized the 32-year-old Elizabeth into The Church of Jesus Christ of Latter-day Saints. I visualized her struggling out of her sickbed and going into the river to begin a new life with the Saints. A few miles from Iowa City I strolled around the site where the wagons and handcarts had begun the fateful journey that brought Elizabeth and her family to Utah in 1856. I thought about the trials of the Martin handcart and Hodgett wagon trains as they traveled together in the snow through Wyoming and into Utah late in the year.

Later, upon my return to Utah, I went to the Salt Lake City Cemetery, very near the spot where Elizabeth had buried her mother and several children. I remembered reading in a Relief Society minute book something Elizabeth had said about her faith in the face of the deaths of her little ones. A secretary notes in 1878: "Sister Elizabeth Higgs said she could bear testimony . . . she heard Pres. Young say a good faithful Brother and Sister should have their children again. She had a trial with her own children's [deaths] but lived to over come."[6] On a visit to the Manti Temple, I contemplated Elizabeth's call to be among the first temple workers in 1888. I wondered how many times she had walked those halls or stood at the altar in the terrestrial room in prayer. I stood under a canopy of tree branches in the cemetery across the road from that sacred building and examined the headstone with her name on it. At that moment I said silently, "God bless you, Elizabeth," and thanked the Lord for such a disciple as this little Christian Saint.

Now, years later, I have nearly completed this quilt—patch by patch—of her life story. Though not complete, each part of the quilt helps warm me with the history of a courageous woman whose activities, sacrifices, and testimony have proven to be particularly meaningful to me. A secretary reported remarks Elizabeth had made while attending a Relief Society meeting in Payson, and I try always to remember and live by their message: "Sister Higgs felt glad that the Lord had opened the way that the children might be taught the things of God. She was thankful that she was here in these valleys. Said the Lord had answered her prayers and she would not complain if her lot was ever hard. [She said] May God bless us in all we do in righteousness."[7]

I am thankful the Lord has allowed for the preservation of the priceless records that note the words and deeds of my great-great-grandmother Elizabeth Stowe Higgs, a heroine of the Restoration.

NOTES

1. John Van Cott, journal, 21 May 1856, Special Collections, Harold B. Lee Library, Brigham Young University, Provo, Utah.
2. Patriarchal Blessing of Elizabeth Stowe Higgs, 12 January 1862, Archives Division, Church Historical Department, The Church of Jesus Christ of Latter-day Saints, Salt Lake City, Utah (hereafter cited as LDSCA).
3. See Endowment House Baptism Book A., LDSCA.
4. See St. George Temple Records, LDSCA.
5. J. Hatten Carpenter, journal, 1909, Special Collections, BYU.
6. Payson Ward, Utah Stake Relief Society Minute Book (1877–85), 6 June 1878, LDSCA.
7. Ibid., 1 October 1878.

꙳

Jeni Broberg Holzapfel, a native of Glendale, California, now lives in Woodland, Utah, with her husband, Richard, and their five children. She is the coauthor of several articles and books, including *Women of Nauvoo* and *Sisters at the Well: Women and the Life and Teachings of Jesus,* and is the author of a forthcoming book, *A Woman's View: Helen Mar Whitney's Reminiscences of Early Church History.* Jeni wrote this essay to honor one of the "unsung Saints" and to encourage others to recover the life stories of their ancestors.

13

"She Did What She Could"
Caroline R. Smoot
1827–1915

*E*ach Memorial Day our extended family is invited to go as a group to the historic Salt Lake City Cemetery and to the county's Elysian Burial Gardens to place flowers on our ancestral graves. Tombstone inscriptions and dates are read, and we share remembered experiences in tribute to those who have gone before us. The present generation is annually ensuring that this tradition is carried on to our growing posterity, who must also know the forebears who left them the great legacy they enjoy today.

A part of this routine has provided annual amusement for our family members. Found on our largest family tombstone in the Salt Lake City Cemetery, etched in black marble, is my great-grandmother's epitaph:

> CAROLINE R. SMOOOT
> Daughter of
> David W. & Martha Collins Rogers
> BORN: MARCH 20, 1827
> DIED: MARCH 14, 1915
> "She Did What She Could"

Caroline R. Smoot

"She did what she could." Through

the years we have never really known why such an epitaph was appropriate for Great-Grandmother Smoot, but her epitaph has become part of the lives of the female members of the family, bringing humor and solace to moments when one thinks she didn't quite measure up, but tried. At such times out comes the personalized version, voiced with a certain amount of ancestral pride and dignity—"I did what I could"—and thus the merriment persists.

I never realized until recently that this serviceable epitaph has a scriptural foundation. In the New Testament I came across these words: *"She hath done what she could:* and the which she has done unto me, shall be had in remembrance in generations to come" (JST, Mark 14:8, emphasis added). The tone and content of that scripture now have particular meaning for me as I contemplate my great-grandmother's legacy to me personally and to my family generationally. Great-Grandmother Smoot's life is certainly "had in remembrance" in the generations that have come, but I think few of us until now have given consideration to more than the humor we discovered in her scripture-based epitaph. My research into her life and times has unalterably changed that for me.

I had heard stories about my maternal great-grandmother throughout my childhood. Now, late into adulthood, I have finally learned for myself what a feisty, faithful little woman of endurance I had laid claim to by birthright. Knowing of the hardships and tragedies in the life of Hannah Caroline Rogers Daniels Smoot, I have come to realize that a lesser woman would never have remained true to her faith under such circumstances. The fact that Great-Grandmother Smoot did bears no small mark upon her posterity, down to the present generation.

This is not to say that all her life was one of grim endurance; in fact, much of her childhood reads almost idyllic. For example, when Caroline was a young child her family lived on the Hudson River shores of Caldwell's Landing, New York City. Of that home Caroline recorded in her journal: "We could see West Point from our house. The home itself was an old revolutionary wartime building with three verandas running around the house, one above the other. It was a large roomy edifice standing on the brow of the river near the shore, a lovely place indeed."[1]

Living on the banks of the Hudson River made life interesting for young Caroline; something was constantly going on. She could watch the steamers dock, look over the bridge railing and see the running river, and notice the changing color of the water with its quiet ripples or the restless, rushing waves breaking into white caps.

When her youngest brother was born in 1833, Caroline wrote that she could hardly wait until he was old enough to be taken outdoors. Later she and her older sister, Hester, often took him to the park so that the baby could be in the open air and feel the sea breezes. Caroline summarized, "That was a happy time of my life."[2]

Another of Caroline's childhood recollections finds her in New York City, where she was to know splendid as well as anxious times. Even though she was only five years old in 1832, she vividly recalled that as "the great cholera year in New York City."[3] The "dead wagons," as they were called, could be heard night and day carrying away those who had not survived the epidemic. At that time her mother became very sick with typhus fever. Caroline remembered her mother mustering all the strength she had to daily call her children together to ask, "How do you feel?" "Does your head ache?" "Do you feel sick anywhere?"[4] She was so afraid the children would contract the dreaded cholera.

That year of early childhood was stamped clearly on Caroline's mind, not, however, because of her mother's illness or the cholera epidemic specifically, but because of the freedom she enjoyed from her mother's omnipresent supervision. Susanna, Caroline's not much older sister, was given the responsibility of caring for Caroline during their mother's illness. Time and time again impish Caroline would run off to play with her neighbor friend, in spite of instructions to stay home. Susanna would dutifully retrieve her little sister, only to have her run off again. Finally, in desperation Susanna took Caroline's dress off so she would stay home. That worked! Those happy, teasing days were part of a clear remembrance that never dimmed for Caroline.[5]

One Sunday in 1837, 10-year-old Caroline's father, David White Rogers, was on his way home from church. He stopped at a place where he and some friends frequently gathered to have discussions or hold meetings. When he got there, someone was speaking. The first words he heard were, "Is it possible that I shall have to go back to those that sent me and say that in all the great city of New York, there was not one person willing to open their house for me to preach in?" At the close of the meeting Caroline's father arose and offered the use of his house to Elders Parley P. Pratt and Elijah Fordham.[6]

This was no small decision for David Rogers. He was an ardent teacher in the Methodist faith. When he offered his home for their preaching, he didn't realize that the missionaries were Mormons. Had he known, one wonders if he would have spoken up. But his heart had been touched, which did not go unnoticed by Elder Pratt. What David also did not know was that the two missionaries had previously received a special witness that many in New York, including himself, were ready to hear the gospel message. According to Parley P. Pratt's autobiography:

> We had retired to our private room up stairs with the few members we had, to hold a last prayer meeting, as I was about taking leave for New Orleans. We had prayed all round in turn, when, on a sudden, the room was filled with the Holy Spirit, and so was each one present. . . . Many marvelous things were manifested which I cannot write. . . .
>
> The Lord said . . . our prayers were heard, and our labors and sacrifices were accepted. We should tarry in the city, and go not thence as yet; for the Lord had many people in that city. . . . And from that very day forward . . . there should be more doors open for preaching than we could fill; crowds, who could not get in, should stand in the streets and about the entrance to try to hear us; and we should know that the Almighty could open a door and no man could shut it. . . .
>
> . . . Now there was in this little meeting a man named David Rogers, whose heart was touched. He, being a chairmaker, fitted up a large room, and seated it with the chairs of his ware house, and invited us to preach in the same. This room was crowded. He then joined with one of our members, who was a joiner, and rented a small place, and seated it for a regular place of meeting; this was generally crowded.[7]

Caroline was another who was ready for the truths of the restored gospel. Even though she was quite young, she was already a student of the scriptures: "I always attended Sabbath school at the Methodist church and loved to learn whole chapters from the testament to repeat each week. I often wished I could have lived in the days of Christ and his apostles. And, when the new and everlasting covenant was preached again to us, my heart rejoiced and I looked on those men that brought the glad tidings of salvation to us, with reverence and awe."[8]

As Elder Pratt taught the gospel to the Rogers family, Caroline "took an uncommon interest in everything" she saw and heard.[9] She later wrote of that time: "I never thought of doubting anything he said. When he spoke of the apostles and prophets, I said to my sister that it was just like it was when Christ and his apostles were on the earth."[10] Everything he said rang true to her. Her faith-filled response of childhood would be further refined in the critical hardships she would be called upon to endure as an adult.

Of that time of conversion Caroline particularly remembered the morning when her father did not come to breakfast and she went to his bedroom to find him. There she saw her father kneeling in prayer by the side of his bed, so she shut the door carefully and went away. Every little while she returned to look through the door to see if her father was still there. He was. He stayed there four days and nights, seeking a testimony of the truth of the restored gospel which he had been taught by the missionaries and by the scriptures brought forth by the Prophet Joseph Smith.[11]

I can imagine Caroline's intent interest when her father shared with the family the vision he had received during those four days of fervent prayer, which was given in witness of the divinity of the restored gospel and of the calling of Joseph Smith Jr. as the Prophet of the Restoration. Her father recounted, "During that time, the room was a blaze of light as bright as the noon day sun. I saw Joseph Smith sitting . . . in the corner of the room with a Book of Mormon in his hand." Later, after describing the man he saw in his vision to Parley P. Pratt, the Apostle said he could not have described the Prophet better himself—and he knew the Prophet, whereas her father had never seen him.[12]

Caroline's mother also bore convincing testimony of the truthfulness of the gospel, detailing a dream she had had two years before Pratt and Fordham came to New York City as missionaries. She indicated that in her dream two men had come to the Rogerses' home bringing a book with them, which they told her was of great importance. She later recognized Parley P. Pratt and Elijah Fordham when they came to the Rogers house together, Book of Mormon in hand.[13]

These were the witnesses borne to young Caroline by her parents. Because of their testimonies and because she felt the truthfulness of the gospel of Jesus Christ as she heard it taught, she remained a strong advocate of the gospel throughout her life. To further bolster her early faith, her father had amazing, faith-promoting experiences as he fulfilled responsibilities given to him by Church leaders.

One such experience occurred when David Rogers was asked to return to Jackson County, Missouri, after the family had journeyed there and then left with the persecuted Saints to go to Illinois. Actually, Church authorities were looking for someone familiar with the area who could sell the Church lands that the Saints had left without recompense. Not a soul volunteered, so Caroline's father was personally approached and he accepted the assignment, in spite of the Missouri mob threats made against any Mormons who might came back to try to sell or repossess their lands. In accepting the responsibility, her father replied, "If it is the will of the Lord . . . I will go and do the business or be found dead trying."[14]

Her father could not have known how close he would actually come to being "found dead trying." The next month, March 1839, he did go to Independence, Missouri, and, assisted by a man familiar with the area, sold the Whitmer farm. The following day, as they crossed the public square, the two men were surrounded "by a posse of about forty men. Soon the square was congested with three hundred people."[15] The spokesman for the posse told the two men that they had to give up the money and any other bills of sale they had for property in that area and leave the county before sunset—or be killed.

Caroline's father asked if he could first speak in their own defense and was allowed to do so. He told the mob he had been sent in the name and power of God to accomplish his business. "And in no way can I be prevented only by commiting wilful, cold-blooded murder." At this point, unbuttoning his coat and vest, he bared his chest to them and challenged the mob: "And if any one present is prepared for that, now is the best time you can ever have, in the blaze of this beautiful, morning sun and in the presence of this large concourse of witnesses, that the honor and glory of the deed may descend to the latest posterity. That is all I wish to say."[16]

The crowd suddenly grew silent. David Rogers's partner had disappeared. Others began to walk away. Soon David White Rogers was totally alone. He returned to his task of selling the lands, staying in the county for over a month and amassing nearly $3,000.[17]

I recognize that Hannah Caroline Rogers Daniels Smoot's own life is a clear reflection of the continuity of that noble legacy from her early youth to her last days. I know now that only her early life was pleasant; throughout adulthood she would have to draw upon that legacy of faith as she was forced to endure nearly unbearable anguish and heartache, portions of which even she thought she "could not live through."[18]

When the call came to go to Zion, Caroline's parents did not hesitate. In 1839 preparations were made for the Rogers family to move to Far West, where the Saints were gathered in Missouri. Their route would take them through Quincy, Illinois. Before they had completed their journey, however, they met several wagon trains crossing from Missouri. They were told the Saints had been driven from the state. Caroline saw the terrible suffering of the newly converted Saints who had fled to Quincy, but she was not persuaded to do other than join with them.

It was there in Quincy that Caroline met and shortly after married Aaron Daniels, on 14 December 1845. The Daniels family had joined the Church in its earliest days, Aaron's father being one of its first 30 members. By the time they headed in earnest for the Salt Lake Valley, Aaron and Caroline had two children. For the trek west they joined with Captain Milo Andrera, who commanded 52 wagons divided into groups of 10. Six weeks after their arrival in the Valley in 1850, Caroline gave birth to their third child.

Caroline and Aaron were among those called to settle Utah Valley in the area now known as Provo. Aaron now had gold fever, however, and wanted to try his luck in California. Refusing to leave the body of the Saints, Caroline went to live with her brother in Provo. Aaron told Caroline that if she would not go with him, he would marry a second wife. She told him she would rather he married a dozen than have him go. Aaron did enter plural marriage and moved to California.

Polygamy deeply troubled Caroline and she sought divine intervention to keep herself from grieving over the polygamous union. "I need not say I did not have trouble. I used sometimes to wish I would not wake up in the morning but sleep the last long sleep."[19] It took some time until she realized that she should not worry over a principle that was calculated to elevate and exalt mankind if rightly lived.

In spite of Aaron's continual pursuit of gold, Caroline had 11 children by him, although she lost four of them. One of these was two-year-old Henry, who died the year Aaron married the second wife. "Losing my child was worse than losing my husband had been," she said.[20] Little Henry died about two hours before her next son was born. Aaron was still gone in search of gold.

Caroline moved into a log room adjoining her brother's home in Provo. It was very uncomfortable, with no door and no chinking between the logs. She put in the chinking herself, filling up the cracks to make the place warmer for herself and her three children. She also made hinges of leather from old boots for the door, put boards down for a floor in front of the fireplace, and lived there for some time. Then there was an accident that compelled her to move again.

The mishap occurred on 11 February 1852, her brother's birthday. He had bought a wild goose from the Indians, which she was cooking. Her brother had a sawmill on the Provo River a short distance from the house, where he and a number of men were working that day. Dinner was about ready to be served, and the older children were collecting wood for the night. Caroline had just left her room and gone around to the door of her brother's home, when she heard an awful noise. She ran back to her room to find that half of the sod roof had broken down and that none of her children—buried under a foot or more of dirt—was to be seen or heard. She never expected to find one of them alive.

Her cries attracted the men at the mill, who came running. They began to dig, although they could only guess where to begin. Soon they found three-year-old Maria. They didn't think she was hurt much. Next they dug out David. They thought he was dead, for he was limp and his face was black. His rescuer said that David could not have lived another minute. It was a miracle that he found him just when he did. Caroline's 16-month-old baby was still missing. All were certain that she was dead until Caroline's nephew called out, "Here she is sitting behind a large pile of wood away from the house." During all the commotion little Maria sat on the knee of the man who had found her. She never moaned or cried, but they later found that her leg was broken in two places. Caroline knew that the Lord had been merciful to her children and to her.[21]

After living 17 years in polygamy, Caroline's husband apostatized from the faith. But when Aaron's second wife left him, Caroline had not only her own children to care for but a young foster Indian girl named Rose from the second marriage, whom Aaron left in her charge. Compassionate and cultured Caroline accepted Rose as her own. She taught her the rudiments of homemaking, cooking, cleaning, weaving, spinning, sewing, and all the tasks necessary to make a comfortable pioneer home. Caroline also gave Rose the opportunity to have an education in the Provo public schools along with her own children.

Caroline counseled with President Young about what to do "as I had a large family of children and no means of support for them."[22] President Young encouraged her to stay with Aaron if he would support her. He told her she might be able to encourage him to come back into the Church. Instead, Aaron said he would turn all their children away from the Church. He succeeded in turning seven of her eight boys away, and one girl. Her youngest son was nine years old. Aaron said that just as soon as the boy was old enough, he would take him away from her, too. "But the Lord showed him he could not have everything his own way and he took my son to himself. My son was a sweet spirit and a saint," said

Caroline. "He had been baptized when he was eight years old. It was hard to part with him, but how much better the Lord should take him than to have had him turn away from the truth."[23] Caroline got a divorce.

In 1886 Caroline married Abraham Owen Smoot in the Logan Temple, later stating, "It was necessary to my salvation and exaltation."[24] His first wife had died the preceding year. In 1895 Abraham Smoot died, and Caroline was alone again.

Regardless of the havoc and heartache that was too often present in Caroline's personal life, her faith and commitment to the gospel remained firm and found continuity in her posterity, even to the latest generation. Caroline's legacy of Relief Society service as well has extended down the generations to and beyond me. Following her own mother's early example of membership in the Female Relief Society of Nauvoo, Caroline gave years of dedicated service and leadership in the Provo Relief Society. Her daughter Caroline Amelia and all succeeding generations have been stalwarts in Relief Society. I have no doubt that this heritage of leadership service in the women's organization of the Church had direct bearing on my eventual call as Relief Society general president. My nearly 10 years of consecrated service I proffered in gratitude and love to the women worldwide I served and as my part of the continuing legacy of faith that was entrusted to me.

In her later years Caroline lived with her daughter Caroline Amelia Daniels Mills, my grandmother. Because of the sound education she'd received, and in response to the Brethren's encouragement that women become doctors, Caroline Amelia pursued that goal. Mother Caroline assisted her daughter through medical school by going to Iowa with her to tend the children. It was this Dr. C. A. Mills who later delivered me, her baby granddaughter.

After 88 years of valiant living, Caroline herself was finally delivered from this life to the eternities on 14 March 1915.

Caroline's courageous life and marvelous heritage can be appreciated by today's generation because she recorded much of her life in her autobiography. In that record she bore vivid testimony of the Prophet Joseph Smith. In part, she recounted:

I well remember the day spoken of in history when Joseph accompanied by other brethren came to Montrose healing the sick and raising them from their beds of affliction. I was personally acquainted with Elijah Fordham, spoken of in [the] history of that day, who came from New York City and was a personal friend of my father. I can testify to the truth of that event of the healing of the sick, at that time.

I well remember too when Joseph was hiding at Brother Hancock's. He lived just back of Montrose on the bluff, as it was called. Of course it was whispered around where he was, but everyone did not know it.

How sorrowful the saints felt, many of them, when he gave himself up to his foes. Of course there were some who advised and almost insisted that he should give himself up to be tried yet another time, which he did to satisfy those doubtful friends. But oh, I well remember the sorrow, grief and lamentations when a few days after came the heartrending news that our Prophet and Patriarch were slain, martyred by a furious mob. All Israel mourned as they never mourned before and as they have never mourned since. Very few eyes closed that night in sleep.

I saw the Prophet and Patriarch in their coffins. I saw the wives and aged mother gazing on the lifeless clay of their loved ones. I saw the bullet hole in Hyrum's face and I saw the clothes that had been taken from their bodies, saturated with their life's blood. I have also seen and handled many a time the six-shooter that Joseph put through the door of the jail and fired at the mob before he attempted to get out of the window. I have also had the watch in my hand that John Taylor had on at that time and which was stopped by the bullet striking it and showing the time of the day the deed was done. I saw and handled those relics in Nauvoo and those events are very clear and vivid in my mind. Many other things transpired which time will not permit being mentioned here.

Soon the old timers will have passed away and as Job says, "The places that have known us will know us no more," and the coming generations will speak of these events long passed by in the history of the Saints of God.[25]

Caroline dealt with "the stern realities of life," as she expressed it, with a resolute faith, if not always a happy heart. In summarizing her life, she asserted: "My faith in Mormonism has never wavered and I hope it never will. I want to bear my testimony to whoever may read this that the gospel is true. Joseph Smith was a prophet of God and I do pray that all my children may be brought to a knowledge of the truth and be saved in His kingdom, which will be the case [if] a Mother's prayers are of any avail before the throne of God, which may God grant for Christ's sake, Amen."[26]

Amen to Caroline's final words, and blessed amen to the life of one who, in dignity, grace, and full faith, "did what she could." I will never view that marble gravestone in the Salt Lake City Cemetery the same again. What was once a seemingly humorous epitaph now draws from the very wellspring of my heart the utmost of respect, awe, reverence, and love.

How honored I am that this is part of my heritage, my noble lineage, this life of Great-Grandmother Caroline Rogers Smoot. How infused I am with a sense of noblesse oblige—to live my life with the same generosity of spirit, the same maternal love, the same conviction of soul, the same integrity of heart, the same faith-filled response to priesthood authority, the same steadfast service and testimony as that of my revered progenitor. How I fervently desire that my life reflect as clearly the continuity of that noble legacy, even from my earliest youth to my last day. The fulfillment of that soul-deep desire in Caroline's life is evidenced in those simple words: "She did what she could." Now knowing their meaning, I would be immeasurably honored if the same were one day said of me.

NOTES

1. Caroline R. Smoot, journal, as quoted in Caroline Strong, "A Proud Heritage," vol. 2 (Mills family history, n.d.), p. 474.
2. Ibid.
3. Ibid.
4. Ibid.
5. See ibid.

6. See ibid.

7. Parley P. Pratt, *Autobiography of Parley P. Pratt,* ed. Parley P. Pratt Jr. (Salt Lake City: Deseret Book Co., 1985), pp. 145, 146.

8. Smoot, journal, in Strong, *A Proud Heritage,* p. 467.

9. Ibid., p. 476.

10. Ibid.

11. See ibid.

12. David White Rogers, as quoted in Strong, *A Proud Heritage,* p. 476.

13. See ibid.

14. David White Rogers, Report, typescript, p. 1, as quoted in Naida R. Williamson, "David White Rogers of New York," *BYU Studies* 35, no. 2 (1995), p. 73. See also *History of the Church* 3:260.

15. Williamson, "David White Rogers," p. 78.

16. Rogers, Report, pp. 2–3, as quoted in ibid., p. 79.

17. See Williamson, "David White Rogers," p. 79

18. Smoot, journal, in Strong, *A Proud Heritage,* p. 470.

19. Ibid.

20. Ibid.

21. See Strong, *A Proud Heritage,* p. 483.

22. Smoot, journal, in ibid., p. 470.

23. Ibid., pp. 470–71.

24. Davis Bitton, *Guide to Mormon Diaries and Autobiographies* (Provo, Utah: Brigham Young University Press, 1977), p. 328.

25. Smoot, "Testimony of Knowing Joseph Smith," as quoted in Strong, *A Proud Heritage,* pp. 486–87.

26. Ibid., p. 468.

Barbara B. Smith was general Relief Society president from 1974 to 1984. She serves on Utah's sesquicentennial committee, the national board of American Mothers, Inc., Governor Mike Leavitt's GIFT committee for the advancement of families, and many other associations. She is married to Douglas H. Smith and has seven children, 39 grandchildren, and eight great-grandchildren. Barbara chose to write about Caroline Rogers Daniels Smoot because of Caroline's profound influence on and example to the generations that followed her.

14

"Believing in the Light After Darkness"
Emmeline B. Wells
1828–1921

*O*n 28 February 1921 the Relief Society general board hosted a grand birthday celebration at the Hotel Utah for President Emmeline B. Wells. She was 93. Dressed in a blue and pink brocade dress with a blue tulle scarf—what the *Deseret News* called "her official costume for which she had become famous"—Emmeline greeted her hundreds of friends "of all creeds and circles who called to pay their respects." When asked to make a wish, Emmeline responded that she hoped her birthdays would continue for years to come, "brim full of happiness and comfort."[1]

Emmeline B. Wells

Only three months later, 25 April 1921, "Aunt Em," as she was affectionately known, died at the home of her daughter. For the first time in the history of Salt Lake City, the flags in front of the Bishops' Building, Deseret News building, and other prominent structures flew at half-mast. They were lowered in tribute to the diminutive pioneer Emmeline Blanche Woodward Harris Whitney Wells, who for 70 years had carried high her banner for Mormonism and its women.

She was the last of those pioneer women whose testimonies had been solidified by knowing the Prophet Joseph Smith. She remembered first meeting him: "His majestic bearing [was] so entirely different from any one I had ever seen. . . . It was as if I beheld a vision. . . . Before I was aware of it he came to me, and when he took my hand, I was simply electrified,—thrilled through and through to the tips of my fingers, and every part of my body, as if some magic elixir had given me new life and vitality. . . . The one thought that stilled my soul was, I have seen the Prophet of God, he has taken me by the hand."[2]

Many aspects of her life fulfilled the blessing given her by her husband, Bishop Newel K. Whitney, that she would have a "tremendous influence in the building of the kingdom in the west."[3] She made extraordinary contributions: she served as president of the general Relief Society, edited the *Woman's Exponent,* established the wheat-saving program, directed the Silver Jubilee anniversary of the Relief Society, received an honorary degree from Brigham Young University, and was memorialized in the Utah State Capitol with a statue recognizing her lifelong offerings.

Emmeline's legacy was far-reaching. In an editorial tribute to this physically frail yet unyielding pioneer the *Deseret News* said, "Having lived a unique and glorious life, she has gone to claim a faithful Saint's reward, leaving a name and memory that will live forever in the hearts of all who knew her."[4]

I feel like I know her. As I have served in Relief Society, I have felt a tie to Emmeline. In tracing her life for this essay I have gained an even broader picture of her influence, her stature, her personal strength. Three things strike me about Emmeline B. Wells: her hope, her belief in women, and her commitment to Relief Society.

First, her sense of hope. I am drawn to her because of her ability to maintain a positive and progressive outlook when things were not easy or smooth or fair. Her positive outlook, her hope, is one of the resounding themes of her life.

While we often pay homage to accomplishments—Emmeline's list is impressive—it is the fact that hers were achieved in the face of great odds that makes them worthy of emulation. In 1874 she wrote in her journal, "When I look back it seems incredible that I should have passed through such hard and thorny places. I have always been . . . hopeful believing in the light after darkness."[5]

Second, Emmeline's belief in women of the Church. Her statement "I believe in women, especially thinking women" resonates within me.[6] In her closing editorial of the *Exponent* she wrote, "We love women, and shall ever strive to uplift and help them attain their ideals."[7] Her journal entry of 31 March 1875 stated that she "was alone nearly all the evening reading and thinking."[8] She believed in women's minds and in their abilities, valued their individual efforts, and praised their work.

Third, her commitment to Relief Society. On 1 April 1875 Emmeline wrote of her feelings when she returned from a Relief Society meeting, feelings that mirror those I have had in my Relief Society calling: "I feel deeply the great responsibility resting upon me in being called to fill this public office; but hope to be guided and sustained by the Holy Spirit in this calling and duty that I may keep humble and be qualified to do all things that are required of me."[9]

As I have looked closely at her Relief Society administration I have seen similarities in the challenges facing women at the first of this century and at the end. Emmeline's fervent desire to maintain the essence of Relief Society in a changing world provided a pattern for future members to follow. We, too, are faced with holding firm the unchanging purposes of Relief Society—to relieve the poor and to save souls—while looking to the education and general development of women. This was a challenge for Emmeline; it has been for me as well.

Many women who are new to membership in the Church attend Relief Society meetings regularly, yet, not knowing the historical background of this divine organization, regard it as "just another class we attend on Sunday." It is so much more. It is the Lord's organization for women!

While I have isolated three elements of Emmeline's life here, I recognize that during most of her years they were interwoven. For example, her love for women and her confidence in their abilities gave her hope. Hope hinged her life together. Emmeline's experiences reveal a constant battle to balance the difficult with the exulting, the needs of the Lord with the abilities of his people, the desires of the heart with the practicalities of what must be done. One of my favorite scriptures applies to her so well: "Wherefore, ye must press forward with a steadfastness in Christ, having a perfect brightness of hope" (2 Nephi 31:20). "A perfect brightness of hope"—what a light, ebullient phrase that is! How well it represents Emmeline! How well it reminds us that "all these things shall give thee experience and shall be for thy good" (D&C 122:7).

Emmeline's last wish for a life "brim full of happiness and comfort" was to ask for a life she had never known. Her life had not been easy. She was persecuted by her friends when she joined the Church; her first child and only son died as a baby; her young husband abandoned her in Nauvoo; his letters to her were never forwarded by his mother; her own mother died at Winter Quarters. Emmeline married again and was widowed in only a few short years, this time with two small girls to raise. Her third marriage, though to a pillar of the Mormon community, never fulfilled her hopes for companionship.

The *Deseret News* noted in its eulogy at her death that Emmeline "had her full share of bitter sorrows, but these only served to test and refine the pure gold in her nature."[10] Indeed, this one-time schoolteacher had been schooled by the Lord, and her grasp of the eternal plan sustained her.

In an autobiographical poem, "Faith and Fidelity," she wrote:

And so some lives go on in tragedies, each part
To be sustained by human effort grand;
Though 'neath the outward seeming lies the broken heart,
That only One above can understand.[11]

When I was called as general president of the Relief Society I brought with me the fervent desire that women feel and acknowledge hope. I cannot imagine life without hope. I learned early that the personal quality of hope is essential for righteous living. Hope comes from a knowledge that the Lord's promises are true, that he will fill our souls with his Spirit, and that we will have the strength to carry on. As Emmeline rebounded from personal rejection and disappointment, she put her faith in the future, reflecting Moroni's teaching that we cannot be saved in the kingdom of God "if [we] have no hope" (Moroni 10:21).

The Apostle Paul helps us understand hope when he counsels

us to be "fervent in spirit; serving the Lord; rejoicing in hope" (Romans 12:11-12). To me, "rejoicing in hope" is a godlike characteristic. Great comfort comes from hope. I find that I measure hope by those things that have spiritual roots: my relationship with the Lord; the precious time I spend in prayer, in study, in service; my relationship with my husband, my friends, my children, and my sisters and brothers with whom I share this glorious gospel. All these sustain my hope.

Emmeline did not view hope as an abstract thought or a nebulous quality. She bolstered it with hard work and commitment, indicating her belief that "there is no excellence without labor."[12]

Born in the small community of Petersham, Massachusetts, Emmeline had the distinction of having been born in a leap year, 29 February 1828. She was the seventh child and fifth daughter of David and Diadama Woodward. Her father died when she was young. Descended from a long line of New England landowners of comfortable means, Emmeline exhibited literary talent as a girl and was admitted to the private New Salem Academy to further her studies. All her life she found joy and expression in writing. Her mother and younger siblings had already joined the Church when Emmeline was baptized 1 March 1842.

Emmeline's personal life reads almost like a tragedy. Her journals give us a glimpse of a life replete with the pain of being alone, the loss of three husbands, the early deaths of three of her children, the struggle with disappointment and discouragement. Through her many trials she grew self-reliant, determined, and diligent. She never gave up hope.

Emmeline's written words flowed with idealism, faith, and high expectations. Her belief in the promises of the Lord is indicated by this notation in her journal: "I have been afflicted and troubled. . . . Thou has promised me days of joy and gladness and O Lord send not more affliction than I can bear."[13]

She was introspective and thoughtful in her personal writings, musing over the events of the day, analyzing their significance and her feelings about them, turning finally to the Lord for guidance and comfort. In her diary entry for 1 September 1874 she wrote of her first and only son Eugene: "He would have been thirty today. If he were living how much happiness he might bring to me."[14] Of her third husband, Daniel H. Wells, father of Emma, Elizabeth Ann, and Louisa, Emmeline said, "[He] is not in want of me for a companion or in any sense, he does not need me at all."[15]

Her struggles with the harsh nature of pioneer life may have prompted her delicate, flowery verse so popular at the time. It may have been her way of making the desert "blossom as a rose," just as her penchant for soft scarves and delicate brocades created a delicacy in her countenance. She published many of her expressions in a volume, *Musings and Memories,* in 1896, with a second edition in 1915. In her poem "October" comes her recurrent theme of hope: "There's beauty and grace in brown October."[16] Other poems describe dreams shattered, happy days of the past, her delight in wild flowers, her "mountain home so dear," and her hope in immortality.

I remember looking out of my schoolroom window to the brown, windswept prairies of Canada while listening to my English teacher explain the poetry that still brings me hope, recurrent pleasure, and motivating thoughts—verses like Browning's "Ah, but a man's reach should exceed his grasp, or what's a heaven for,"[17] Gerard Manley Hopkins's "Glory be to God for dappled things,"[18] and Oliver Wendell Holmes's "Build thee more stately mansions, O my soul."[19]

Emmeline's ability to transfer her thoughts to paper became one of her greatest contributions. In the *Woman's Exponent,* established in 1872 to discuss "every subject interesting and valuable to women,"[20] she wrote of the vitality of women, their ability to do great good, and their responsibility in the community and to their families.

Progression in the eternal plan was a central theme of Emmeline's messages to women, which she expounded upon often in the pages of the paper. The *Exponent* sought to broaden women's understanding of the world and to clarify the doctrines of the kingdom of God.

I, too, have a passion for the power of the word. At the close of this century that Emmeline so capably helped open, we see women again turning to words for expression and understanding through the literacy effort of the Church. The literacy program helps women use this skill to lift others, to teach their children, and, most of all, to help them draw closer to their Father in Heaven. Literacy is a step-by-step process which, when embraced, means not only reading but comprehending and taking action.

When Brigham Young reestablished the Relief Society in 1867, Emmeline was involved quickly. She loved Relief Society. She revered the many great women in the Church whose contributions were so important—women like her beloved sister-wife Elizabeth Ann Whitney, charter member in Nauvoo and counselor to Emma Smith and Zina Young. Emmeline believed Relief Society lifted women's spirituality and gave them hope.

I, too, love Relief Society. My mother, my grandmother, my aunts, and my neighbors were all involved in Relief Society in our town of Cardston, Canada. When I was 12 I read the Relief Society magazine every month, sometimes at night by the light from the hall that streaked under the door to my room. Relief Society was my anchor as a young bride in Boston, in New York City, and again when we moved to the frontiers of Alaska several years later.

In 1876 President Brigham Young called Emmeline to organize the women in a grain-saving program that was a signature activity of Relief Society for almost 40 years. For four years Emmeline chaired the central grain committee until 1880, when the Relief Society assumed full management of the project.

From those years of sisters gathering and storing wheat came a work ethic synonymous with Relief Society. It became such a significant symbol that wheat sheaves were added to the Relief Society emblem which we still use today.

Emmeline was in charge of the Silver Jubilee celebration of Relief Society in 1892. At that great event in the Tabernacle, Apostle Abraham Cannon read a talk, "Work of the Relief Society Since Nauvoo," prepared by Emmeline. President Joseph F. Smith, then a counselor in the First Presidency, led the women of the Church in an official prayer. More than 50,000 Relief Society sisters in countries around the world gathered together for that singular event and held prayers in their local units.

One hundred years later, in 1992, the Relief Society again celebrated in the Tabernacle. What a thrill it was to be a part of this event! Relief Society membership numbered more than 3.5 million, and again, sisters in 137 countries around the world gathered, this time for a satellite broadcast received practically simultaneously around the world. The sesquicentennial featured tributes to Relief Society from women representing countries on five different continents—Zimbabwe, Mexico, South Korea, Australia, and Germany. Emmeline and her sisters would have surely joined with us as I invited the sisters to follow Isaiah's supplication: "Let us go up to the mountain of the Lord, to the house of the God of Jacob; and he will teach us of his ways, and we will walk in his paths" (Isaiah 2:3).

When President Joseph F. Smith called Emmeline as the fifth president of the Relief Society on 3 October 1910, she was 82 years old. She had been corresponding secretary from 1888 to 1892 and then general secretary since 1892. She described herself as "the last leaf upon the tree,"[21] for she had spent her adolescent years in Nauvoo, had helped to settle Zion with many sisters familiar to us from Church history, and was now the only one left. With Emmeline's calling came the challenge to lead in a new century, relying upon the strength of the Relief Society and its promise of "future greatness" that had been extolled from the beginnings in Nauvoo.

Much of what we know as Relief Society was introduced during Emmeline B. Wells's administration. "Charity Never Faileth" became the motto; visiting teaching was formally initiated; standardized lessons for four meetings a month were circulated, some even corresponding directly with priesthood lessons. In addition, an emphasis was given to genealogy, public health, home economics, and charity work.

A study of Emmeline's presidency shows a series of breaks with long-standing traditions she had helped institute or maintain. The challenge of her 11-year presidency was to preserve the essence of Relief Society while shaping new directions. Each step seemed to distance the organization from some established practices and to require the adoption of new ones. In many ways it was a difficult era.

Through a decade of change, Relief Society tried to respond to a growing sense of social consciousness among younger sisters and yet still hold fast to its spiritual charge. Emmeline openly expressed her concern that "we are getting too far away from the spiritual side

of our great work, and from the thought that inspired the first organization of the Relief Society." She emphasized, "The Society stands
first for spirituality, and then for charity and mercy."[22]

I have wrestled with how to keep Relief Society balanced and
focused. The challenge of the 1990s has been to meet the needs of a
world in turmoil in a rapidly growing church, and to bring women
representing many cultures and traditions into the circle of our
presidency and board. I have worked to maintain the essence of Relief Society—its identity and contribution—when the women in
high-growth areas have no connections to its past role. This organization for women, established by a prophet, is an essential part of
their gospel experience.

Building the personal testimony of every woman is foundational
to developing and exercising the charity for which Relief Society is
known. Membership has the responsibility to care for each other,
the opportunity to learn together, and the joys of a unified sisterhood. Because it was organized under the direction of and after the
pattern of the priesthood, it has a divine identity. It continues to
function with this guiding power.

What we learn from Emmeline's era is that the Relief Society is
not based on a collection of programs or good ideas put in motion.
Methods and policies have changed with time and emphasis. The
strength of Relief Society comes from being grounded in spirituality
and service, as identified by the Prophet Joseph Smith when he
charged the women "not only to relieve the poor, but to save
souls."[23]

In the past seven years as I have worked with our priesthood
leaders in directing Relief Society, I often have reflected on Emmeline's pioneer role. During her 11-year tenure as Relief Society president, Emmeline faced tough issues. Stepping forward to disband
the grain storage program when many women were so vested in the
assignment—having built granaries, organized accounting procedures, and encouraged this as a hallmark activity—was a bold yet
humble act. Bold as a leader, humble as a follower, Emmeline
moved Relief Society into the order of the Church.

I have also tried to lead the Relief Society according to that pattern described in the Doctrine and Covenants: "Hearken unto my

voice, and unto the voice of my servants whom I have appointed to lead my people" (D&C 124:45).

On 29 February 1928, on the 100th birthday anniversary of Emmeline B. Wells, the women of Utah placed a marble bust of this great woman in the rotunda of the Utah State Capitol. The inscription is simple: "A Fine Soul Who Served Us." What a tribute this is to her life, her dignity, her contributions, her love of women and Relief Society, and, most of all, her remarkable hope, "believing in the light after darkness."

NOTES

1. "Emmeline B. Wells," *Deseret News*, 25 April 1921.

2. *Young Woman's Journal,* December 1905, pp. 554–55.

3. Augusta Joyce Crocheron, ed., *Representative Women of Deseret: A Book of Biographical Sketches* (Salt Lake City: J. C. Graham and Co., 1884), p. 65.

4. "Emmeline B. Wells," *Deseret News*.

5. Emmeline B. Wells, diary, 1 September 1874, Special Collections, Harold B. Lee Library, Brigham Young University, Provo, Utah.

6. Emmeline B. Wells, *Woman's Exponent,* 1 October 1874, p. 67.

7. Wells, *Woman's Exponent,* February 1914, p. 100.

8. Wells, diary, 31 March 1875.

9. Ibid., 1 April 1875.

10. "Emmeline B. Wells," *Deseret News*.

11. Wells, "Faith and Fidelity," *Musings and Memories,* 2d ed. (Salt Lake City: The Deseret News, 1915), p. 221.

12. Wells, *Woman's Exponent,* 15 April 1880, pp. 75–76.

13. Wells, diary, 20 February 1845.

14. Ibid., 1 September 1874.

15. Ibid., 13 September 1874.

16. Wells, "October," *Musings and Memories,* p. 75.

17. Robert Browning, "Andrea del Sarto," in James Dalton Morrison, ed., *Masterpieces of Religious Verse* (New York: Harper and Row, 1948), p. 604.

18. Gerard Manley Hopkins, "Pied Beauty," in Arthur Quiller-Couch, ed., *The Oxford Book of English Verse* (Oxford: Clarendon Press, 1939), p. 1011.

19. Oliver Wendell Holmes, "The Chambered Nautilus," in Morrison, *Masterpieces,* p. 370.

20. Wells, *Woman's Exponent,* 15 July 1872, p. 32.

21. Annie Wells Cannon, "Mothers in Israel," *Relief Society Magazine,* 3 February 1916, p. 68.

22. Relief Society General Board Minutes, 10 December 1913, Archives Division, Church Historical Department, The Church of Jesus Christ of Latter-day Saints, Salt Lake City, Utah.

23. *History of the Church* 5:25.

&

Elaine L. Jack, general president of the Relief Society since 1990, was born and raised in Cardston, Alberta, Canada. She was a member of the Relief Society general board for 11 years and served as a counselor in the Young Women general presidency. She is the author of *Eye to Eye, Heart to Heart,* as well as several articles for Church publications. She and her husband, Joseph E. Jack, have four sons and 13 grandchildren. Elaine says that in writing this essay she has renewed her appreciation for Emmeline's bold leadership, which she hopes to emulate.

15

Wherever You Are, Emma Turner

Emma Turner Stayner

1833–1875

*Y*ou come for me, Great-Grandmother Emma. Dreaming or waking I sense you, in my blood, in my looks, in my perceptions and perspectives. How can this be when I know so little about you?

My only connection for most of my life was a yellowed photo of you, hand colored, I imagine, by my artistic mother with her cotton rolled on a toothpick and dipped in her oils. Subtle, inviting, it was in her scrapbook beside my grandmother, also, like you and me, an Emma. Your hair pulled into a thick bob is dark brown, like your deepset eyes hugged by your dark eyebrows. Even though you're scarcely smiling, the clarity of your gaze and the turn of your mouth below your slender nose and high-boned cheeks invite me to listen for you and expect your eyes to turn and meet mine. But there is a sadness about you, a drawn immersion in something behind your eyes as they look beyond me into some space, and a yearning contradicted by your velvet-trimmed, lace-collared dress and jawline set to take on childbirth or dispose of chagrin. A beauty born of resolution and expectation lights kindness in your eyes.

Emma Turner Stayner

And something else of you talks to me.

Hanging in the same lighted corner of what used to be my mother's room in our home, where she lived with us for 15 years, is a sampler, rather large, 10 by 17 inches, stitched by you. On it you cross-stitched meticulously the alphabet in capital and small letters, each a different color, above numbers to 14, and a verse:

> When daily I kneel down to pray
> As I am taught to do
> God does not care for what I say
> Unless I feel it too.

You stitched geometrics and trees, a flowered border, and, most important:

> Emma Turner,
> aged seven years,
> September, 1840

There are mended tears in the ochre linen, breaks in some of the dividing borders, and your initials *ET* toward a middle edge. Concerned about its weathering for more than 150 years, I had it framed and covered with glare-free glass. I pass it daily going in and out of our bedroom. But only recently have you come after me to find you. You have become a real presence. About two years ago I began to ask, Who were you? How did you live? When? Where? And why do you want me, a non-genealogist, to find you, know you?

Finally, one day, after a *Deseret News* board meeting in the Church Administration Building on South Temple, I thought, Why not? Why not pay a very novice visit to the Family History Library next door in the Joseph Smith Memorial Building and find that Emma Turner? Amazing. A young sister missionary from Brazil fed me a keyboard, some instructions—and lo, unto me were delivered some 15 pages identifying you, my great-grandmother Emma Turner. In the Ancestral File, backward and forward run your lines, from four generations back to 1721, and a pedigree chart from your birth in 1833 in Malvern, England, to your marriage to Arthur Stayner in 1857 in Salt Lake City, and finally to your death in 1875 in Farmington, Utah. The lines then run on the descendency chart from you to oldest child, Emma Louise Stayner, my grandmother; to my mother, Grace Richards; to me, Emma Lou Warner. Bonanza! I was thrilled. I had found you.

But had I? I knew your years, your coming to Deseret, your marriage at 24, your 10 children's births, your death at 42, my genetic connections to you. But what did I know of *you*? Not one thing. I longed to have beside me my historian friend, Laurel Thatcher Ulrich. She, a detective of fabric and its relation to women's lives, could have found you in the material of your sampler, in the letters and figures of your writing, in a history of Farmington, or in a recipe book handed down to my grandmother to my mother to me. She might even find a connection between your birthplace, Malvern, England, and Malvern Avenue that leads into solid Tudor Highland Park Ward in Salt Lake City, where I housed my first 25 years and where I am in the cornerstone as the first baby blessed there in 1924. Into the skeleton lines on those pages I needed to have injected so much more of your story than lines and dates on a chart. I longed suddenly to know about your laughing and tears, passions and frustrations, dreams and disaffections. I needed to be brought into the picture knowing why you and I hang there on those lines I punched up on a computer in the Joseph Smith Memorial Building.

Since then, after that first tantalizing taste of your history, you have become an enigma. Daughters of Utah Pioneers, with their extensive records, had little to offer me. The youngest of your 10 children, my great-aunt Katherine Elizabeth Stayner, who was four when you died, never married, and became like my second mother. She tells in her written story only that you were a beautiful seamstress and a meticulous homemaker, that you made all of your sons' suits out of broadcloth from your husband's cast-off trousers, and that you wanted him, Arthur Stayner, to have lots of land in Farmington. When he was secretary-treasurer to the Union Pacific Railroad, you saved a little box full of $20 gold pieces to enable him to buy that land. More, you were the "Malvern nightingale" in Farmington. You had a beautiful voice and a "smile that lighted the world." And you were Arthur's first wife.

Whatever might erupt from your story, Emma Turner, could be spun like flax as the linen of your sampler. I want that story. What kind of woman grew up from that little seven-year-old who knew how to read and write in a time when so few girls did? A cousin said you resisted joining the Church with the rest of your family because you were away in Ireland in a "finishing school," that you wanted an education. Rumor? And what did you do with that learning? Ten babies in 14 years? Did you ever read or ruminate on what you were about? Or laugh with neighbors? Maybe question how a doctrine or an edict might affect your days? Were you hardy? Sickly? Why dead at 42?

I asked my older cousin's wife, who lived with Aunt Kate till she died at 95, what Emma Turner died of. "The family legend is that she died of a broken heart when Arthur took another wife." True, Emma? Aunt Kate adored her father, Arthur Stayner, with his aristocratic English background, his fluency in four languages, and his bringing sugar-making from France to Utah. She faithfully cared for him until he died at 64. Fascinating that in January of 1935, on the back of her typed pages, she painstakingly wrote by hand, "Sometime *after Emma died*—he married Alice Turner, Emma's sister, had 2 children. And after she died—he married Helen Hyde, had 6 children. And later he married Clara Miller, had 3 children." (Emphasis added.) Did Aunt Kate, like you, Emma, need desperately for him not to be polygamous? Because not a word of her statement about his marriages was true.

I ache that the charts tell such a different story: By the time you died, he had married and divorced Mary Elizabeth Clark and married Helen Hyde. A third wife, Clarissa Ruth Miller, he had married the January before you died in March. He did wait until the November after you died to marry your sister, Alice Turner.

As you elude me in the tangles of contradicting facts and rumor, I only want to know more about you, Emma. What were you drawn to in that finishing school at 15? What did you sing about? Get angry over? Who taught you the prayer about God in your sampler? Did you go on believing it? What finally led you, unmarried, to join the Mormons, cross the Atlantic and the plains? In whose company? Did you believe in a prophet and revelation? Where did you meet Arthur? How did he, at 27, attract you at 24 to be his first wife?

What was life like in Farmington as you bore 10 children in 14 years, lost two before they were two? Where was your fire? Your solace? Did you keep that meticulous household to keep your husband? Why were you eager for land? And how did you save that box of $20 gold pieces? I hope that, like Mother and Grandma, you laughed as well as you worked. Was my grandmother, your first child, primed by 17 to raise the other seven when you died? Did you teach her to stitch as a child as you had? Did she choose her role or run from it to marry at 21 a man four years younger, to have 12 children of her own, tailor their suits and dresses as you did, and give a home to your youngest, Katie, when her beloved father, your Arthur, died 19 years after you?

What pride made Kate sign formally her careful story that her father was never polygamous? Why the family legend about your death from a broken heart at 42 from his taking other wives? I need you to be real, to speak with your own voice. Did you have options without chains, opportunities without strings? Did you retain your ability to question your own or anyone else's assumptions about your history, your education, your church, your relationships? What did you feel? Know? Were you comfortable with *not* knowing some things? Were you comfortable with yourself?

Your oldest daughter, my grandmother Emma Louise, who lived with us as we grew up, could make the ordinary extraordinary. From what my mother, Grace, told me, with no deep, self-conscious search for self-expression Grandma Emma Louise, my namesake, read hungrily, loved sociability, and was her surgeon husband's scrub nurse in their kitchen; she simply took enjoyment in everything she did. What could she have told me of you, her mother? I slept with her till she died there when I was 12. *"We slept with breaths that matched. I went to sleep every night restraining deliberately one extra breath in five to let her slower time teach mine to wait."*[1] Could your story have come through her—not only her genes but her breath teaching me?

I want to imagine a journal kept nightly by you, Great-Grandmother Emma, as I have grown into keeping mine just before I sleep. If I had done a sampler, it likely would have been of Mother's truism, "Pray at night and plan in the morning." In that night, I yearn to derive who you were, beg for you to come alive. Under the exquisitely tuned eye of what I find the night provides, you visit me and invite me into your world. I picture you like Laurel Thatcher Ulrich's Martha Ballard, "mustering grease and ashes, shaking feather beds and pillows to attention, scrubbing floors and lines into subjection, [to restore] a fragile order to a fallen world."[2] And singing as you muster.

It may be that only in my life to come will I hear your singing, maybe me singing with you in the voice you never bequeathed me, as we join Mother and Grandma, we three Emmas and a Grace, eyes meeting and holding, hands clasped in each other's, knowing everything there is to know.

NOTES

1.   Emma Lou Thayne, *Until Another Day for Butterflies* (Salt Lake City: Bookcraft, 1973), p. 28.

2.   Laurel Thatcher Ulrich, *A Midwife's Tale* (New York: Alfred A. Knopf, 1991), p. 219.

Emma Lou Thayne, a lifetime resident of Salt Lake City, has taught secondary and college-level English and served on the University of Utah alumni board of directors and the Pioneer State Theatre Foundation. She is a 1996 recipient of the People of Vision award from the National Society to Prevent Blindness. She and her husband, Melvin E. Thayne, have five daughters and 18 grandchildren. Emma Lou's essay expresses her recognition of the bond that draws spirit and heart to previous generations.

16

"All That Is Wanting Is Faith Sufficient"
Aurelia Spencer Rogers
1834–1922

*I*t has been said that no woman was ever really a little girl. Perhaps this observation is what prompted Louisa May Alcott to write about girls as "little women," a phrase that could describe Aurelia Spencer Rogers, the first Primary president, as a child. Aurelia's childhood seems to have been very brief indeed.

Aurelia Spencer Rogers was born into a world that was physically and emotionally demanding. She would be submitted to the rigors of a persecuted people establishing Zion and colonizing a desert. Yet her faith, her optimism, and her industry, as well as what she considered to be a natural affinity for children, would give her a vision of possibilities for the children of a fledgling Church organization, and the courage and tenacity to carry out that vision.

My admiration for Sister Rogers began when I was a member of the Primary general board and we were preparing for the Primary centennial in 1978. Primary general president Naomi M. Shumway and her counselors wanted board members to understand the background and motivations of the woman who deliberated about the future of the children of the Church and asked the questions that would turn the wheels for

Aurelia Spencer Rogers

the beginning of Primary. President Shumway accomplished her goal, because I am in awe of Sister Rogers's ability to face and execute faithfully and cheerfully the burdensome responsibilities that fell upon her.

Through all time, little girls of tender ages have rocked the cradle and swept the floors. It was not unusual that I, the eldest of six children, tended babies, cooked a little, and swept a floor once in a while. But Aurelia's girlhood duties quickly advanced to full-fledged mothering when her mother died during the exodus from Nauvoo, leaving Aurelia, her older sister, Ellen, and four younger children. Aurelia was then 10 years old.

Her believing heart would help carry her through. She wrote later that in her very early childhood, "I remember having been told that God lived in Heaven, above us. So one day I went outdoors and looked up in the sky, thinking I might see Him walking among the clouds. And I was quite disappointed, that He did not make Himself visible."[1] Her faith, born early, sustained her throughout her life.

While the Saints were at Winter Quarters, Aurelia's father, Orson Spencer, left to serve a mission in England. Ellen, age 14, and Aurelia, age 12, were in charge of the family for three years, with neighbors, a Brother Bullock and his wife, counseled to look in on them when they could. After two years in Winter Quarters the little family of children crossed the plains to Salt Lake City in Brigham Young's company.

Today all this seems appalling—indeed, I can hardly bear to think about it—but sacrifices such as Aurelia's and her sister's are the foundation of strength that made heroines of our mothers of the Restoration. Sister Rogers's story is much the same as that of my own heritage. Some of my ancestors were in Nauvoo and Winter Quarters. Like Aurelia, they saw the bodies of Joseph and Hyrum as they were brought from Carthage. They, too, suffered persecution, deprivation, and expulsion. I feel a genuine kinship to Aurelia.

I have developed a love for these people who cut a swath through the wilderness to settle even more wilderness because of their love of God and the restored gospel of Jesus Christ. They made it possible for me to grow up in the gospel in relative peace and security.

The Spencer children were hungry, cold, and shoeless much of the time their father was away, and their suffering caused him to suffer as much or more than they did. Brother Spencer wrote to his children of his love and concern for them: "Dearly Beloved Children: . . . Elder Hyde wrote me . . . [that] you had seen rather straitened circumstances, which made me weep with sorrow. . . . "2 "My dear Children . . . whom I love with the most inexpressible fondness. You are my dearest treasures upon the earth. . . . "3

Brother Spencer gave strength to his children through occasional money he was able to send and through his letters: "I knew that you were suffering for Christ's sake, which gave me some comfort. . . ."4 "Thus far, your lives are full of promise, your minds are all intelligent and your hearts innocent and pure. . . . I desire so to live that my example and teaching shall tend to give you a mould and polish which will make heaven happier at your approach, and angels to rejoice over you. . . ."5 "My dear children, I trust God, who counsels us to walk the narrow way, will be your shield and defence, and provide for your wants and keep you all alive till we meet again. . . . I shall plead for your lives to be spared, and your minds kept unpolluted. Love one another and bear each other's faults. Cherish the spirit of God by patience and kindness. Never yield to sin or do anything that you would be ashamed to ask God about or tell me of. . . . Believe that God can hear and help you when you need it. . . ."6

Orson Spencer was a constant and stable light to Aurelia throughout her life. Later she wrote of his spiritual influence and of his testimony and wisdom being a strength to her during hard times. As I have matured and contemplated my love for my children and my extended family and how I can help them the most, I have come to realize the importance of the example of constant faith in rearing children and helping them in their adulthood.

In our Gospel Doctrine class during a discussion of Job and the responses of his family and friends to his trials, class members shared the most helpful responses they had received from others as they met their own challenges. We had a good discussion, with people sharing many positive observations. Then one young man said something that struck me as being obviously simple, yet most significant—something that describes the influence of my own parents. He said, "What has helped me the most in difficult times is that my parents and others whom I admire continue to be strong and confident in their faith and their courage. I look at them and think, 'If they can have faith, so can I. If they can have courage, so can I.'"

Orson Spencer did this for his daughter Aurelia. She truly needed to draw on his strength, faith, and courage, because she had a physically and emotionally rigorous existence all her life.

Aurelia matured in Salt Lake City and married Thomas Rogers, whom she had met on the trek across the plains. She later buried five of the 12 children she bore, as well as many friends and relatives. Her first home as a wife was a two-room log house with a roof of willows and dirt. Besides the bed, her furniture consisted of a table, four chairs, and a cupboard made of unpainted wood, all of which, along with her wood floor, she scoured once or twice a week. "Having no scrubbing brush I had to use sand and a cloth," she wrote.[7] She carried water in a bucket up a hill from a stream, swept with a homemade willow broom, and cooked over a fire. She was 16.

Later she wrote about "how lovely and romantic the [Valley] looked, with high mountains on the east and the Great Salt Lake on the west. . . . There was nothing for me but the bright side to look upon, and I imagined myself equal to the emergency. . . . I would not like the reader to imagine that I was unhappy; far from it; with the exception of certain times of trial, . . . 'I was happy as a bird.'"[8]

When she reported hardship in her history, it was often followed with similarly positive observations. Of witnessing the death of a friend, which happened frequently, she wrote, "These things caused a sad feeling to come over me; but such is life. . . . We partook of a nice warm supper. . . . Took train for home, . . . feeling much benefitted by the journey and visits."[9] In assessing her life Sister Rogers later wrote, "My blessings have exceeded all my trials."[10]

Her positive responses to a hard life motivate me. I have wanted to weather my challenges, including my time in the general Primary presidency, in a cheerful and hopeful way. Along with experiencing the joy of serving with other leaders and the stimulation of constant challenge and growth, I also spent long hours and encountered frequent roadblocks. Traveling during the time I was a Primary counselor and president was particularly taxing for the domestic soul that I am. I felt much was expected of me. I missed my husband and children, my bed, and familiar food. I sometimes felt frustrated when people didn't understand my feeling about children and what we needed to be doing for them. Like Aurelia, I needed to return feeling "benefitted." And I did. What I learned far exceeded my sacrifice.

Aurelia was not afraid of hard work. Her industry, learned of necessity in her childhood, was part of her success and helped her know that children needed direction and training. She had deliberated considerably about the children and youth around her, when her bishop, John W. Hess, challenged the mothers of his ward to teach their children the way they should believe and behave. She pondered for some time that such training required the united efforts of the parents in their community. Similarly, haven't we all wished at times that parents in our neighborhoods would commit to adhering to the same standards of morality and behavior that have been set for our children?

Aurelia was rather shy and did not act on her impulse for some time, but continued to ponder the matter. One summer afternoon during a visit at her Farmington, Utah, home with Emmeline B. Wells, Eliza R. Snow, Mary S. Clark, Nancy Clark, and Lorinda Robinson, the discussion turned to the disgraceful state of the young people. They were particularly concerned about the "rough, careless ways many of the young men and boys had at the time."[11] Many of them were allowed out late at night, and Aurelia referred to them as "hoodlums."[12]

"It may seem strange," Aurelia wrote later, "that in a community calling themselves Latter-day Saints, children should be allowed to indulge in anything approaching rowdyism. . . . In many instances our people have been driven about and persecuted on every hand, until it has seemed to be all they could do to make a living for their children. . . . Yet why should anything be allowed to come before the most sacred duty of parentage, that of looking after the spiritual welfare of the children? was the question which burdened my mind."13

During her discussion with her friends, Aurelia asked, "What will our daughters do for good husbands, if this state of things continues? . . . Could there not be an organization for little boys, and have them trained to make better men?"14 Eliza R. Snow, who also had been concerned about the children, was deeply impressed and agreed with Aurelia.

While Sister Snow proceded to meet with Church authorities about the matter, Aurelia contemplated what needed to be done. As usual, the simple faith that carried her through hardship sustained her during this time. As she reflected on the challenges that lay ahead, she received a spiritual witness that what was about to happen was the will of the Lord. She wrote: "While thinking over what was to be done for the best good of the children, I seemed to be carried away in the spirit, or at least I experienced a feeling of untold happiness which lasted three days and nights. During that time nothing could worry or irritate me; if my little ones were fretful, or the work went wrong, I had patience, could control in kindness, and manage my household affairs easily. This was a testimony to me that what was being done was from God."15

Eliza obtained authorization from President John Taylor, then President of the Council of the Twelve and presiding authority at the time, and Bishop Hess. Then Sister Rogers proceeded to organize the very first Primary.

As she spoke to the group of women called to serve in the first Primary, she expressed her confidence that Primary would benefit the children and the Church. She said, "When little children pray it will avail much. While they are running loose, the Adversary will feel that he can instill into their tender minds such influences that in their youth will make them subject to him. But I feel that in this he will be baffled." She added, obviously sensing what would influence children the most, "My intentions are to speak and act with the Spirit of the Lord." 16

The children met for the first time on 25 August 1878 in a little rock chapel in Farmington. There were 224 children enrolled in the first Primary, and 115 attended the first meeting.

Sister Rogers worked tirelessly to organize and edify the children. At one time she had a little business of teaching pattern cutting, but she gave it up because it interfered with her Primary work. She did sometimes become discouraged when her optimistic expectations were not always realized. After the first meeting she felt that "it was not quite a success on account of unforseen hindrances and some of the children not knowing the hour of the meeting."[17] After seven years as Primary president she wrote that she felt she had failed because not very many little boys were attending at the time. But "I made up my mind not to worry any more, but leave them in the hands of the Lord."[18]

Later she went to a Relief Society conference in Kaysville, following which some of the sisters met in a home and "had a good visit in talking over the things of the Kingdom. I had often wondered whether Jesus could know anything about the pains of women. Sister Eliza happened to say at that time, that God in order to be God, must know the suffering of woman as well as man. Why had I not thought of this before? It opened up a new train of thought. . . . Does not God understand our organization? . . . All that is wanting is faith sufficient. . . . By keeping His commandments, our faith is always strengthened."[19] Sister Rogers was willing to put her trust in the Lord and to wait upon him to make a success of Primary.

However, she learned another important lesson soon afterward. While attending a young people's meeting, she was called upon to speak. As she was speaking she remembered that Oliver Cowdery, "when called upon to translate, had an idea that the Lord would dictate, and he would have nothing else to do but write it down. The Lord told him by way of revelation, this was not what He wanted; He expected Oliver to think for himself, and if what came into his mind was pleasing to the Lord, his bosom would burn within him, and he would feel that it was right; and if it were not right, he would have a stupor of thought."[20] (See D&C 9.)

She mentioned this to the congregation, and afterward recognized that she had received inspiration from the Lord for herself and for Primary. "It was made plain to me that we must think for ourselves, and if we fail in one thing, try another. I felt determined to be more diligent in my duties ever after, and upon returning home went to work with a will and had good success with the Primary children."[21] She exercised her agency, used her initiative, and moved forward with new plans.

Primary did succeed and has endured. Membership has grown to include well over a million children today because of the Lord's inspiration to and support of Aurelia Spencer Rogers, and because of many leaders and teachers who have taken on Sister Rogers's cause by responding to calls from the Lord to serve children.

Today leaders are teaching children the gospel of Jesus Christ and helping them learn to live it. A peek into today's Primary finds teachers in classrooms with children busily engaged in meaningful gospel learning activities. Members of the bishopric teach children when they give messages in Primary opening exercises. Primary presidencies teach children in opening exercises and sharing time. Music leaders teach children the gospel of Jesus Christ through song. Nursery leaders are teachers who help give little ones their first feelings that Church is a safe and happy place. All Primary leaders today teach and inspire by the example of their behavior, their love for and attention to each child, and the quality of their performance in their callings.

Sister Rogers would be pleased to know that Primary has thrived and that teaching truth is at its heart. She undoubtedly knew that helping children develop testimonies of Jesus Christ and his Church is a sacred trust.

When Moses was called by the Lord and entrusted with assisting in the Lord's work, he was shown the earth from beginning to end. He saw all the inhabitants of the earth, as well as of numerous other worlds. (See Moses 1.) When Moses saw all this, he was able to understand that his task was not just to lead one group of people from one land to another but to help prepare a people who would receive the Savior, who would redeem the world.

Like Moses, Sister Rogers seemed to have a broad view of the future of the children of the Church. Today's Primary leaders and teachers are doing more than leading a song, marking a roll, making a visual aid, or setting up chairs. They are helping children find their places in eternity.

Their task, as Aurelia Spencer Rogers hoped to do, is to create an atmosphere in which children can feel a happy spirit as they learn the principles of the gospel. The spiritual preparation that lifts and builds a teacher or leader is the foundation that will enable them to help a child feel the Spirit of the Lord.

Why was Aurelia Spencer Rogers successful? What are her lessons to us?

As she concluded her personal history near the end of her life, she wrote of her faith:

> In the sad experiences related, the sacrifices which have been made, I sincerely hope there is nothing which might have a tendency to weaken the faith of any Latter-day Saint, or discourage those who may be investigating our religion. And I wish to bear my testimony, that with all that the members of our family have passed through, I have not doubted the truth of the Gospel which I have embraced, and feel that I have great cause to be zealous in testifying that I do know that God lives, and that the Church of Jesus Christ of Latter-day Saints is His true Church.
>
> The one time in my life . . . when my children were taken from me by death, and I did almost question the existence of a God, was momentary. The words of my father comforted me, and the seeming doubt when cleared away never returned.[22]

Her faith was her strength. It gave her the will to continue, the brightness of hope and its resulting optimism. It allowed her to channel her industry and vision into the righteous cause of providing children with an environment in which they might feel the Spirit of the Lord.

We can keep the same kind of faith. We can be energetic and dependable in our duties. We can radiate the light of the gospel of Jesus Christ as we, like Sister Rogers, "speak and act with the Spirit of the Lord."

With the other hardy pioneers, the child Aurelia trudged forward at the pace of a rolling, rocking wagon. The growth of the Church during her lifetime was steady but as slow as those wagons. The relative ease of our lives today is a blessing that is allowing today's Church to race forward at breakneck speed. Children we care for in our families and in Primary need to be prepared not only to keep up with that rapid pace, but to lead it as they seek to find their places in eternity.

NOTES

1. Aurelia Spencer Rogers, *Life Sketches of Orson Spencer and Others, and History of Primary Work* (Salt Lake City: George Q. Cannon and Sons, 1898), p. 13.

2. Ibid., p. 57.

3. Ibid., pp. 66–67.

4. Ibid., p. 57.

5. Ibid., p. 67.

6. Ibid., pp. 69, 70.

7. Ibid., p. 126.

8. Ibid., pp. 123, 124, 126.

9. Ibid., pp. 253–54.

10. Ibid., p. 330.

11. Carol Cornwall Madsen and Susan Staker Oman, *Sisters and Little Saints* (Salt Lake City: Deseret Book Co., 1979), p. 1.

12. Rogers, *Life Sketches*, pp. 205–6.

13. Ibid., p. 206.

14. Ibid., p. 208.

15. Ibid., p. 212.

16. Madsen and Oman, *Sisters*, p. 6.

17. *Woman's Exponent* 7 (1 September 1878): 53, as quoted in ibid.

18. Rogers, *Life Sketches*, p. 230.

19. Ibid., pp. 245–46.

20. Ibid., pp. 231–32.

21. Ibid., p. 232.

22. Ibid., pp. 230–31.

❧

Michaelene P. Grassli served as Primary general president from April 1988 to October 1994, having previously served as second counselor to President Dwan J. Young for eight years and for five years as a board member. She is the author of two books, *What I Have Learned from Children* and *LeaderTalk*. She and her husband, Leonard, live in Pleasant View, Utah, and have three daughters and eight grandchildren. In writing this chapter Michaelene looked at Aurelia Rogers not just as the organizer of Primary but as a loving, caring woman of vision who knew the needs of children.

17

"We Were a Happy Band"
Mary Goble Pay
1843–1913

A trip to the woods of northern Minnesota triggered in me a deepened understanding of how it is that Mary Goble Pay, a woman who suffered so much, could identify herself and her fellows as a "happy band." With my family on a lake in those woods, I anxiously watched an evening rainstorm swirl toward us as our fishing boat zoomed to safety. I secured our tackle while my brothers began putting up the rain protection. We beat the storm to shore, and the instant we docked, the welcoming committee of mosquitoes swarmed around us in a ferocious attack.

Fighting the bugs, we sweated and struggled to secure the boat and its contents as the first drops pelted us. With a final whoosh, the last canvas went up, and we sprinted to safety. It was then that I felt the strength of our bond of family camaraderie and mutual goals. It was good to work on a project, even that minuscule one, with my brothers and nephew.

Maybe, I thought as I slipped into bed late that night, maybe being put to a test with one's family and other loved ones, be the task great or small, does brings out the

Mary Goble Pay

best in people.

I first read Mary Goble Pay's life history

more than 20 years ago. It has seemed to me since then that the tests Polly (as her mother called her), her family, and associates endured are quite beyond my comprehension. Her writing is plain, so straightforward and understated that, like the words of Nephi, it moves me every reading.

Born in England in 1843, Mary Goble started her journey to Utah in 1856, less than six months after her baptism, by boarding a "sailing vessel" in Liverpool with her family. Before they even left the river "the crew mutinied but they were put ashore and another crew came on board. They were a good set of men."[1]

She reports that a shark followed the ship. After one of the 900 "souls on board" died and was buried at sea, "we never saw the shark any more." She tells about what they did during the six weeks of their voyage. "After we got over our sea sickness we had a nice time. We would play games, and sing songs of zion. We held meetings and the time passed happily" (p. 1).

She records a miraculous incident: "When we were sailing through the banks of Newfoundland we were in a dense fog for several days. The sailors were kept night and day ringing bells and blowing fog horns. One day I was on deck with my father when I saw a mountain of ice in the sea close to the ship. I said, 'Look, father look.' He went as white as a ghost and said, 'Oh, my girl.' At that moment the fog parted the sun shone bright till the ship was out of danger when the fog closed on us again" (p. 1).

All of that was mere adventure compared with the tragedies that lay ahead. From Boston the family went with the Saints to Iowa City. Purchasing two unbroken yoke of oxen, one yoke of cows, a wagon, and a tent, the family, who "did not know a thing about driving oxen" (p. 1), made their way to Council Bluffs. En route the first casualty occurred. A sister, Fanny, had contracted measles on the ship. In her characteristic, matter-of-fact style, Mary Goble Pay tells us, "There came up a thunder storm that blew down our shelter, made with hand carts and some quilts. My sister got wet and died the 19th of July 1856. She would have been two years old the 23rd. The day we started on our journey we visited her grave. We felt very bad to leave our little sister there" (pp. 1-2).

They arrived in Council Bluffs on the first of September. They continued to move west 15 to 25 miles a day, a thousand miles between them and other Saints. The Indians, "on the war path and . . . very hostile," and the wilderness itself necessitated that "the men had to travel all day and guard every other night" (p. 2).

At the Platte River "it was bitter cold" and I wonder if those wanderers felt like the "great lumps of ice floating down the river" about which Mary wrote. At camp, they "went to prayers" and "sang 'Come, Come, Ye Saints No Toil Nor Labor Fear.'" Mary, sounding so young and vulnerable, wrote, "I wondered what made my mother cry. That night my mother took sick and the next morning my little sister was born. . . . We named her Edith. She lived six weeks and died for the want of nourishment" (p. 2).

This tale reminds me of my own forebears. In my living room I daily look at a portrait of Jane Alder Bourne, my great-great-grand-mother. She is very real to me. On my coffee table I keep her crystal wine decanter, the only wedding present she was able to bring with her from England. On the ship, in a handcart, in a tent, she protected that gift. My paternal grandmother, who gave it to me, was her oldest granddaughter. It makes me wonder, what might young Mary have then protected on the ship, in her handcart, or under those flimsy quilts, that has been passed down to succeeding generations?

Once in Utah, my great-great-grandmother Jane and her family took shelter in a cave along the foothills outside of Kaysville. She gave birth to a child in those circumstances. When her brother George came to visit her, he saw that as the baby suckled, blood trickled from its mouth. As my grandmother told me the story, he immediately left for Ogden, some 25 miles away, where he traded his greatcoat for a bag of flour. Carrying the flour on his back, he returned to his sister's shelter with what proved the gift of nourishment and life. The child lived.

Mary tells one of the most poignant stories in her life as follows:

We had been without water for several days just drinking snow water. The captain said there was a spring of fresh water just a few miles away. It was snowing hard, but my mother begged me to go and get her a drink. Another lady went with me. We were about half way to the spring when we found an old man who had fallen in the snow. He was frozen so stiff we could not lift him, so the lady told me where to go and she would go back to camp for help for we knew he would soon be frozen if we left him. When she had gone I began to think of the Indians and looking and looking in all directions I became confused and forgot the way I should go. I waded around in the snow up to my knees and I became lost. Later when I did not return to camp the men started out after me. It was 11:00 o'clock before they found me. My feet and legs were frozen. They carried me to camp and rubbed me with snow. They put my feet in a bucket of water. The pain was terrible. The frost came out of my legs and feet but not out of my toes (p. 2).

After their last crossing of the Platte River, they journeyed in snow. Mary's group traveled in wagons and so they helped handcart companies they came across on their way. Lack of food, in part caused by the grazing of enormous buffalo herds, made cattle give out. The company inched along, moving only a few miles a day. The snow became so deep and the cattle so weary that the "brethren would shovel the snow to make a track for our cattle" (p. 3).

At Devil's Gate they left a wagon and "lots of our things." Mary's "brother James ate a hearty supper and was as well as he ever was when he went to bed. In the morning he was dead" (p. 3).

The journey was "nothing but snow." Unable to drive the pegs in their tents, they had to pile the snow to keep the tents in place. Mary wrote, "We could not get enough flour for bread as we got only a quarter of a pound per head a day so we would make it like thin gruel" (p. 3).

Four companies dragged across the plains. "We did not know what would become of us," wrote Mary. Finally, help and hope arrived in the form of Eph. Hanks, "a living Santa Claus." He told the camp "there would be plenty of flour in the morning for Brother Brigham Young had sent men and teams to help us. There was rejoicing that night" (p. 3).

The rejoicing was short-lived for the Gobles. "My mother had never got well, she lingered until . . . the day we arrived in Salt Lake

City. . . . Three out of four that were living were frozen. My mother was dead in the wagon" (p. 4).

So began life in Zion:

> Bishop Hardy had us taken to a house in his ward and the brethren and sisters brought us plenty of food. We had to be careful and not eat too much as it might kill us we were so hungry.
>
> Early next morning Brother Brigham Young and a doctor came. . . . When Brigham Young came in he shook hands with all of us. When he saw our condition, our feet frozen and our mother dead, tears rolled down his cheeks.
>
> The doctor wanted to cut my feet off at the ankles. But President Young said no, just cut off the toes and I promise you, you will never have to take them off any farther. The pieces of bone that must come out will work out through the skin themselves.
>
> The doctor amputated my toes using a saw and a butcher knife. The sisters were dressing my mother for her grave. My poor father walked in the room where mother was then back to us. He could not shed a tear. When my feet were fixed they packed us in to see our mother for the last time. Oh how did we stand it. That afternoon she was buried (p. 3).

They stayed with relatives; some months later Mary's father remarried. In July 1857 Mary went to live with Dr. Wiseman so she could work off medical services. As she put it, "instead of my feet getting better they got worse. . . . But it was no use he said he could do no more for me unless I could consent to have them cut off at the ankle. I told him what Brigham Young had promised me. He said all right sit there and rot and I will do nothing more until you come to your senses."

The story takes a miraculous twist here:

> One day I sat there crying my feet were hurting me so, when a little old woman knocked at the door she said she had felt that someone needed her there for a number of days. When she saw me crying she came and asked what was the matter. I showed

her my feet and told her the promise Brother Brigham Young had given me. She said, "Yes, and with the help of the Lord we will save them yet." She made a poultice and put on my feet and every day after the Doctor had gone she would come and change the poultice. At the end of three months my feet were well.

One day Doctor Wiseman said "Well, Mary, I must say you have grit. I suppose your feet have rotted to the knees by this time."

I said, "Oh no, my feet are well."

He said, "I know better. It could never be."

So I took off my stockings and showed him my feet. He said that it was surely a miracle and wanted me to tell him what I had been doing. I told him never to mind that they were now healed.

I have never had to have any more taken from them. The promise of Brother Brigham Young has been fulfilled and the pieces of bone have worked out (p. 4).

Having sat so long, her legs had become stiff and she could not straighten them. She returned to her father's home. "When he saw how my legs were we both cried. He rubbed the cords of my legs with oil and tried every way to straighten them, but it was no use. One day he said 'Mary, I have thought of a plan to help you. I will nail a shelf on the wall and while I am away to work you try to reach it.' I tried all day and for several days. At last I could reach it and how pleased we were. Then he would put the shelf a little higher and in about three months my legs were straight and then I had to learn to walk again" (p. 4).

Mary moved to Nephi and became reacquainted with Richard Pay, who had traveled with Mary's group and was now a widower. When Richard Pay and Mary Goble married, "it was very hard times. My husband bought a one room adobe house. For the window we had sack. That did all right until one day it rained and that spoiled our glass. We then put up factory (unbleached muslin). We had a bed stead, three chairs, a table, a box for our flour. Our bed tick we filled with straw. We had two sheets, two pillow slips and one quilt. I used to take them off the bed and wash them and put them on again. For dishes we had three tin plates, three cups, a pan or two to cook in and a spider (a flat iron skillet) to bake our bread" (p. 5).

Richard and Mary made a living ranching in Nephi, Utah. Mary described where the couple resided: "The people all lived inside of a large mud wall with a north and south gate. At night our cattle and sheep were brought home and we were all locked inside the fort for safety from Indians. Guards were at both gates to see that no one came in or went out of the gates. They were locked at eight o'clock every night. If you did not get in by then you were locked out. We were a happy band of brothers and sisters. We felt safe locked inside the fort walls" (pp. 5-6).

That clause, "We were a happy band," tells so much about Mary and her fellow Saints and about the nature of unity and faith. I have never been one to compare the here and now with the there and then. I have no idea what it might have been like to live before airplanes and automobiles. I've never sent a husband to war or watched a child die. I've never even made soap. Yet in my own way, I know what it is like to feel safe inside the fort, to relish moments of unity with my fellow travelers.

Several years ago I attended church in Rio de Janeiro. A guard sat at the front door, supposedly to keep armed gangs from robbing all of us. I went to the youth Sunday School class, which was also the seminary class, only to find that their teacher hadn't shown up. With the help of a missionary, I asked the five young men and women present about their lives. They told me about the daily struggle to stay pure, to remain faithful. I learned much from a single mother who stopped me after church to tell me about her errant son. I needed no interpreter to know of her angst over this boy, or to sense how difficult putting bread on the table was for her.

Later my friend and I talked about these good souls, and she said something that has profoundly stayed with me: "To have the fulness of the gospel and not to appreciate it is so ungrateful." She was right, of course.

Mary Goble Pay, five Sunday School/seminary students, and a single mother in Rio understood that, I believe. I suppose that understanding within Mary was why she could call her group a "happy band." They had the truth, they had faith, and they had each other—a potent combination that could overshadow much privation.

Life demanded a great deal of the Pays. Native Americans and daily survival loomed large in Mary's life. "My husband took his turn on guard and when the Black Hawk war broke out he was a minute man called out any moment night or day. . . . I got to know the rap of Brother Peter Sutton. He would say, 'Brother Pay, I want you on the march as quick as possible.' He would kiss his wife and babies and be gone. We did not know if we would ever see each other again. All we could do was pray" (p. 6).

From the wife of the chief of a "small tribe of Indians call[ed] Pagwats that stayed around Nephi," Mary learned their language. "I well remember one day," she wrote, "when I was dressing my baby and two of the boys were playing on the floor when the door opened and two Indians came in. One was the meanest looking Indian I have ever seen. They started to talk. He said, 'Let's kill them, see there are four scalps.' The old chief said, 'No, you cannot kill them.' He talked a little while trying to get his consent but when I looked at the chief I knew he was my true friend. He said, 'No, you cannot kill them for she and her husband are my friends.' He got mad and said, 'I would like to cut their throats.' Then I answered him. I tell you he was a frightened Indian for he didn't know I knew what he said. He stood there ramming his gun. I told him to go. The old chief laughed and made fun of him because he did not know I understood him. I loaded the old chief down with something to eat because he had saved my life and my children" (pp. 6-7).

My own maternal grandmother told stories of being the oldest daughter in charge of 10 siblings on a Moroni, Utah, farm. One day while my great-grandmother was in Mt. Pleasant on Relief Society business, Native Americans came seeking food. Grandma Colt had all the children crawl under the bed, and when the men knocked again, she called from under the bed, "Nobody home."

Mary Goble Pay had a remarkable capacity to take counsel. Obedience saved her life more than once. "I could relate many more incidents of our dealings with the Indians, but we followed President Young's advice to be good to them, feed them and not fight them. An Indian never forgets a kindness and he never forgets a wrong. They are truthful. If they say they will do a thing, they will do it" (p. 8).

Mary Goble Pay's life revolved around church and family. She served in Primary and Relief Society. She bore 13 children, 10 sons and three daughters. Two died in infancy; she also lost "one little son two years old." She outlived several other children and her husband. Richard Pay left her "with nine children, two were married" and little else. "It looked pretty dark with nothing coming in. I had to depend on my boys and they did not get much work, so I started to nurse the sick. In this I had good success" (p. 9).

Fifty years after they had "left their homes over the sea for Utah," Mary Goble Pay and "quite a few of us that are left" went to Salt Lake City "to celebrate our Jubilee. . . . We met the captain of our company, Brother John Hunt, and some of the people that came in our company. We were very happy to see one another and talk of the times that are gone" (p. 10).

While in Salt Lake City she looked up cousins and, poignantly, with members of her family, found her mother's grave. "It was the first time I had seen it, for when she was buried our feet were so we could not go to the funeral and later we moved south. No one knows how I felt as we stopped there by her grave. . . . There were three generations and our mother was a martyr for the truth. I thought of her words, 'Polly, I want to go to Zion while my children are small, so they can be raised in the Gospel of Christ for I know this is the true church.' . . . I think my mother had her wish" (p. 10).

Later in life, writing her remarkable story brought painful reminiscences:

> October 24, 1909. I went to Sunday School and was asked to relate a few incidents of our journey across the plains. I told them we had the first snow storms the 22nd of September in 1856. There were fifteen who died through the cold and exposure while crossing the Platte River. Sister McPherson sat by me and she said her mother was the fifteenth to die. They were all laid side by side and a little dirt thrown over them.

November. I have been to the reunion. I met Brother Langly Bailey and had a good time talking over incidents of our trip across the plains. It made me feel bad. It brought it all up again. Is it wise for our children to see what their parents passed through for the gospel? Yes, I think it is (p. 11).

President Gordon B. Hinckley wrote of Mary Goble Pay, his wife's grandmother:

> [Her] story is representative of the stories of thousands. It is an expression of a marvelous but simple faith, an unquestioning conviction, that the God of Heaven in his power will make all things right and bring to pass his eternal purposes in the lives of his children.
>
> We need so very, very much a strong burning of that faith in the living God and in his living, resurrected Son, for this was the great, moving faith of our gospel forebears.
>
> Theirs was a vision, transcendent and overriding all other considerations. When they came west they were a thousand miles, a thousand tedious miles, from the nearest settlements to the east and eight hundred miles from those to the west. A personal and individual recognition of God their Eternal Father to whom they could look in faith was of the very essence of their strength. They believed in that great scriptural mandate: "Look to God and live" (Alma 37:47). With faith they sought to do his will. With faith they read and accepted divine teaching. With faith they labored until they dropped, always with a conviction that there would be an accounting to him who was their Father and their God. . . .
>
> Let us look again to the power of faith in ourselves, faith in our associates, and faith in God our Eternal Father. Let us prayerfully implement such faith in our lives.[2]

My personal feeling is to echo President Hinckley and to add from my woman's heart that Mary Goble Pay blesses me as surely as she must bless her direct descendants. A consummate model of faith and faithfulness, she reminds me how good my life is even when it isn't going well. She calls to me, just as my forebears do, "You have the fulness of the gospel. Have faith. Be true."

Edgar Lee Masters wrote in his wonderful poem "Lucinda Matlock," "Degenerate sons and daughters, life is too strong for you—it takes life to love Life."[3] Of that truth the lives of Mary Goble Pay and her happy band bear witness.

NOTES

1. Mary Goble Pay, *Life of Mary Goble Pay,* typescript, p. 1, Church Historical Department, The Church of Jesus Christ of Latter-day Saints, Salt Lake City, Utah.

2. Gordon B. Hinckley, "The Faith of the Pioneers," *Ensign,* July 1984, p. 6.

3. Edgar Lee Masters, "Lucinda Matlock," *Spoon River Anthology* (New York: Macmillan, 1916), p. 221.

Carol L. Clark, who resides in Salt Lake City, earned her Ph.D. from the University of Utah and is the chief operating officer of a financial corporation. She has received many honors for her consumer and other professional work, including the National Council of Women's Leaders of the Future award. She served for almost 14 years on the Relief Society general board and is the author or editor of several books and articles. Carol gained an increased appreciation for the positive attitude born of faith as exemplified in the life of Mary Goble Pay.

18

"Up the Rugged Hill of Knowledge"
Romania Pratt Penrose
1839–1932

$\mathcal{T}$he summer before I left my childhood home in Salt Lake City to attend faraway Harvard University was a difficult, worrisome one. I had never been apart from other family members for more than five days, and then only to attend a girls camp some 30 miles away. It hardly compared to the 2,400 miles I would soon be traveling. As I packed up my belongings and prepared to relinquish my bedroom to my too-excited younger sister, I nervously wondered how I would fare on the East Coast. For me, Harvard represented the geographical, cultural, even religious antithesis of my Utah upbringing.

"You need to move your stuff out of your closet by Monday," my younger sister suddenly informed me one morning in mid-July. "The carpenter will be coming over on Tuesday to measure the closet for shelves." She sighed to express her sorrow, whether real or feigned, at my fast-approaching departure. "It will be *so* quiet here after you leave," she added, gathering up the wallpaper samples she had been scrutinizing against my walls. As soon as I left, she planned to strip my bedroom walls of my navy print and replace it with a new floral

Romania Pratt Penrose

pattern. Six weeks remained before I left for Boston, but already I felt displaced.

As the weeks dwindled into days, my apprehension grew. Would my high school preparation be enough? Suppose I didn't measure up to the university's expectations. Suppose the brigade of prep school graduates knew more than I. Would the roommate horror stories I had heard prove all-too-painfully true?

As I prepared myself physically and psychologically for college, I began to liken myself to the pioneer women about whom I'd recently been studying. I had spent the summer researching some Mormon heroines as part of the preliminary work needed to establish the William and Patricia Child Chair at the University of Utah Hospital and School of Medicine. This chair recognizes and honors Utah's early women doctors. Those female medical practitioners had journeyed outside the center of Mormondom to obtain an education, just as I would now journey to Harvard. Their personal and academic successes both comforted and inspired me.

That summer Romania Penrose, Ellis Shipp, Margaret Roberts, and Martha Cannon, all early Utah doctors, had become familiar names, like those of old, beloved friends. Yet even from the beginning of my research I felt an especial kinship with Romania. True, Romania lived a century ago and was 16 years older than I when she left the Salt Lake Valley to attend the Woman's Medical College in New York. Nevertheless, I felt a link because she, like me, went east for her education, and she, like me, came from a Mormon background. So it seemed natural that, as a soon-to-be college freshman, I would look to Romania as a role model, as the epitome of the woman of "nerve, energy, and ambition" I needed to be.[1]

Now that I'm a junior in college, I still find Romania Pratt Penrose to be a wonderful example of survival and success in the micro-world of college life. Her distinguishing characteristics of hard work and persistence are becoming my own. I now understand firsthand what Romania meant when she spoke of "plodding daily up the rugged hill of knowledge." Accounts of how she studied up to 16 hours a day in medical school inspire me to follow uncomplainingly in her tracks.[2]

Even as a child Romania exhibited the insatiable thirst for knowledge that characterized her in later life. As a young girl she attended the Western Agricultural School, a Quaker institution in Ohio, and later boarded at the Female Seminary in Crawfordsville, Indiana. In addition to the basic subjects of education at the time, Romania studied German, painting, and piano. She claimed that she "should have obtained a very finished education; but my blooming woman-hood began to draw around me admirers which warned my mother to flee from Babylon before I became fastened by Gentile bonds."[3]

Romania's mother had long wanted to join the Saints in Utah. Concern that teenaged Romania might marry one of her many non-Mormon admirers hastened that move. Six years earlier, Romania's father, Luther Bunnell, had traveled to California during the gold rush, hoping to "get rich quick." He did, but at too great a personal sacrifice. After amassing a small fortune in the gold mines, Luther contracted typhoid fever and died.[4]

Romania's mother, Esther, used some of Luther's reclaimed gold to purchase oxen, a wagon, and other supplies for the family's west-ward trek. Romania, her mother, and three siblings joined the John Hindley company and journeyed to Utah in 1855, basically without incident. They arrived in the Salt Lake Valley, however, during a se-vere famine caused by drought and crop-eating grasshoppers. "Now for the first time in life did I face its stern realities," Romania solemnly recalled in her *Memoirs*.[5] The knowledge and skills she had acquired from her early schooling suddenly also became her livelihood. While her mother took in laundry, 16-year-old Romania taught day-school to Brigham Young's children. She also gave music lessons on the side.

Whenever she could, Romania read and reread her treasured books from her early school days in Ohio. Even after her marriage to her first husband, Parley P. Pratt Jr., in 1859 and the subsequent births of their children, Romania continued to be a self-appointed student. Sharing her love of learning with her children, Romania taught her five sons how to read and write and play their prized piano. But 16 years after her marriage to Parley Jr., Romania's edu-cation would far exceed the fundamentals she learned as a child and later passed on to her own children. Her decision to study medicine marked her biggest step and greatest challenge in pursuing her for-mal education.

Leaving home to attend medical school was not an easy decision for Romania. She was 34 years old and the mother of five boys who ranged in age from nine months to 14 years. It pained her to leave her young children behind, even in the care of her own mother. But Romania sadly remembered how two of her children had died in infancy: a son, Luther, who died just days after birth, and a daughter, Corinne, who died shortly before the age of two. Their deaths left scars in Romania's memory that strengthened her resolve. She did not want other mothers to suffer such losses. Unfortunately, the deaths of her own babies were not isolated instances. Infant mortality was high at that time in Utah, as in other places. Romania had also witnessed the death of a friend who died for lack of medical assistance. Watching her friend die and feeling her own inability to save her or even relieve her pain had affected Romania deeply: "I saw her lying on her bed, her life slowly ebbing away, and no one near knew how to ease her pain or prevent her death; it was a natural enough case, and a little knowledge might have saved her. Oh, how I longed to know something to do, and at that moment I solemnly vowed to myself never to be found in such a position again, and it was my aim ever afterward to arrange my life work that I might study the science which would relieve suffering, appease pain, prevent death."[6] *Never*, Romania promised herself, never again would she allow anyone within her sphere, especially women and children, to die for lack of medical care. It was then that she resolved to go east and study medicine.

In her decision to become a doctor, Romania knew she had an ally in President Brigham Young. In a general conference address three years earlier President Young had called for women to venture into the professional world and fill those jobs vacated by the men. Because Utah and the Church were still in their early stages of growth, men were needed to serve missions or perform manual labor. Women could therefore best be spared to perform professional services. "We believe," the prophet had declared, "that women are useful, not only to sweep houses, wash dishes, make beds, and raise babies, but that they should . . . study law or physic[s]. . .and all this to enlarge their sphere of usefulness for the benefit of society at large."[7] Of primary concern to Brigham Young was Utah's lack of doctors. Most of the outlying settlements had no access to doctors, and the core settlements could barely boast of better medical conditions.

One of Eliza R. Snow's first responsibilities as central board Relief Society president was to ensure that every ward had at least three women skilled in midwifery and nursing. Most of these women, however, had no formal training. They learned from textbooks, memories of their own labor, or, as was more often the case, trial and error. Brigham Young knew only too well of Utah's health care crisis, and he called upon women to remedy it. Eliza R. Snow echoed President Young's call, rallying women of "nerve, energy and ambition" to go east to become doctors.[8] With her natural curiosity, intellect, and hard-work ethic, Romania Pratt fit Sister Snow's description perfectly.

To pay her high tuition Romania sold her treasured piano, one of the first pianos brought across the plains to Utah. She and her husband also sold their home and a small farm that Parley Jr. had inherited. Romania's mother recognized the educational motivation and frontier necessity fueling her daughter's ambition. She generously offered to care for Romania's children during her absence.

Bidding her mother and children a tearful farewell, Romania boarded the train that would take her to New York City. Once there, she joined her husband and helped him edit and prepare for publication the autobiography of his celebrated father, Elder Parley P. Pratt.[9] After they submitted the book for publication several weeks later, Romania enrolled at the Woman's Medical College in New York City.

Romania's transition to eastern life and the pressures of medical school were difficult at first. Like me, Romania suffered from culture shock and homesickness. A week before my own freshman year began, my father flew with me to Boston to help me get settled into my new life. Any excitement about my new surroundings or new-made friends quickly vanished when he left to return to Utah. I felt like Remus and Romulus of Roman mythology when they were abandoned to the wolves. Romania, in writing of similiar feelings as a new college student far from home, described herself as "a stranger in a strange land, beside being almost a 'hiss and a byword' on account of my religion."[10]

Romania was a new student but certainly not an ordinary one. She was older and a mother. She enrolled at the Woman's Medical College very late in the term. On her first day of class, Romania lagged weeks behind the other students in her medical readings and course work. She felt ignorant, different, and alienated from her more homogeneous peers. During her first term at medical school, she audited her classes, trying to grasp the basics of the very unfamiliar material.

Shortly after her enrollment at the college, one professor, forgetting that Romania was a new, auditing student, called upon her during an oral exam. As he directed his question at her, 50 pairs of eyes fastened upon an embarrassed Romania. Unable to answer the question correctly, Romania explained her predicament to the professor. He apologized for his oversight and moved on to question another student. Flushed and flustered, Romania leaned back in her seat. Out of the corner of her eye she noticed the "mischievous smiles" of the other students gloating in her "extreme confusion"[11] and "total rout."[12] Those knowing smiles became the last straw. Never would she suffer such humiliation again. Romania silently resolved that she would learn the material, would never be unprepared, would be *over*prepared if need be. In her *Memoirs* she recounted: "During the summer vacation, while [the other students] were recreating, sea bathing and visiting with friends, I daily plodded studiously up the rugged hill of knowledge; reciting as a private student every day to the professor of physiology. I also took lessons in opthalmology of Dr. Wm. Little . . . also a course under Dr. P. A. Callan and finally by special permission I joined a class taught by Prof. H. D. Noyes in Bellevue College. Dr. Little said I was the first woman ever admitted to Bellevue." With evident satisfaction Romania added, "My revenge was more than complete at the beginning of the next term in witnessing their astonishment because of my advancement."[13] On her first day of class for the new term, Romania marched confidently into the lecture hall and took her seat at the front. Her ready answers to the professor's questions astounded the other students who remembered her only as the "quivering mouse" of the previous year.[14] Romania continued to excel in her studies, especially in her dissections, which received praise from students and professors alike. One of Romania's fellow students confided to her that a certain professor "would go to her table every day after she had left, and calling his class to him, would show them the model and style of [Romania's] dissection, using it as an example for the other students to pattern after."[15]

Overcoming her academic hurdles did not end all Romania's obstacles to earning her medical degree. As for most college students in any era, money was a constant worry and did not come easily. For just $1 a week Romania rented a small room and "lived much of her time on insufficient food for days together" in order to save enough money to pay for her costly tuition fee of $1 per hour.[16] In spite of her economy, Romania's funds ran so low after her first year that, without more money, she could not afford to remain another term at the medical college. Romania returned to Salt Lake City that summer and applied to Brigham Young for financial assistance. President Young listened to Romania's account of her poverty and medical ambition. He then alerted Eliza R. Snow, still central board president of the Relief Society, to Romania's financial plight. "She must continue her studies in the east," President Young told Eliza. "We need her here, and her talents will be of great use to this people."[17] Sister Snow collected enough money from the Relief Society sisters to help Romania meet her college expenses. After her graduation, Romania repaid this debt by teaching free midwifery classes to the Relief Society sisters for many years.

Financially secure, Romania returned to medical school that autumn. This time she attended the Woman's Medical College of Philadelphia, which was less costly. Clinics, dissections, and lectures in chemistry, anatomy, physiology, surgery, hygiene, obstetrics, and diseases of women filled her busy school schedule.[18] "The days all seemed so much alike that it was as one long day," Romania wrote of her years at medical school. "I was ever ready to do extra work that I might add to my store of knowledge."[19] Clearly Romania did just that, spending one summer working at the New England Hospital for Women and Children in order to put her textbook knowledge to hands-on use. Her senior year she wrote a thesis entitled "Puerperal Hemorrhage, Its Cause and Cure." Finally, on 3 March 1877, Romania passed her academic "golden gate."[20] She described her long-awaited graduation day as "one of the most eventful days of my life."[21]

Not content with just a medical degree, Romania later completed her postgraduate studies in Philadelphia and New York in order to specialize in diseases of the eye, ear, nose, and throat. She attended classes at the Wills' Hospital and Philadelphia Dispensary and later at the New York Eye and Ear Infirmary. With her specialized medical knowledge, Romania subsequently performed numerous surgeries, including Utah's first cataract operation.

After completing her medical and postgraduate studies, Romania happily returned home to her much-missed children. She soon opened an office on Main Street and established a busy medical practice. Sick women and mothers with sick children flocked to her for treatment. To accommodate all of her patients, Romania purchased a horse and buggy so she could travel quickly and safely to visit them over long distances and even during the night. In addition to running her medical practice, Romania taught two midwifery courses each year. Most of her pupils were women from rural settlements who, often supported financially by their towns, came to certify as midwives under Dr. Penrose and then return home to practice as such. The *Woman's Exponent* heavily advertised her obstetrics courses:

> We are pleased to notice that Dr. Pratt commences a new class in obstetrics during the winter. She has been requested to teach this branch of medicine by the leading sisters who are constantly visiting through the Territory and witnessing the painful lack of knowledge in this department. Her office is central, and she has the necessary charts, mannikin, etc., requisite to teach as thoroughly as can be expected in such a partial course. Not only are the sisters interested in these classes, but the brethren of the highest authority have extended their approval and expressed their desire that the people take advantage of the opportunity opened to them.[22]

Romania's professional skills proved particularly valuable when circumstances forced her to live by them. Four years after her return from medical school, Romania obtained a Church-sanctioned divorce from her husband, Parley P. Pratt Jr. Reasons for their divorce are unclear. The couple's many years apart, first while Parley Jr. was serving missions for the Church and later while Romania was attending medical school, helped to estrange them. Parley's polygamous marriage to a second wife during Romania's absence may have provided the crowning blow. For the next five years until her second marriage to Charles W. Penrose, Romania single-handedly supported her aging mother and five growing sons. During those struggling years of single parenthood and growing professional responsibility, Romania sometimes worked literally around the clock caring for both her patients and children.

Romania, driven to learn, never acquired enough knowledge to satisfy herself. Over a decade after her graduation the *Woman's Exponent* remarked, "Her desire for knowledge compels her to devote much time to study, that she may improve every passing hour."[23] Graduating from medical school proved only one of Romania's academic plateaus, not the peak of her "rugged hill of knowledge." Her thirst for knowledge reminds me of the importance of making my own education a lifelong pursuit. One semester during finals, friends and I commiserated about our heavy work loads. Some commented on how eagerly they anticipated tossing aside their textbooks. I disagreed. Although none of us relished the stress of final examinations, I could not imagine ever reaching a day when I would no longer want to learn. I cannot imagine such a day was ever a part of Romania's life.

Romania's education greatly enhanced the effectiveness of her service in Church and community. Romania played an active role in the Deseret Hospital for nearly 14 years, from the time it opened to the time it closed, and it "owed its existence largely to her enthusiastic labors."[24] Since her graduation from medical school, Romania had dreamt of opening a hospital that would care for the poor and prosperous alike. With the prophet's approval, she and other Relief Society sisters set about raising the necessary funds and renovating their small quarters into a well-equipped institution. At the dedication of the hospital in 1882 President John Taylor praised the Relief Society sisters for "their labors of love" in establishing a hospital where "the sick of the Lord's people could be attended and have the benefit of the ordinances of the Church as well as skillful treatment."[25] The completed Deseret Hospital became Utah's fourth hospital after the Williams, a small, family-run facility, and the Catholic-sponsored St. Mark's and Holy Cross Hospitals. It was the first LDS hospital in the state.[26]

Romania served on the hospital's board of directors from the very beginning, volunteering her time and services as a visiting physician. She later served as resident physician. This full-time position entailed a hectic schedule: "calls daily to all parts of the city and county, as well as all the details and heavy labors of the hospital work to superintend; then up at night and off, perhaps to some distant country place, and never knowing one moment what she may be called to perform in the next."[27] For eight years Romania served in this tiring position until the hospital closed, presumably for lack of funds, in 1895.

Romania championed the woman suffrage movement, rallying at not just local but national and even international conventions. "Why not let capacity and ability be the test of eligibility and not sex?" she demanded of *Exponent* readers.[28] "It is high time woman set a high price on all her works and abilities, and see which bill foots up the highest," a daunting challenge for her day.[29] Utah men and women, however, did set a "high price on all [woman's] works and abilities." In 1870 the Utah territory's legislature passed a statute granting women the right to vote. Utah women enjoyed that right for the next 17 years. In 1887, on the wave of an anti-polygamy crusade, the national Congress passed the Edmunds-Tucker Bill, which, among other things, revoked woman suffrage. In the 1890s, the United States government finally concluded to admit Utah into the Union. During Utah's Constitutional Convention, Utah lawmakers inserted a provision reinstating woman suffrage. The United States ultimately approved Utah's constitution, woman suffrage provision and all. It was years later before they passed the Nineteenth Amendment, which guaranteed that right to other women in the nation.

During these decades of woman suffrage and revocation of woman suffrage, Romania was among those who enthusiastically pursued the cause. She addressed many gatherings on the benefits of woman suffrage, including one suffrage meeting held at the Ogden Tabernacle. While completing her postgraduate studies in New York, Romania attended the National Woman's Suffrage Convention in Washington, D.C. There she met the legendary suffragette Susan B. Anthony, with whom she became friends. Years later, while she presided with her second husband, Charles W. Penrose, over the European Mission, Utah governor John C. Cutler asked Romania to represent Utah women as a speaker and delegate at a convention of the International Woman Suffrage Alliance in Amsterdam, Holland. Standing there before a crowd of thousands from around the world, Romania extolled the advantages of woman suffrage in Utah.[30] The following year Romania again attended the convention of the International Woman Suffrage Alliance, this time in London, England, where she represented the Church's Relief Society.

Romania's love of learning applied to her religious as well as secular education. Perhaps it is because of Romania's love of knowledge that she so readily embraced the gospel, which offered her the most perfect source of truth. "It has been a matter of great satisfaction to me to remember how fully and easily I received all the principles of the Gospel," Romania later wrote. "I can truly say I do not remember when I did not believe."[31]

From the outset of her medical schooling Romania perceived her profession as a sacred calling, always conscious of the divine assistance she was given. While a medical student in New York, she wrote, "I was not wholly deprived of hearing the sound of the Gospel in New York, for there was a branch of the Church in Williamsburgh to which I repaired each Sunday to partake of the sacrament for I felt it gave me more strength and power to perform my daily duties."[32] Like Romania, I, too, have found that partaking of the sacrament and attending Church strengthen me and help me in my studies.

Romania was certainly blessed in her medical work. During her 35 years of practice she successfully delivered hundreds of babies, including many of her own grandchildren and great-grandchildren. During her 28 years of teaching she trained hundreds of midwives, who in turn delivered thousands of other babies.

For more than 30 years Romania served as a member of the Relief Society central board (now general board), mostly as the assistant secretary. In her *Memoirs* Romania speaks of her spiritual education, the spiritual "feasts," as she calls them, that she experienced with other Relief Society sisters.

Romania continued to serve on that board while she and her second husband, Charles W. Penrose, presided over the European Mission. While President Penrose inspected the missionary work among the brethren, Sister Penrose organized the European sisters into Relief Societies. "There are over forty Relief Society organizations in the British Isles, with an average enrollment of twenty each, and an average attendance of ten or twelve," Romania wrote in an "Address to the Relief Society in the British Isles." However, Romania later wrote that "many of them soon broke up, on account of the members emigrating, and the scattered condition of the Saints."[33]

By the time of her death in 1932, Romania had acquired dozens of textbooks on countless subjects. Even more remarkable, she had learned their contents mostly on her own. After the age of 60 she painstakingly taught herself two languages: French and Spanish. She was one of the few, if not the sole, pupils to graduate from a private French class offered in the Salt Lake Valley. Having studied French since the age of six myself, I am amazed that Romania possessed the ability and self-discipline to learn the language so fluently during her later years. Her knowledge of French and Spanish, and the German she had acquired as a young girl, ultimately proved to be of practical as well as intrinsical worth. Romania was 67 and Charles was 74 when he was called to preside over the European Mission. In this capacity he served as president of the British Mission and oversaw the Scandinavian, Swedish, Netherlands, Swiss, German, French, and South African Missions. Fortunately, with Romania as interpreter, President Penrose functioned ably in many of these foreign countries.

An amusing incident reveals the practical value of Romania's knowledge of foreign languages. While visiting France with her husband, Romania decided one day to take a taxi by herself to visit a friend who resided in Paris. When the taxicab arrived, Romania, perhaps a little insecure about her French, handed the driver a slip of paper with the friend's address and, without saying a word, climbed into the backseat. After a few minutes en route, Romania felt that the ride was taking longer than it should and that the driver wasn't following a direct course. Her speculations were confirmed when the taxi pulled up next to another cab and the two drivers momentarily conversed in French.

"Where are you going?" the first inquired in French.

"I've got a stupid American woman in the backseat," replied the other driver, "and when the meter gets high enough, I'll take her to her destination."

Romania understood clearly what the unsuspecting driver had said and, in perfect French, ordered the cab driver to take her immediately to her destination or she would report him to the police. Astounded, the driver quickly obeyed.[34]

After returning home from Europe, Romania retired from her medical practice at the age of 72. Her teaching now shifted from the Relief Society sisters to her own grandchildren. She taught many of her grandchildren and even great-grandchildren to read from a large-print primer specially ordered so that her failing eyes could still see it. Her grandchildren and great-grandchildren recalled sitting next to Romania's big leather lounge chair, sounding out the words in her primer and printing out the longer words such as *butterfly* over and over again beneath Romania's stern gaze. Romania even organized a Spanish class for her older grandchildren so that she could teach them the language she had painstakingly learned from her textbooks.

If all of this sounds as if Romania lived a phenomenally long and busy life, it is because she did. In 1881, at the age of 42, Romania wrote her *Memoirs*—since she lived to be 93, she had not yet passed her life's halfway point when she sat down to write her reminiscences!

As I read Romania's rather intimidating list of accomplishments, I took comfort in Susa Young Gates's praise of Romania. More than highlighting her material achievements, Susa lauds Romania as a good mother and daughter, a religious woman, and a kind, gentle friend. In an 1891 article published in the *Young Woman's Journal*, Susa describes her longtime friend Romania as:

. . . a wonderful woman. Not because she has done anything impossible to be done by other women, but because in becoming a doctor able to sever a limb, or take out an eye, now delivering with gentlest care the sick bed of some poor old man at the hospital, yet with it all she has a home on another street where she keeps a corner warm and cosy for her mother and her unmarried boys; also is she a woman with religious duties devolving upon her shoulders, and with it all she is the same sweet, quiet-voiced, gentle lady that my childish memory so vividly produces. . . . She is honored and loved by all who have the pleasure of her acquaintance and their name is legion.[35]

"Not because she has done anything impossible to be done by other women . . ." That phrase strikes me most in Susa's commendation of Romania. It says to me that Romania exemplified the possibilities in all men and women. These several generations later, she exemplifies the possibilities present in me, particularly as I now pursue my own education. I see Romania having done what I am currently preparing to do—venture out to fulfill the possible.

Romania's life also reminds me of the importance of taking my own life in stages. "To every thing there is a season, and a time to every purpose under the heaven" (Ecclesiastes 3:1). Right now my scale tilts towards school and Church. At times I feel frustrated and a little guilty that studying consumes so much of my time. I don't have enough time to participate in as much community service as I would like, my family genealogy doesn't head my to-do list, and domestic chores like sewing on buttons or taking out the trash frequently come dead last. I am hopeful that this season and the succeeding seasons in my life will eventually fit together as harmoniously as did Romania's.

In an art history course I attended the professor classified as a 20th century fallacy the idea that great people are born great. Michelangelo, he noted, employed an apprentice, Ascanio Condivi, to rewrite his biography and to deliberately exclude certain references to his early artistic schooling and years as a struggling sculptor. Before Michelangelo's death, the great artist destroyed many of his early, technically imperfect pieces in order to hide traces of his early workings and reworkings. The professor cited Michelangelo as a prime example of his theory that individuals, even legendary geniuses, achieve success primarily through hard work.

Just as Michelangelo reminds my professor of the benefits of hard work, Romania Penrose inspires me to persevere. "It is a trite but true saying," she wrote, "that 'There is no excellence without great labor.' God virtually says to each of us, The world is before you; be as good and great as you will and I will assist you."[36] Romania was not born accomplished or successful. With practical realism, she diligently applied herself and sacrificed in order to achieve her objectives.

There is a clear message in all this for me. I may not become a doctor; I need not become a suffragette. The Lord may have experiences in store for me far different from Romania's. Yet through Romania's example I recognize that if I possess "nerve, energy, and ambition," if I dare to dream, and work hard enough to achieve my dreams, my possibilities can become realities.

NOTES

1. *Women's Exponent,* as quoted in Lori L. Nickerson, *Women of Nerve, Energy, and Ambition: The Relief Society's Commitment to Frontier Health Care* (Provo, Utah: Women's Research Institute, Brigham Young University, 1992), p. 1.

2. See Romania Pratt Penrose, *Memoirs,* 1881, p. 12, Archives Division, Church Historical Department, The Church of Jesus Christ of Latter-day Saints, Salt Lake City, Utah.

3. Ibid., p. 3.

4. See Orson F. Whitney, *History of Utah,* vol. 4 (Salt Lake City: George Q. Cannon and Sons, 1904), p. 600.

5. Pratt, *Memoirs,* p. 5.

6. *Woman's Exponent,* 1 September 1888, p. 49.

7. Brigham Young, in *Journal of Discourses* 13:61.

8. *Woman's Exponent,* as quoted in Nickerson, *Women of Nerve, Energy, and Ambition.*

9. See Parley P. Pratt, *Autobiography of Parley P. Pratt,* ed. Parley P. Pratt Jr. (Salt Lake City: Deseret Book Co., 1985).

10. Pratt, *Memoirs,* p. 16.

11. Ibid., p. 11.

12. Susa Young Gates, in *Young Woman's Journal,* September 1891, p. 533.

13. Pratt, *Memoirs,* pp. 11–12.

14. Gates, in *Young Woman's Journal,* p. 533.

15. Ibid., p. 534.

16. Ibid., pp. 533–34.

17. Ibid., p. 534.

18. Romania Pratt Penrose Papers, Archives Division, Church Historical Department, The Church of Jesus Christ of Latter-day Saints, Salt Lake City, Utah.

19. Pratt, *Memoirs,* p. 15.

20. Ibid., p. 17

21. Ibid., p. 16.

22. *Woman's Exponent,* 15 September 1880, p. 59.

23. *Woman's Exponent,* 1 September 1888, p. 49.

24. Gates, in *Young Woman's Journal,* p. 535.

25. *History of the Relief Society 1842–1966* (Salt Lake City: General Board of the Relief Society, 1966), p. 33.

26. Ralph T. Richards, *Of Medicine, Hospitals and Doctors* (Salt Lake City: University of Utah Press, 1953), p. 232.

27. Gates, in *Young Woman's Journal,* p. 535.

28. *Woman's Exponent,* 15 August 1890, p. 331.

29. *Woman's Exponent,* 1 October 1880, p. 65.

30. See Journal History, 15 June 1908, Church Historical Department, The Church of Jesus Christ of Latter-day Saints, Salt Lake City, Utah.

31. Pratt, *Memoirs,* p. 5.

32. Ibid., p. 13.

33. Romania Pratt Penrose Papers.

34. See William C. Sutherland, letter, 21 June 1996, in author's possession.

35. Gates, in *Young Woman's Journal,* p. 535.

36. Pratt, *Memoirs,* p. 7.

੭ৡ

Marie W. Mackey is a junior at Harvard University majoring in English. She was born in Oxford, England, and spent most of her childhood in Utah. While attending high school she worked for two years as an intern for the *New Era* magazine and was first runner-up in Utah's Sterling Scholar foreign language category. Through her research Marie has come to feel a special sisterhood with Romania, whose life provides a wonderful example of persistence, dedication, and faithfulness.

19

"No Prophet Is Greater Than His Mother"

Jennette Eveline Evans McKay

1850–1905

*O*ne of my favorite scenes in early Utah history is a simple one. It is after dark in April 1883, and Jennette and David McKay are sitting in front of the fireplace in their rock home in Huntsville, Utah. Their four children, David O., age nine; Thomas, seven; Elizabeth, four; and Annie, two; are sitting with them on the floor, probably on a homemade braided rug.

David senior has just returned from a two-year proselyting mission to his native Scotland. After arriving back in Huntsville, it was with great emotion that David toured "the old home" and farm that had been so faithfully cared for by his wife and children during his absence. He tenderly began making friends with little Annie, who was born 10 days after his departure for Scotland.

The McKay children are anxious to hear about their father's adventures in such a faraway land. He describes to them the magnificent castles he saw, the heather that covered the landscape, and the kilts and bagpipes that are so much a part of

Jennette Eveline Evans McKay

the family's Scottish heritage. But children usually want more than descriptions of landscapes. Children want stories, events—a miracle would be wonderful. So one of the young sons gets right to the point and asks that very question: "Father, did you see any miracles while you were in Scotland?" David McKay pauses a minute, looks over at his beautiful Welsh wife, and puts his arm around her shoulders, which had borne such a heavy load as a single parent during his absence. He then turns to the children and says with a quiver in his voice, "Your mother is the greatest miracle that one could ever find."[1]

The older McKay children never forgot the tribute their father paid to Jennette that evening in Huntsville: their mother, the miracle. It would influence forever their feelings for family, marriage, and womanhood.

What exactly was it that made David believe that Jennette was the greatest miracle he had ever found? In reflecting on that question I remember two more recent occurrences. The first memory is an experience with my own mother when I was very young.

I was always the shortest student in my class at school. As the daughter of parents who were both under five feet six inches tall, I had little chance of a career in basketball, or of reaching dishes on the top shelf in the kitchen, or of ever seeing the top of a refrigerator. In a society that places so much importance on physical stature and appearance, it would have been easy for me to grow up feeling less important than the other children, or at least less capable.

During a recent visit to Salt Lake City I saw my first-grade teacher, Mrs. Mavis Hilton. She had brought her grandchildren, and I had brought my children, to see the Ringling Brothers Barnum and Bailey Circus. Mavis had taught me more than 35 years earlier at Adams Elementary School in Logan, Utah.

After exchanging hugs and pleasantries, she smiled and shared an incident she still remembered from the year I was in her class. Mavis said that on the first day of school I walked right up to her, standing straight and confident, and said, "My mother says I'm the cutest thing she's ever seen." The incident says less about me than it does about the love my mother, Grace Fort Arrington, invested in her children.

Years later, now the mother of four daughters, I think about this incident frequently and pray that I might instill that same confidence and self-esteem in my own girls. That kind of love for one's children is a magnificent and powerful thing. From what I know about the lives of Jennette Evans McKay's children, there must have been many such interchanges, day in and day out, in the McKay home. Indeed, when coupled with love for God, such maternal love almost defines what it means to be an exceptional woman.

I say "almost defines" because there is another ingredient as well, which brings me to the second memory I would like to relate.

In October of 1990 my husband, Dean, and I attended general conference in Salt Lake City. One incident that caught my full attention was an off-camera drama, unseen by those watching by television. I will never forget it.

At this particular session Elder Helvécio Martins gave one of the most beautiful and stirring addresses on the importance of testimony that I have ever heard. He had been sustained as a member of the Second Quorum of the Seventy six months prior to this conference, making him the first black General Authority in the history of the Church. And now we were there to hear his first conference address.

I had noticed the wives of the General Authorities sitting in a section to the right of the pulpit. It was not difficult to pick out Elder Martins's wife, not just because of the color of her skin but because she was the one sitting on the edge of her seat, closely watching the monitor as her sweetheart spoke. She was hanging on every word, perhaps reliving his description of their journey together to find the truth in their native Brazil. I was impressed that his address was filled with the pronouns *we, our,* and *us.* Together they had searched, pondered, prayed. Together they received confirmation of the truth of the gospel. Together they joined the Church and began a lifetime of service to their Heavenly Father, each supporting the other.

Theirs is an especially remarkable story, for they had joined the Church in 1972, six years before anyone knew that Elder Martins would one day be able to receive the priesthood. Nonetheless, their hearts were filled with joy when President Spencer W. Kimball announced the construction of the São Paulo Temple in 1975. Brother

Martins served on the publicity committee for the temple and Sister Martins sold her jewelry to help with fund-raising—all the while not knowing if they would be able to enter the house of the Lord in this lifetime.[2] Can we begin to imagine the strength of their faith?

As Elder Martins ended his conference address, I watched as his wife gave in to a rush of uninhibited emotion, weeping tears of joy as her sweetheart completed what must have been one of the most challenging sermons of his life. She was with him all the way. His accomplishment was obviously hers also. Elder Martins and his wife, Rudá, impressed me as a "team." One flesh. One purpose. One goal. The strength of this partnership was written on Sister Martins's face, just as I see it written in the daily lives of Jennette and David McKay. Along with love of God and unconditional, selfless maternal love, it is love for and singular devotion to one's eternal spouse that completes the definition of what I believe it means to be a magnificent and holy man or woman. In Jennette's love for David McKay, I see this definition fulfilled in its completeness. Here is more of their story.

To appreciate David's calling Jennette "the greatest miracle that one could ever find," it is helpful to understand the circumstances under which David left for his mission to Scotland. The call had come in 1881 at a most inconvenient time for the little family. Jennette was expecting a baby right away, and her husband was reluctant to leave her home alone with responsibility for the baby to come, the other children, the house, and the crops and livestock. Their dream of enlarging their small home seemed now within reach if David stayed home. Otherwise it would have to be delayed.

David and Jennette still felt the pangs of grief from the loss just one year earlier of their two oldest children. Margaret, age 11, had died of rheumatic fever on 28 March 1880, and Ellena, age nine, died on 1 April of pneumonia. The two girls were buried in the same grave.

When the mission call arrived, young David O., age seven, observed what was the first and only open disagreement he ever saw between his parents. His father's reaction was, "Of course I cannot go." Jennette's reply, firmly delivered without hesitation, was, "Of course you must accept; you need not worry about me. David O. and I will manage things nicely."[3]

And manage they did. With the considerable help and support of friends and neighbors, Jennette quickly set about supervising David O. and his younger brother, Thomas, in learning more about running the farm and helping with household chores. Priesthood quorums did the spring planting, and by summer an excellent crop of hay and grain was ready for harvest. But grain prices were low, so Jennette wisely stored her grain until spring. Because prices were good by then, she realized a healthy profit.

Encouraged, she and her sons worked even harder the next season and after harvest the second year were able to afford the addition to the house Jennette and David had planned before he left. Without writing a word of it to her husband, Jennette arranged to have several new bedrooms added on to the house, and the dining room and kitchen were enlarged. Jennette took special pride in the new, wide, and straight stairway leading up to the boys' bedrooms. Many a winter night before this stairway was built, she had dressed warmly, gone outside, and climbed a ladder up the side of the house into the second story to tuck her children in bed and have evening prayers.

Jennette's willingness to encourage her husband to serve a mission for the Lord that required he be gone for this length of time surely reflected her own personal gratitude for two missionaries who had knocked on the door of her parents' home in 1850 in southern Wales, changed their lives, and ultimately sent them and their family a third of the way around the world. I believe Jennette's origins explain much of her strength, her love, and her commitment to the gospel.

Jennette's life began 28 August 1850 near Merthyr Tydfil, Glamorganshire, Wales. The village was in the very heart of the coal mining region of Wales, and thus its lovely, broad, low mountains and lush, deep valleys were tempered in beauty by what Thomas Rees described in 1815 in *The Beauties of England and Wales* as "the perpetual smoke and constant din of the forges."[4] "At night, when the furnaces were opened," one visitor observed, "the sky looked as if a blazing volcano were erupting."[5] It was in these mines that Jennette's father, Thomas, earned the family's income as an ironstone miner.

While her father spent long hours amid the hot furnaces of the ironworks, Jennette's mother, Margaret, fought to provide pleasant and healthy living conditions for her 11 children. It wasn't an easy task. The 1849 *Public Health Reports* of the Merthyr area paint a grim picture of the sanitary conditions the Evans family contended with. The rapidly growing industrial region had poor drainage and no sewage system, with little or no access to fresh water. All of this dramatically affected the incidence of sickness and death. Major epidemics of scarlet fever, typhoid, measles, and whooping cough raged through Merthyr, with the greatest toll among the young.[6] The 1854 *Public Health Reports* read: "More than half of the funerals which took place are of children less than five years of age, more than one-fourth are infants under one year."[7] The biggest killer was cholera, which claimed 824 lives in 1854 alone. Jennette was four years old at the time, and the Evans family buried three children that year—a two-year-old daughter and infant twins, a boy and a girl. Two years after this terrible experience Thomas and Margaret decided to pack up their belongings and seek a better life for Jennette and their other children.

They did not depart alone. Four years before the death of the three children, a few months before Jennette was born, her parents had heard the restored gospel and received a testimony of its truthfulness. They were baptized in May 1850. A determined and active member, Jennette's father, Thomas, served as president of the Merthyr Tydfil conference of the Church. Family members later felt it was more than just coincidence that William and Ellen Oman McKay, parents of Jennette's future husband, David McKay, were baptized members of the Church the same year in Scotland. The Evanses of Wales and the McKays of Scotland were among the 4,300 European Saints who sold their property and gathered to America in 1856.

Before they left, Jennette's mother, Margaret, paid one last visit to the graves of five of her children. Then she and her husband, Thomas, journeyed to Liverpool, England, where they boarded the ship *Horizon* with their six remaining children: Ann, age 16; Thomas, 14; Evan, 12; Howell, 10; Jennette, six; and Elizabeth (Lizzie), an infant.

The family set sail 25 May 1856 and were among 856 members

of the Church under the leadership of Edward Martin. All were eager to join the Saints in Utah. About 600 of this group later became members of the second handcart company to be caught in a terrible early storm on the prairie in late 1856, and some 145 of them perished. But the Evans family had decided not to travel all the way to Utah that year. They remained in Iowa for three years while Thomas accumulated provisions, equipment, and clothing. The McKay family also waited in Iowa. By 1859 Thomas and Margaret Evans had obtained wagons, teams, and a milk cow, and joined Philip Buzzard's Utah-bound company. They arrived in Salt Lake City on 25 August. They were four days ahead of young Jennette's future in-laws, the McKays, who arrived in the Valley on Jennette's ninth birthday. Shortly thereafter both families moved to Ogden.[8]

In spite of their surprisingly parallel travels, the Evans and McKay families never met, as far as we know, until, shortly after the Evanses arrived in Ogden, 15-year-old David McKay saw the attractive nine-year-old Jennette sitting on the tongue of her family's wagon.[9] He later confessed he could not forget the large brown eyes under her pink sunbonnet.[10] As Jennette grew she became one of the most attractive and popular young women in Ogden, and David's interest in her increased.

By the time he proposed marriage, years later, David had been courting Jennette for many months and had earned enough money to pay for a small farm in Huntsville, in Ogden Valley east of Ogden. Even though Jennette was not yet 17 years old, David persuaded her parents to let her marry him. The marriage was performed by Elder Wilford Woodruff of the Council of the Twelve on 9 April 1867 in the Endowment House in Salt Lake City. Jennette was 16 and David was 22.

Their first home was a log cabin David had built in Huntsville. Jennette was considered to be one of the prettiest girls in the region, and David wanted her to stay that way, so he preferred not to let her work in the fields. It is not accidental that the McKay boys acquired the reputation of being handsome, and the McKay girls, strikingly beautiful.

One of the things Jennette had to adjust to as a new bride was frequent visits of Indians to their farm. President Brigham Young had counseled the Church members to "feed them rather than fight with them," and Jennette tried her best to be friendly and generous, but she was always somewhat nervous. On one occasion an Indian man decided that Jennette would make a lovely bride for him. He came into the McKay cabin one morning while she was washing clothes and startled her with the announcement, "You be my squaw!" She grabbed a wet towel from the washtub, struck the surprised man in the face, and ran to the room where her husband was sleeping. As soon as the Indian realized Jennette was not alone in the cabin, he hurried to his horse and disappeared.[11]

Two daughters, Margaret and Ellena, were born to Jennette and David while they were living in the log cabin. When the front part of their new rock house was completed, they moved into it. The new home was affectionately called "The Old Home." It was there that the future prophet David Oman McKay was born on 8 September 1873. Seven more children followed: Thomas Evans, Jeanette Isabel, Ann Powell, Elizabeth Odette, William Monroe, Katherine Favourite, and Morgan Powell.

Motherhood seemed to be a role that fit Jennette just fine. The children remember the home atmosphere to be one of tenderness, patience, and unconditional love. Surely the many hundreds of sermons President McKay would give later in his life can be traced to his childhood experiences in "The Old Home," which he often referred to as "the dearest, sweetest spot on earth."[12] He once described a nostalgic visit to the family home in 1938, in a letter to his brother Thomas, who was then serving as president of the Swiss-German Mission. He closed with these lines: "It is only an old country home, but no palace was ever filled with truer love and devotion on the part of the parents, brothers, and sisters, than those which pervaded the hearts of the loved ones in that family circle. [When] I walked out of the front door, as the night-latch clicked, I thought it might have been the click of the lid of a treasure chest that held the wealth of memories that no money could buy."[13]

Jennette and her husband made great financial sacrifices to ensure a good education for each of their children. They maintained a separate home on Madison Avenue in Ogden, where they lived during the winter so their children could attend school there. Then they returned to the farm for the summer months. With financial assistance from Grandmother Evans and by mortgaging their farm, they were able to send each of their eight surviving children to a university and all eight graduated with college degrees. Their children's educational accomplishments are impressive.

Jennette served in the Relief Society and Young Ladies Mutual Improvement Association in the Huntsville Ward, but most of her energy was spent rearing her family and supporting her husband as he served as bishop of both the Eden and Huntsville wards, as stake patriarch, and later as a member of the Weber Stake high council. He also served in the Utah territorial legislature, being elected a state senator for three four-year terms.

Jennette frequently hosted Church leaders visiting the Huntsville area since the town had no restaurant or hotel. The table in their large dining room was always extended to full length, and guest rooms were nearly always occupied, especially on weekends. The McKay children met and ate dinner with members of the First Presidency, many other General Authorities, and general officers and board members of the Church auxiliaries. At times when there were many guests for dinner, Jennette had a special code, "FHB," which stood for "family hold back." The children were encouraged to "hold back" from taking too much food, to be sure everyone at the table got enough.[14]

The weight of her responsibilities eventually took a toll on Jennette's health. She experienced health problems at a relatively young age. She died at her home following a stroke at the age of 54 on 6 January 1905 and was buried in Huntsville by her grieving family and a host of heartbroken friends.

The *Salt Lake Tribune* said of her, "Few women in Weber County were more widely known or more universally loved than Mrs. David McKay, and the announcement of her death has caused a gloom of sorrow not only throughout Ogden City and Weber County, but over the entire state."[15]

President McKay and other members of the family visited Wales on several occasions to see the village and home where Jennette McKay was born. In March 1961 President McKay returned to Wales to break ground for a new Latter-day Saint chapel in Merthyr

Tydfil and to unveil a commemorative plaque he was given permission to have placed at his mother's birthplace.

If Jennette succeeded in building self-confidence in her children, she also wanted to keep them humble. President McKay once told a congregation in Wales: "I [am] reminded of a visit I made home when I was in college. Mother was sitting on my left where she always sat at dinner and I said 'Mother, I have found that I am the only member of your children whom you have switched [whipped, as with a willow shoot].' She said, 'Yes, David O., I made such a failure of you I didn't want to use the same method on the other children.' "16

Such is the beautiful story of the motherhood, the magnificent womanhood, of Jennette Evans McKay.

It becomes increasingly clear to me that life is a partnership. We are partners with God in working out our salvation. We are partners with our spouses and children in building eternal families. We are partners with our fellow Saints in building the kingdom of God. Relationships thrive when the strengths and contributions of one partner complement and complete the strengths of another.

My husband, Dean, and I had been married only a few months when an incident took place that set the tone for our partnership and for our service in the Church for the years to come. One September afternoon we decided to bottle a bushel of tomatoes. We had both canned fruits and vegetables with our mothers while growing up, but it had been many years since either of us had undertaken such a task. It turned out to be a hot, messy, time-consuming project.

The phone rang while we were both up to our elbows in tomatoes. It was our Logan 20th Ward Young Women president, Brigitta Clyde. I was her counselor. She was reminding me there was a stake Young Women's leadership training meeting in half an hour. Could she come by and pick me up? I turned to Dean with a combination of fear and sympathy. "Should I go? Do I dare leave you in this mess?" His answer, like Jennette McKay's, was an unequivocable "Yes—go ahead. I'll take care of things here." Hesitantly I got cleaned up and left for the meeting. When I came home a couple of hours later, the kitchen was clean, the dishes were washed, and two dozen beautiful quart jars of tomatoes sat gleaming on the counter.

His willingness to support me in my callings and projects has enabled me to serve (gracefully, I hope) for five years as a bishop's wife, and now as the wife of a stake president.

I have long sought inspiration in the lives of the heroines of the Restoration. In researching material for my first book, *Sunbonnet Sisters: True Stories of Mormon Women and Frontier Life,* I became acquainted with many remarkable women in the history of The Church of Jesus Christ of Latter-day Saints. They include an impressive list of politicians, midwives and doctors, journalists, Relief Society presidents, artists, ranchers, actresses, and administrators. Jennette Evans McKay lacks the long list of societal accomplishments that often accompany women "of note," but she resoundingly accomplished the greatest feat of all: she gave everything she was and all she had in striving to raise a most remarkable family, including a son, David O. McKay, who would influence the way the entire membership of the Church revered home and family for generation after generation after generation.

As I devote most of my life to the rewarding challenges of rearing a family (slipping in the writing of a book here and there when possible), my heart and soul resonate most to the life of Jennette Evans McKay, my own personal heroine from Church history, the woman who was simply a magnificent mother.

An early 20th-century novelist, Will Levington Comfort, succeeded in putting "greatness" into proper perspective with these words, framed and hanging on the wall of our living room:

"I believe that mothering is the loveliest of the arts: that great mothers are hand-maidens of the Spirit, to whom are entrusted God's avatars; that no prophet is greater than his mother."[17]

NOTES

1. Llewelyn R. McKay, *Home Memories of President David O. McKay* (Salt Lake City: Deseret Book Co., 1956), p. 6.

2. See "Elder Helvécio Martins of the Seventy," *Ensign,* May 1990, p. 106.

3. McKay, *Home Memories,* p. 6.

4. Thomas Rees, *The Beauties of England and Wales,* vol. 28 (1815), as

quoted in *Recollections of Merthyr's Past* (Risca, Wales: The Starling Press, 1979), p. 5.

5. *Recollections,* p. 6.

6. See J. J. Dyke, *1849 Public Health Reports,* as quoted in *Recollections,* pp. 20–21.

7. *1854 Public Health Reports,* as quoted in *Recollections,* p. 21.

8. See James B. Allen, "David O. McKay," in Leonard J. Arrington, ed., *The Presidents of the Church* (Salt Lake City: Deseret Book Co., 1986), pp. 276–77.

9. See ibid., p. 277.

10. See Francis M. Gibbons, *David O. McKay: Apostle to the World, Prophet of God* (Salt Lake City: Deseret Book Co., 1986), p. 3.

11. See Leonard J. Arrington and Susan Arrington Madsen, *Mothers of the Prophets* (Salt Lake City: Deseret Book Co., 1987), p. 143.

12. Jeanette Morrell, *Highlights in the Life of President David O. McKay* (Salt Lake City: Deseret Book Co., 1971), p. 31.

13. David O. McKay, letter to Thomas E. McKay, 12 December 1938, as quoted in Morrell, *Highlights,* p. 31.

14. Arrington and Madsen, *Mothers,* 145–46.

15. *Salt Lake Tribune,* as quoted in ibid., pp. 148–49.

16. Gibbons, *David O. McKay,* p. 370.

17. Will Levington Comfort, as quoted in Arrington and Madsen, *Mothers,* p. 1.

꩜

Susan Arrington Madsen earned a bachelor's degree in journalism from Utah State University and served for four years as an adjunct faculty member at the Logan LDS Institute of Religion. Her previous books include *Growing Up in Zion: True Stories of Young Pioneers Building the Kingdom, The Lord Needed a Prophet,* and *I Walked to Zion: True Stories of Young Pioneers on the Mormon Trail.* She and her husband, Dean, are the parents of four daughters and live in Hyde Park, Utah. Susan sees in Jennette Evans McKay the hallmarks of character and faith that make for a heroine in any era.

20

"An Extraordinary Initiative Power"

Susa Young Gates

1856–1933

*M*ost of us have a sincere curiosity concerning the children of famous people; all the more so with Brigham Young, whose sons and daughters numbered 57. How did it work? Did the principles he expounded as a prophet find practical application within his own home?

After I became a docent, or tour guide, at Brigham's Beehive House over 30 years ago I was afforded insights into the structure and spirit of a family where the needs and feelings of each individual were regarded with tender, almost sacred care. Brigham's daughter and 51st child Clarissa grew up believing she was her father's absolute favorite until she became old enough to realize that, in his wisdom, he had made each child to feel the same way. At one time, after learning of the illness of one of his children, Brigham "stopped a council meeting declaring to the assembly that the meeting could wait, but his sick child could not."[1] He encouraged his daughters as well as his sons to obtain an education—to educate their minds and spirits in all ways possible—teaching that in educating a man, you educate an individual; in educating a

Susa Young Gates

232

woman, you educate an entire household. His daughters exercised implicit trust in him, mindful as they were of his gentle dealings with their mothers and with themselves.

"His beautiful courtesy," daughter Susa Young Gates wrote, "was never more in evidence than when he approached any one of his wives whom he loved and who loved him."[2] In candid yet nevertheless nearly incredulous appraisal she added, "In all my life in that beloved home I never heard my father speak an unkind or irritable word to one of his wives."[3] From the viewpoint of a daughter, she added, "His presence was like light and sunshine and 'benediction after prayer.' "[4]

Despite the inevitable confusion inherent in so large a family as Brigham's, his daughters were raised in an atmosphere of diversity, encouraged to educate their minds and develop their talents as well as to perfect their housewifery skills. Physical exercise was stressed (Brigham installed a gymnasium on the west corner porch of the Lion House fitted up with "wooden steps, trapeze, vaulting and climbing poles, hoops, backboards, jumping ropes, and the like"), and a harmony or balance between the physical, mental, and spiritual was an openly stated goal.[5] Nurtured and encouraged, all of the children grew up with a lively awareness of their potential, and a firm assurance that they were valued and loved, that the great man who, to them, was a tender and interested father believed in the ability of each to make a place in the world, a contribution to the kingdom.

All well and good, as long as it lasted. What then, when the storms of life beat upon the spiritual structures that had dwelt so long beneath the powerful, nurturing sunlight of such a father's protection and love?

Susa attended the University of Deseret (later the University of Utah) and was there appointed associate editor of one of the first western college publications, the *College Lantern*. By the age of 14 she was expert in the fields of stenography and telegraphy. But at this time Brigham moved Susa's mother, Lucy Bigelow, down to St. George, partly to remove her daughter Dora from an unwelcome relationship with a young man who was given to drinking and weak-willed ways. The attempt was to no avail. On 3 October 1870—her mother's birthday—shortly before they were to start for St. George, Dora "slipped out of a party in the school house, met the young man, and was secretly married."[6]

Banished from the city and society she loved, with the shadow of her sister's disgrace hovering above her, Susa could have become discouraged and despondent. But she possessed an inner vitality that came to her aid, an "extraordinary initiative power . . . inherited from her father."[7] She taught music lessons, joined the dramatic club, and organized a club of her own "which promoted social graces and self-improvement."[8]

What possessed her to marry the cousin of her sister's handsome but dissolute husband? At the age of 16 she became the wife of Alma Dunford. Alma was a dentist, but he was also a drunkard, and the match was a most unfortunate one. Both Susa and her sister Dora returned to Salt Lake and had babies born during the same month, August of 1875, and Susa returned to St. George that fall. On a personal level both young women were struggling and unhappy. Several months later Dora left her husband and rejoined her mother and two of her sisters, Susa and Mabel, and surely the contrast between their present existence and the gentle happiness of their childhood must have been keenly felt. But here we see coming into play one of the strengths Brigham taught his children, both by precept and example. Keep your troubles to yourself, in the sacred privacy of your own bosom—that was how Brigham lived, even within the intimacy of his own home, never imposing his difficulties upon others. Eliza R. Snow had inspired Brigham's daughters with the same admonition. "Never tell any body if you are sick or sorry," she was wont to say. "Don't make others weary with your complainings."[9] Indeed, Susa had seen Brigham's wives exercise this high level of control. Writing about the quality years later, as editor of the *Young Woman's Journal,* she told the girls of the Church: "Words are the weakest as well as the strongest things on earth. They are weak when they betray our spirits, and they are strong when they obey an intelligent will."[10]

So in June of 1876, when Brigham turned 75 years old, mother and daughters put their cares aside. Lucy prepared an outstanding dinner for her husband, and Susa wrote and delivered an address in the new tabernacle where the people of St. George had arranged a public celebration. Lucy was chosen as president of the sister workers in the temple, and both Dora and Susa were called as ordinance workers. Half a year later, on New Year's Day, 1877, the preliminary dedication of the new temple took place. The April conference of the entire Church was held in St. George the following spring, as well as the formal dedication of the sacred building. Less than five months later Brigham lay dying in the Lion House—the light, the strength, the loving presence suddenly removed from their lives.

Dora's husband died, but when she married for a second time it was to a Catholic judge. Mabel married twice, and her second husband was also a non-Mormon. Susa sought a divorce from her husband in 1877, probably feeling the dark emptiness of her father's support and counsel, being only 21 years old at the time. After heartrending battles she was able to obtain custody of her son, Bailey, but never permanent care of her two-year-old daughter, Leah. During the time of these struggles she confided to her mother: "God help me to be worthy of the good opinion of all of the true Saints. For verily I want to be as near what father would wish me to be, as it is possible for my weak queer disposition to be. Oh mother, don't you long to see father, to clasp his arms around your neck, and hear his blessed voice pronounce those sweet words 'Welcome, my beloved, to your home.' Oh I know I am young and have a destiny in this Church to fulfill, but how I would love to go to father!"[11]

She had made mistakes, and she was paying for them, feeling the anguished weight of her mortal condition—and making vital choices that would greatly determine the remainder of her life. With every reason to abandon hope and give way to despair, she yet fought her way upward. She returned to Provo and the Brigham Young Academy, determined to learn and grow and make herself useful. There she taught voice and piano, directed the choir, and, in 1878, organized a department of music.

Susa had never expected to marry again and had reconciled herself to a patient existence of sustaining her family and serving others. But in 1880, when she was nearly 24, she married Jacob Gates and enjoyed a fulfillment she had not allowed herself to dream of. Five years later she traveled with him to the Sandwich

Islands (Hawaii), where they served a four-year mission. Three of her children were born during these challenging years, away from home and the conveniences to which she was accustomed. It must have challenged her powers to the utmost to be almost continually pregnant, with little ones to care for, while at the same time doing all in her power to support her husband's work and serve the local Saints. Of the 11 children born to this marriage, only four lived to adulthood. This, with the haunting sorrow of separation from her first daughter, kept Susa's heart tender and empathetic to the sufferings of others.

Susa lived a life of service by choice, trying to achieve the balance her father had taught her. Her diversity of talents led her into many fields of endeavor, from politics to science, writing to nursing and women's health, and one of her great loves, genealogy and temple work. She helped establish the domestic science department at Brigham Young Academy; founded many organizations, including the Daughters of Utah Pioneers and the first state chapter of Daughters of the Revolution; established the *Young Woman's Journal* in 1889; and wrote extensively for Church periodicals and purposes and authored half a dozen books, both fiction and nonfiction. She was a powerful figure in the women's rights movement, being selected by the National Council of Women to serve as chair of the powerful press committee for three years, to speak at the International Council of Women in London in 1889, and to serve as sole delegate for that council in Denmark in 1902, penning a pamphlet setting forth the views of both men and women in the state of Utah on the issue of women's rights. Susa taught theology, domestic science, and music at the Brigham Young Academy and was a member of its board of directors for 25 years; she became a member of the general Relief Society board in 1911 and organized and edited the *Relief Society Magazine* in 1914. In private life she was known as an excellent cook and charming hostess, skilled at conversation and the art of putting those around her at ease.

In her "Notes for the Day's Work" we gain powerful insight into how she brought all this work to pass:

Notes for the Day's Work: Provo, Utah, August 19, 1895

Go down cellar with Emma Lucy [later, a world-famous coloratura soprano] and show her how to clean it.

Go to Aunt Corneel's and take her to Eikens and get hers and my fruit. Darn Dan's stockings. Boil over the bottle of spoiled fruit.

Practice on my bicycle. Write down plan of altering the house which came to me in the night.

Clean my office. Answer Leah's, Sterling's, Sis. Taylor's, and Mrs. Grey's letters, and Carlos's. Prepare talk on 'Women and Literature' and go to the [Brigham Young] Academy's opening exercises at 10 o'clock.

Talk to Aretta Young about her story. Write to Pres. Joseph F. Smith, Pres. George Q. Cannon, Apostle Franklin D. Richards, and Elder B. H. Roberts about writing for *Young Woman's Journal*. Also write Mrs. M. E. Potter and Marie D.

Write and thank Carol for her lovely gift. Get the cloth for Dan's pants and boys' clothes and send them to the tailor. Finish the last chapter of "John Stevens' Courtship" for *The Contributor*. Sketch out editorials for *Young Woman's Journal*.

Wash my head. Get the kitchen carpet and have the girl and Dan put it down. Get cot and crib from store. Also washstand and glass and wardrobe. Get vegetables and fruit for dinner. Take my bicycle dress over to Polly and have it fixed. Take clothes to the Relief Society. Get consecrated oil. Bless Cecil [B. Cecil Gates, later director of the Mormon Tabernacle Choir] to do his chores well. Administer to baby Franklin [later an outstanding figure in the early days of radio].[12]

Such an exhaustive list could not be accomplished in today's world where television and other entertainments divert us. Brigham had taught his daughters that work was ennobling; Susa had proven the truth of his words for herself.

What about the balance? What of the motivation behind all the activity? From what I have gleaned about Susa, she struggled daily to do what her father had done: to live what she preached. Very early Brigham had given her the special mission of uplifting the youth of the Mormon people with her pen. Yet at the same time he had gravely admonished: "You may become the finest writer in the whole world; you might be the most famous and gifted woman of your day, and you might be of great use to thousands of your fellow beings, but if you should fail in your duty as wife and mother, you would find in the morning of the first resurrection that your whole life upon the earth had been a failure."[13]

His words are withering, all-pervading; they leave us nowhere to hide, no loose ends we can hold forth as excuses. I believe Susa possessed her own testimony of this deep, challenging counsel. She had lost her children to death, she had been denied the blessing of raising her first precious daughter, she had seen the tragic effects of her sisters' marriages and felt her mother's anguish at their weak and unwise choices. She *knew* from personal experience where true power and true peace could be found.

Susa's own daughter Emma Lucy was a living example of this great truth. Having performed and won musical honors from the age of 14, at 18 Lucy traveled to Germany with Elder John A. Widtsoe and his wife, Lucy's half-sister Leah Dunford. While there she first studied piano and then voice. She made her debut as Anchen in *Der Freischuetz* in the Royal Opera House in Berlin, very possibly being the first American woman to debut there. During her four years in Germany she sang over 50 roles and was invited to perform at Kaiser Wilhelm's palaces. With the advent of World War I she concentrated on performing in the United States only, at length organizing her own opera company in Salt Lake City. Her marriage, somewhat late in life, was to a widower with two young twin boys. Once the experience of wife and mother came to her, she said: "Looking back on my life now, if I had to choose between home and children and a career, I'd take the home and children."[14]

These testimonies stand as beacon lights for us to follow amid the confusion of worldly voices that beckon us away from those paths which lead us to true fulfillment and true joy, both in this life and the next.

Not merely endurance but *obedience* was the hallmark of Susa Gates's life, and a love for others that was based on a firm foundation of testimony—not the borrowed light of the father she adored, but her own hard-won conviction. In a special publication for the Deseret News Press she told at length how she had obtained her testimony of gospel truths. As a young girl she had confided her desires to Brigham and he had advised her to obtain her testimony the same way he and her mother had obtained theirs—to go down on her knees in prayer to God. "Flesh and blood did not, could not, reveal that truth to Peter, nor to any other man or woman—but only through God the Father can that conversion or testimony come to the human heart,"[15] she later wrote, recalling her father's counsel. She began to pray for light upon this question, delving deeply into every principle of restored truth, examining, questioning, proving it for herself.

It thrilled me to see this process laid forth before me, for it reminded me of my own experience when I began writing for the Church and coming in contact with that class of Saints we sometimes deem "privileged." I remember as a girl believing that it had to be easier for some than for others; surely those born to wealth and ease, or those blessed with strong Latter-day Saint roots and loving examples—surely for them the path to testimony, to perfection was less stony, less uphill. But I soon determined for myself that in this crucial matter the process is a fair one, the same for each individual, no matter what his or her exterior circumstances might be. Brigham's love and strength could not be transferred to his daughter; the inner, very personal struggle must take place for her as well as for him. She must desire, study it out, then seek, in faith and humility, the confirmation of the Spirit to her own heart. Brigham's experiences, powerful though they might have been, could not carry her. He might testify: "Daughter, so precious to me is the testimony of the Gospel as revealed to the Prophet Joseph Smith . . . that I could be cut into inch pieces every night of my life and put together again in the morning to live out that day rather than I would do anything to lose that testimony." But this "spirit of flaming truth" she longed for had to be kindled within her own soul.[16]

I realized this myself when people would come to me with tears in their eyes and tell how some song I had written had blessed them and strengthened their testimony. I realized that having written the "inspiring words" was of no lasting benefit to me—these people had incorporated the principles into their beings more strongly than I, and I must utilize the same sacred process as they if the words were to ever become truly mine.

Susa wrote:

The Holy Ghost was the medium of communicating that testimony to me and to all others—I must pray for that Spirit to rest upon me and to communicate to me, in some way, the actual testimony of the Truth.

During one year when I was nearly 40 years old, I disciplined my taste, my desires and my impulses—severely disciplining my appetite, my tongue, my acts, for one whole year and how I prayed!

Then one day at the close of that year . . . it came to me in the simplest, homeliest environment possible. . . . I was sweeping the floor one day, and a voice within my soul—that same calm, deliberate, yet soul enlightening voice I had heard in the Lion House years before—spoke to my spirit these simple words: "You know it is true! Never doubt it again!"

I never have! All other truths and facts and philosophies which came to my attention, and come today, I measure by one standard only: Does this or that idea or theory agree or does it conflict with the truths of the Gospel . . . if it agrees, it is mine! If it does not, I cast it out, or lay it upon the altar of prayer till God reveals the truth to His Prophet at the head of His Church.[17]

This living testimony which empowered all her deeds is what unites Susa's spirit with ours—this makes us sisters in every true, joyous sense of the word.

"By their fruits ye shall know them. . . ." Susa Young Gates left a bountiful harvest that we, in gratitude, may still garner today.

NOTES

1. Susa Young Gates, with Leah D. Widtsoe, *The Life Story of Brigham Young* (New York, 1930), p. 340.

2. Ibid.

3. Ibid., p. 354.

4. Ibid., p. 337.

5. "How Brigham Young Brought Up His 56 Children," *Physical Culture,* February 1925, p. 141.

6. Susa Young Gates, "From Impulsive Girl to Patient Wife: Lucy Bigelow Young," ed. Miriam G. Murphy, *Utah Historical Quarterly* 45 (Summer 1977): 283.

7. Andrew Jenson, comp., *Latter-day Saint Biographical Encyclopedia,* 4 vols. (1901–36; reprint, Salt Lake City: Western Epics, 1971), 2:629.

8. Susan Evans McCloud, *Mothers: Praising the Daughters of God* (Salt Lake City: Covenant, 1996), p. 20.

9. *Young Woman's Journal* 4 (1893):426.

10. Ibid., p. 427.

11. McCloud, *Mothers,* p. 21.

12. Leonard J. Arrington, "Women as a Force in the History of Utah," *Utah Historical Quarterly* 38 (Winter 1970): 5–6.

13. *Young Women's Journal* 5 (November 1893):91.

14. "Royalty Has Heard Her Voice," *Salt Lake Telegram,* 26 July 1937, as quoted in Raye Price, "Utah's Leading Ladies of the Arts," *Utah Historical Quarterly* 38 (Winter 1970):74.

15. Susa Young Gates, *Why I Believe the Gospel of Jesus Christ* (Salt Lake City: Deseret News Press, n.d.), p. 3.

16. Ibid., p. 27.

17. Ibid.

❧

Susan Evans McCloud is the author of more than 30 books, including *Sunset Across the Waters,* the *Mormon Girls* series, and *Who Goes There?.* She has also written screenplays, biographies, talk tapes, and lyrics, among them the loved "Lord, I Would Follow Thee." She and her husband, James, live in Provo, Utah, and have five daughters, one son, and four grandchildren. In the example of Susa Young Gates, Susan has found a sweet power that has lifted her own sights higher and warmed her paths with its light.

21

"Taking the Great Plan into Consideration"

Martha Hughes Cannon

1857–1932

*W*hen Martha Hughes married Angus Munn Cannon on 6 October 1884, she became the sister-in-law of his brother George Q. Cannon, my husband's grandfather. In the complex family patterns of plural marriages, we can now proudly claim Martha as our "Aunt Mattie."

However, Mattie, as she was familiarly known, was not real to

me until the mid-1960s. That was when Angus's granddaughter Beatrice Cannon Evans asked me to help compile a book later published as the *Cannon Family Historical Treasury*. When I read Martha's minibiography submitted by her only surviving child, Elizabeth McCrimmon, Mattie became my friend and an example to follow—not in her success as a pioneer physician, legislator, and suffragette, but as one who overcame frailties I share and hard circumstances I can scarcely imagine, in order to accomplish noble ends. Her story has also deepened my appreciation for my own pioneer heritage and for those who created it.

Martha Hughes Cannon

Martha was Welsh, born 1 July 1857 in Llandudno to Peter and Elizabeth Evans Hughes. They and their two little girls immigrated to Utah as Mormon convert pioneers, like my own Welsh great-grandparents, John and Martha Cozzens. But the Hughes family was less fortunate than mine. Peter's poor health delayed them for nearly two years in New York, where a baby sister, Annie, was born. They resumed their journey, sharing a covered wagon with another family after leaving Florence, Nebraska. Annie died along the way and was buried beside the trail. Three days after the family finally reached the valley of the Great Salt Lake, Peter also died. Elizabeth was left a widow with two little girls to support.[1]

Elizabeth Hughes was strong. She had walked beside the wagon on the journey west so her little girls and sick husband could ride. Their care must have been an added burden. What mother has not been weary at the end of a day caring for her sick family—even without walking across the plains! My great-grandmother Mary Ann Rich had also driven a covered wagon and walked beside the oxen to the Salt Lake Valley, but without the added burden. Looking back years later, she could remember: "We did not grieve or mourn over it; we had some very nice times when the roads were not so bad. We would make the mountains ring with our songs, and sometimes the company would get together and we would have a dance in the evening on the grass."[2] But Mary Ann had no children to worry about, and her husband, Apostle Charles C. Rich, was firmly in charge of the pioneer company. That made a big difference.

Elizabeth must have known her two little girls needed a father and she needed a husband, not only to help support them but to love them. She soon found one to marry—James Patton Paul, whose wife had died leaving him with four children of his own. James was a carpenter, and a good one; he and Elizabeth soon built a new home for the expanded family. Together they added five more sons and daughters to the six they had brought to the marriage. It was a big family to feed, and everyone needed to help. Martha's daughter Elizabeth (probably named for Martha's mother) described some of their activities: "The family picked the native currants that grew along the creeks. They planted fruit pits and seeds they had brought with them across the plains. The children gleaned in the grain fields to feed the pigs."[3]

Perhaps the necessity of working together helped to lessen the conflicts still inherent today in second-marriage families. At least Martha and her stepfather, James Paul, seem to have developed a real respect for each other. She used Paul as her last name when she was "set apart" to study medicine; James offered to help pay for her schooling. After she married Angus Cannon, Martha named their first son James. I like to think she was honoring her stepfather.

These are real people to me now, deserving of recognition and respect, along with other Mormon pioneers. The tiny body of Annie Hughes is only one of the legendary 6,000 Latter-day Saints who lie buried on the plains and in the mountains between the Mississippi and the Great Salt Lake—mute evidence of the willingness to sacrifice even life itself for the right to practice their unpopular religion. Their sacrifices and their hard-won success in building a Zion "in the tops of the mountains" have been deservedly honored across the world by their fellow members of The Church of Jesus Christ of Latter-day Saints. In 1992 my husband and I took part in a day-long Pioneer Day celebration in Berlin that featured children who had never been to America pulling their handcart replicas around the block singing "Come, Come, Ye Saints"—in German, of course.

The Mormon pioneers made the land fruitful with irrigation and hard work, and built their towns with broad, tree-lined streets for future generations to inherit. The American Indians and other migrants who came before and the non-Mormon immigrants and visitors who came after them—the religious groups, businessmen, miners, and others who contributed to Utah's culture—all deserve a place on the broad stage of Utah's history. But as we survey the grand diversity of that crowd, let us not lose sight of little Annie Hughes or of her parents: Peter, who died three days after successfully crossing the daunting plains, and Elizabeth, who walked that her loved ones might ride, who brought her surviving daughters safely through and then gave them a loving stepfather, and who helped her new husband build the house in the Valley that nurtured 11 children within its sturdy walls and still stood in 1978. Elizabeth Hughes Paul is also a heroine of the Restoration, along with her daughter Martha, for it was her faith in the restored Church that sustained her.

Disease and death were common at the time Martha was a child in Salt Lake City. Healing by faith was often the best resource available, and faith in divine providence the only consolation. "And should we die before our journey's through," the Saints continued to sing, "Happy day! All is well!"[4] The usual healing arts of herbalism and midwifery were truly more art than science, but some common medical practices such as blood-letting were more dangerous. Brigham Young counseled the Saints to rely on faith and natural remedies, and to avoid doctors.

Then medicine took a quantum leap forward, as the discoveries of the French chemist Louis Pasteur, the German bacteriologist Robert Koch, and the English surgeon Joseph Lister began to be taught in the medical schools of eastern America. Some well-trained non-Mormon doctors set up practices in Utah. The astute President Young desired his people's independence in the medical field as well as in economics, and no doubt he also saw the value of the new discoveries. He changed his mind about doctors.

"The time has come," said he in October conference of 1873, "for women to come forth as doctors in these valleys of the mountains." Eliza R. Snow, his wife and then president of the central board of the Relief Society, also called for women of "nerve, energy, and ambition to attend medical school."[5] That same year she announced at a Relief Society conference in Ogden that "President Young is requiring the sisters to get students of Medicine." She then gave information about classes in "physiology, anatomy, and other branches," which young women could attend in Salt Lake City to prepare themselves for further study.[6] The sisters were the logical ones to be called, for they were the traditional caregivers to the sick. Those who took part in Relief Society health programs would be ready to answer the call.

Sixteen-year-old Martha Hughes Paul was ready in her heart and ambitions, even without such a call. She had taught in public school at age 14 and worked as a typesetter for the *Deseret News* and *Woman's Exponent* for several years, saving money for her medical education. Martha knew the road would be long and hard, but she was determined to become a doctor.

The following account appears in the Journal History of the

Church of Jesus Christ of Latter-day Saints on the date of 13 August 1878: "This morning in the Historian's Office the following sisters were blessed and set apart to practice medicine and surgery among the Saints: Romania Bunnell Pratt by John Taylor; Ellie Reynolds Shipp by Geo. Q. Cannon; Margaret Curtis Shipp by John Taylor; Martha Hughes Paul by Geo. Q. Cannon."[7]

Martha would eventually receive her medical degree from the University of Michigan on 1 July 1880, the day she turned 23. But she was not satisfied with that. She wanted to educate others in the principles of public health, such as sanitation, clean water, disease prevention, and other challenges posed by Utah's rapidly growing population. To help achieve that end she went on to get a degree from the National School of Elocution and Oratory (to improve her speaking skills) and a bachelor of science degree from the department of medicine at the University of Pennsylvania.

What had motivated a pretty little teenager to attempt such a demanding goal, and then to pursue it with such tenacity? We know that strong impressions in early youth can affect our later lives. I have heard my grandfather Dr. Edward I. Rich describe some of his experiences growing up in 19th-century Bear Lake, Idaho—suffering a fractured leg, having an infected tooth yanked out by the local blacksmith, being kicked in the chin by a horse. The experiences were not unusual in that pioneer community, and they all helped lead him to his M.D. from Jefferson Medical College at Philadelphia in 1893. He knew the need!

Martha Hughes had seen her little sister die on the trail to the Salt Lake Valley, and her father die at its end. She had witnessed the chills and fevers of the ague, the sufferings and deaths of mothers and children. All of that must have made a profound impression on young Mattie, whose grown-up letters to her husband reveal her as an idealist, sensitive to the pain of others as well as to her own. So it seems likely that her chief motive for becoming a doctor was an honest, even passionate, desire to relieve pain, to teach the principles of hygiene that would help people avoid it, and to supplement with science the healing power of God, in which she truly believed. She had been blessed by a prophet to achieve this goal.

For a short while she was able to use her professional skills in private practice, first in Michigan as part of her training, then in Salt Lake City on her return. Soon she was called to serve as the second resident physician at the Deseret Hospital, which had been started in 1882 by the Relief Society. She served there less than four years but found a new focus for her life during that short time.

That focus was her marriage to Angus Munn Cannon, a member of the Deseret Hospital's board of directors and president of the Salt Lake Stake. He had been the business manager of the *Deseret News* at the time Mattie was working there as a typesetter.

As a prominent Church official, Angus was living the principle of plural marriage when Martha became his fourth wife on 6 October 1884 in the Endowment House in Salt Lake City. No fanfare or festivities accompanied the wedding, for Angus was already targeted to be a test case for the antipolygamy forces. Three months later he was arrested and tried for "cohabitation." He would still be in prison when Martha's child, Elizabeth, was born 13 September 1885.

Why would a beautiful 27-year-old woman, well educated and independent in her medical profession, want to marry a 50-year-old man who already had three wives, thus making her marriage illegal? The first answer is simple—she loved him. Her letters to Angus from England during her exile there from 1886 to 1888 are full of endearing terms and expressions of genuine affection and trust. Just before her return to Utah, she wrote, "I would rather spend one hour in your society, than a whole life time with any other man I know of."[8]

Angus was handsome, financially secure, and prominent in Church and civic circles. More important to Martha were his kindness and spirituality. No doubt she was particularly attracted to certain qualities described by a granddaughter: "In disposition [he] was both frank and genial, . . . noted for his choice use of language and his quickness at repartee."[9]

Martha's reasons are more complex for accepting a plural marriage at a time when polygamy was under determined attack. Perhaps she underestimated the determination; in 1885 the Supreme Court struck down an argument that the federal Edmunds Act prohibiting polygamy was unconstitutional.

Martha firmly believed the principle of plural marriage to be both divinely sanctioned and eugenically sound. Moreover, "the principle" offered some practical advantages. She may not have been entirely facetious in pointing out to a reporter that a plural wife had more freedom than a single one, because "if her husband has four wives, she has three weeks of freedom every month."[10]

Martha evidently had a friendly, if not close, relationship with the three older wives who preceded her. The first two, Sarah Maria and Ann Amanda Mousley, were actual sisters. They had been married to Angus by President Brigham Young in a joint ceremony on the same day, 18 July 1858.

When Angus was being tried for "cohabitation," Martha successfully eluded the summons served on her at the Deseret Hospital and never had to testify. Clarissa Moses Mason, Angus's third wife, was not so lucky and was subjected to the ignominy of being the chief witness against her husband. Angus's conviction was upheld—even though by that time he was only taking meals with his families—under a new court ruling that "cohabiting" included "providing food and shelter on a regular basis for more than one woman."[11] This decision seemed to make it illegal for a man to support even wives he had married before the passage of the Edmunds Act. The determination of the federal government to bring an end to plural marriages could no longer be mistaken. Angus's determination was just as firm. Rather than agree to abandon his wives and children, he paid his fine and went to prison.

Mattie had been prepared to share her husband. "I assure you," she wrote to Angus from England, "taking the great plan into consideration a quarter section, aye! even less, is preferable to none at all of your precious self."[12] She was *not* ready to endure the persecution, the constant dread of discovery on the "underground" evading the federal marshals, or the demeaning need for secrecy about a relationship she deemed worthy of recognition by the law and by society, as well as by the Lord.

In a letter to a close non-Mormon friend she explained another reason for her desire to escape: she had delivered the children of several polygamous wives, and "if it can be proven that these children have actually come into the world, their fathers will be sent to jail for five (5) years. . . .To me it is a serious matter to be the cause of sending to jail a father upon whom a lot of little children are dependent, whether those children were begotten by the same or by different mothers—the fact remains they all have little mouths that must be fed."[13]

What to do? Stay home and chance the game of hide-and-seek she abhored? Flee to Canada or Mexico, as some of the Saints were doing? Martha's solution was to go to England, where relatives would take her in, along with seven-month-old baby Elizabeth. Angus consented sadly, realizing her need. He would continue to send her money and support her emotionally with letters assuring her of his love—to which she responded according to her volatile moods.

Mattie's letters reveal what she calls her "mercurial" temperament in full spate. Reading them is like showering under a high waterfall. She pours out her emotion-laden thoughts in forceful language, often replete with exclamation points and underlinings. A letter to Angus written from her hiding place just before she left Salt Lake is typical. First she inquires about his health, as she often does with real concern. Then she bursts forth: "O dear oh dear!!! If we ever live through this present strait I trust we will be 'wiser and better men' *and women*. I grow heartily sick & disgusted with it. Polygamy in these days reminds me of Bishop Hunter's polygamy in the days of *Nauvoo*. He remarked, 'Polygamy in the days of Nauvoo—*law, law, law!!* Don't talk about it. Law! law! law! Don't talk about it.'"[14]

Presiding Bishop Edward Hunter had suffered the more drastic persecution of suspected polygamists in Nauvoo, and he was noted for his short, often enigmatic exclamations. Mattie relishes quoting his remark, which seems to reflect her own feelings about the antipolygamy laws and the need for secrecy that have caused her approaching exile. Next she becomes abruptly practical, asking Angus to get her horse ready for use, as she has "a little running around" to do before she leaves—Angus had supplied her with her own horse and carriage for her medical practice.

She closes with "Best love, Martha"—probably the last time she will sign her own name to her "letters from exile" or address her husband as "Angus." From then on, as she tries to maintain anonymity, she will usually sign "Maria" or "M" and address her husband by a variety of pet names such as "Dear Old Duck," "My Dear Lover," "Old Chick," "Old Boy," but most often "My Own Loved One" or simply "Dearest." Only once does she break the rule, with "My Dear Husband," and then continues in her impetuous style: "There! now . . . that is a very 'uncautious' heading for these perilous times, but then the thing was running through my mind, and down it came on paper, and as it looks rather nice to me, and will probably sound rather nice to you—I risk the business."[15]

Angus, in his steady, consistent way, usually addresses her as "My Own Dear Martha" and signs himself "A. Munn," "A," or not at all. His letters are full of love and solicitude for her and Lizzie, with offers of help and no complaints. He seems to accept Martha's teasing with good humor and to sympathize with her moods. (In this he reminds me of "my dear husband," his great-nephew.) Martha refers to his "buoyant" spirit and "lightheartedness," as well as to "your own dear pleasant self." No wonder she missed him!"

Fortunately Angus saved all her letters but one, although she often asked him to burn a certain one or "all my letters." The one he burned at her insistence was written toward the end of her exile. In it she evidently accused him in frantic terms of never having loved her, and this hurt him deeply. His reply took all the blame on himself, expressed his true, ardent love, and so moved her that she wrote back: "Oh Papa, Papa— . . . I feel like crying myself sick to think what a wicked girl I have been to hurt your feelings as I have. I did not know what mean things I had written until I read your quotations from my letter. I was half beside myself when I wrote, sobbing & hysterical, and did not know half what I said—but this is a paltry excuse for so grave an error. The only thing I can do now is to humbly ask forgiveness and pray to our Heavenly Father that my petition will be granted. . . . I shall be the happiest woman in the world, if I am permitted to meet you and hear from your own lips I am forgiven."[16]

It is good to know that as proof of his love Angus traveled to New York to meet his "own dear Martha" when she returned from England. He spent several days with her and their child before returning to Utah.

Reading Martha's letters has given me new insight into the power of steadfast faith and endurance. Her writing, so often poured out impetuously under stress, has also confirmed a lesson I learned long ago: candor may be good, but kindness is better. Before I graduated from college I asked a dear cousin and confidante to return any of my girlish letters she had saved. She did, and I found that many of them held complaints or unkind comments. I have never been sorry that I burned them.

Moreover, I have found a theory of the philosopher William James to be true: expressing an emotion may increase it. "A baby doesn't cry only because it's uncomfortable," he said, as I recall. "It's uncomfortable because it's crying." Mattie was certainly uncomfortable long after the end of the distress that prompted the damaging letter. I'm glad Angus burned it. Perhaps another lesson might be: if you think your letter should be burned, do it yourself before you send it.

Martha had some positive experiences during her European exile. She enjoyed trips to France and Switzerland, where she indulged in sightseeing and also visited hospitals and acquired textbooks to be used in the nursing school she helped establish after her return to Utah. In Switzerland she sought her genealogy.

According to her daughter Elizabeth McCrimmon (the sickly "babe" of Martha's letters), Mattie assisted in the British Mission headquarters under Daniel H. Wells. Her baby's frequent illnesses were helped by the faith and administrations of the missionary elders and other Latter-day Saints. In her letters to Angus, Martha details the success of their help with fervent testimony. She was not alone, though often lonely. Yet she did not wish to stay.

So what were the ingredients of Martha's bitter cup of exile? The main factor was illness, both hers and her baby's. "When one is dragged down with a bodily ailment," she writes, "the shadows of life hang more heavily about them."[17] When her headaches and postpartum uterine problems are in abeyance, when Lizzie is not suffering from her frequent colds and fevers, teething, or the aftermath of her near-fatal accidental poisoning, Martha expresses heartfelt joy and gratitude. When illness strikes, depression flows into her letters.

A second disappointment was the continuing need for secrecy, from which she had not escaped. Her efforts to conceal her identity became burdensome, with frequent changes of address and frustrating contacts with certain other Utah "undergrounders." With a dash of jealousy over Angus's younger (by a mere six months!) wife, Maria Bennion, the bitter cup is full. Mattie could not drink it alone, so she shared it with Angus.

Hope for better medical help was one important reason for Martha's decision to return home. They left in December of 1888. After seeing Angus in New York, she went to Michigan, where she had received her medical training, rather than to Salt Lake City. There she stayed for six months, enduring an unusually cold winter and Lizzie's chicken pox, scarlet fever, and pneumonia, with dental work but no corrective surgery for herself. But by spring she was feeling more cheerful and Lizzie was responding to treatment for her bladder inflammation. Mattie was in no hurry to go on west; she was beginning to be aware of the increasing tension there and decided to wait until mid-May. She explains to Angus: "When I left Utah two years ago, it was with the full determination to relieve you of all apprehension on my account—and I have not changed on that point. . . . I might come home now and keep under cover, but another determination on my part would prevent that. That was to breathe the Rocky Mountain air *freely* or not at all."[18]

Meanwhile Angus was in the midst of the increasingly vindictive crusade against polygamy and the fight against the political influence of the Church. The Edmunds Act of 1882 had been supplemented by the more punitive Tucker Amendment, which was being contested in the courts. Some of Angus's property might have been in danger of being confiscated.

Yet he wanted Mattie home and supplied her with her own horse and buggy again when she arrived. He could not give her the home of her own for which she longed, however. She stayed with her mother and stepfather while she set up a school for nurses and began her private practice again.

On 19 May 1890 the United States Supreme Court upheld the seizure of Church property under the Edmunds-Tucker Act. On that same day a son was born to Martha and Angus. James Hughes Cannon was a symbol of the ongoing vitality of their faith.

Soon after that, Martha took her children into exile again, this time to San Francisco. She could not be present in the Salt Lake Tabernacle at the October conference of 1890 to hear the historic announcement of the Manifesto or to raise her hand with that great congregation to sustain it. No doubt she would have done so, even if it put her own situation as a fourth wife in jeopardy, for she had faith in the principle of revelation to a modern prophet. Perhaps hoping the persecution of plural marriage would have subsided, she returned to Salt Lake after two years and resumed her medical practice.

The Manifesto closed the door to future plural marriages, but the status of those already in place was cloudy. Most husbands and fathers of polygamous families, including Angus Cannon, were unwilling to disown them. Some took the route to exile in Canada or Mexico; others decided to possess their souls in patience and maintain contacts with their plural families as much as possible. The fact that a third child, Gwendolyn, was born to Angus and Mattie in 1899 shows that he chose the latter route.

The door was now open to a successful petition for statehood. After much jockeying to realign political parties, that was accomplished in 1896, nearly 50 years after Brigham Young had begun the attempt. The new state constitution included a restoration of Utah women's right to vote. For Martha Cannon that breakthrough also opened up a whole wide field of achievement in the area of her greatest professional concern—public health education and legal enabling acts.

Martha achieved fame—or perhaps notoriety—both in her time and ours by an event that has been popularly misinterpreted. In the first election for the new Utah state legislature, Martha was one of five Democratic candidates for senator. Angus was one of five Republican hopefuls on the open ballot. Theoretically both Angus and Martha could have won senate seats or both lost. As it happened, the top five vote-getters were elected in a Democratic sweep, and Martha was one of them. Angus and his fellow Republicans all lost. Of course Martha became known as "the woman who beat her husband" in that first election. But as she later explained to an English visitor, she should rather be viewed as running against Emmeline B. Wells, the only other woman — and a Republican.[19]

Her husband had wished her well on the eve of the election, Martha said, and was not the least jealous of her success.[20] Judging by his loving, good-humored responses to her unhappy letters, Angus might well have been glad that she now had an outlet for her ambitions, one that could bring her the recognition he honestly felt she deserved. Toward the end of her exile in England she had written that her life was "a failure."[21] She was about to prove it was not.

Martha had no intention of being just a token woman. She began briskly by introducing three significant bills. The first was "An Act providing for the Compulsory Education of Deaf, Dumb, and Blind Children." That one has a unique meaning for me: in 1941 my father was superintendent of the State School for the Deaf and Blind in Ogden (*dumb* had long since been dropped). My husband and I had our wedding reception in the superintendent's home, located on the spacious grounds of that school. I wish I had known about Martha then.

The second bill was even more far-reaching: "An Act Creating a State Board of Health and Defining its Duties." Martha's interest in public health and sanitation was not only related to her medical profession; it was the main reason she had entered politics. Indeed, it was the main reason she had determined as a young girl to become a doctor. Governor Wells appointed her to the new seven-member Board of Health, and her continuing concern for children was shown in two measures she introduced: a law prohibiting school attendance of children with contagious diseases, and rules for the inspection of school buildings.

The third was "An Act to Protect the Health of Women and Girl Employees," which required employers to provide seats for women when they were not working. This bill may seem irrelevant today in the equal opportunity workplace, but Martha had experienced the relationship between fatigue and "female problems." Who can doubt that the women who used the seats appreciated her concern! Other bills that she introduced or supported testify to her ability to represent both the women and the men of Utah. She also gave Utah the distinction of being first in the nation to elect a woman state senator.

Her Utah political career ended with the birth of her youngest child in 1899, but her goals reached beyond that state. Before, during, and after her four years in the Utah senate she traveled and spoke for causes in which she believed, particularly women's right to vote in the whole nation.

Her oratorical skills became well known. The *Salt Lake Tribune* described one of her speeches enthusiastically: "Senator Cannon prefaced her vote with an address so eloquent that despite parliamentary decorum and the rigid rules against demonstrations she was cheered and cheered again at its conclusion."[22] Apparently the same dramatic expression that makes her private letters to Angus so overwhelming was put to effective use in the political arena.

Even during her hectic years this vibrant woman nourished her roots in the Salt Lake City 10th Ward, where she served for eight years as secretary of the Young Women's Retrenchment Association and taught a Gospel Doctrine class. She shared her testimony of the restored gospel with others at home and abroad. Such ways of serving others are available to all of us and can be as healing as a doctor's skills.

After her retirement from public life Martha enjoyed living in Los Angeles, California, with her inventor son, James, and also in West Salt Lake Valley with her daughter Elizabeth and son-in-law on their ranch. Her other daughter, Gwendolyn, died in 1928. Angus died 7 June 1915, 17 years before Martha.

According to Elizabeth, her mother spent the last five years of her life in her own home at last, in Los Angeles. She freely gave her services as a volunteer in the orthopedic department of the Graves Clinic, an adjunct to the University of California. Martha died at age 75 on 10 July 1932.

We can be grateful that the sickly babe Lizzie, whom Martha nursed through countless illnesses during their exile abroad, lived to care for her mother and become her loving biographer. Like her Welsh grandmother Elizabeth Evans, Elizabeth Cannon Porter McCrimmon has brought Martha to life, that we might know her. Would not every mother of a difficult child hope for such a reward!

Martha's life means different things to different people. To some she is the envied model of the independent woman, to others a great lady to admire but impossible to emulate. (No one these days can be the first woman state senator in the United States!) To me she represents the ability to triumph over weaknesses. To me she says: Our Heavenly Father did not send us here to fail, but to learn. We can learn from our mistakes—learn not to repeat them. We can learn from our weaknesses by strengthening them with good deeds. We can turn our uncontrolled emotional waterfalls into channels of living water to irrigate a thirsty land. Mattie did that. We can too. With her we can say, "I know that this is His work and that what we are passing through is for our benefit."[23]

In Salt Lake City on the corner of South Temple and what is now Second West, a simple stone monument honors Martha Hughes Cannon. According to the bronze plaque, her home and office were located nearby. This tribute was erected in 1970 by medical and public health groups who wanted Martha's life remembered. More than a quarter century later she would be remembered as one of the pioneer women doctors honored by a Presidential Endowed Chair in Radiology at the University of Utah School of Medicine, with Dr. Ann Osborn Poelman as the first occupant. In the historic City and County Building, a conference room where Martha's portrait hangs was dedicated to her memory.

On 24 July 1996, following the traditional Pioneer Day parade, the rotunda of the Utah State Capitol gradually filled with relatives and friends, dignitaries and well-wishers. On the wide stairs leading up to the balcony stood the International Children's Choir. In one of the four tall niches a full-length statue waited to be unveiled and dedicated. The children's choir sang. The dignitaries spoke. The bronze statue was unveiled—Dr. Martha Hughes Cannon, first woman state senator in the United States, standing erect, looking confidently to the future.

President Thomas S. Monson, First Counselor in the First Presidency of The Church of Jesus Christ of Latter-day Saints, was one of the speakers. In his dedicatory talk he praised Martha for her worthy goals and pointed out that although she experienced some disappointments and unfulfilled dreams, she never lost her eternal perspective; she endured to the end. With a little smile, he added that he wished she could have been in the parade that morning, leading the way. The thought came to some of the listeners: Perhaps she was!

NOTES

1. See Jean Bickmore White, "Martha H. Cannon," in Vicky Burgess-Olson, ed., *Sister Saints* (Provo, Utah: Brigham Young University Press, 1978), p. 386.

2. Mary Ann Rich, "Autobiography of Mary Ann Phelps Rich" (Logan, Utah: n.p., 1951), p. 20.

3. Elizabeth C. McCrimmon, unpublished manuscript, Utah State Historical Society Library, as quoted in White, "Martha H. Cannon," p. 387.

4. William Clayton, "Come, Come, Ye Saints," in *Hymns,* no. 30.

5. *Church News,* 31 March 1996, p. 7.

6. Jill Mulvay Derr, Janath Russell Cannon, and Maureen Ursenbach Beecher, *Women of Covenant: The Story of Relief Society* (Salt Lake City: Deseret Book Co., 1992), p. 106.

7. Journal History of The Church of Jesus Christ of Latter-day Saints, 13 August 1878, Historical Department, The Church of Jesus Christ of Latter-day Saints, Salt Lake City, Utah.

8. Martha Hughes Cannon, letter to Angus Munn Cannon, 3 February 1888, in Constance L. Lieber and John Sillito, eds., *Letters from Exile: The Correspondence of Martha Hughes Cannon and Angus Munn Cannon, 1886–1888* (Salt Lake City: Signature Books in association with Smith Research Associates, 1989), p. 255.

9. Beatrice Cannon Evans, "Angus Munn Cannon," in Janath R. Cannon, *Cannon Family Historical Treasury,* 2d ed. (n.p.: 1995), p. 215.

10. White, "Martha H. Cannon," p. 391.

11. James B. Allen and Glen Leonard, *The Story of the Latter-day Saints,* 2d ed. (Salt Lake City: Deseret Book Co., 1992), p. 405.

12. Lieber and Sillito, *Letters,* p. 11.

13. Ibid., p. xv.

14. Ibid., p. 3.

15. Ibid., p. 8.

16. Ibid., p. 238.

17. Ibid., p. 202.

18. Ibid., p. 269.

19. See Beatrice Webb, *Beatrice Webb's American Diary,* ed. David A. Shannon (Madison, Wisc.: University of Wisconsin Press, 1963), p. 132.

20. See ibid.

21. Lieber and Sillito, *Letters,* p. 213.

22. *Salt Lake Tribune,* 2 February 1897, as quoted in White, "Martha H. Cannon," p. 389.

23. Lieber and Sillito, *Letters,* p. 65.

❧

Janath Cannon, a graduate of Wellesley College in Massachu-setts, served as first counselor to Barbara B. Smith in the Relief Soci-ety general presidency. She and her husband, Edwin Q. Cannon, presided over the Switzerland Mission, Nauvoo Visitors Center, Germany Hamburg Mission, and the Frankfurt Temple, and, to-gether with the Rendell Mabeys, were the first official Church repre-sentatives in West Africa. They have six children and 25 grandchil-dren. In researching Martha Hughes Cannon, Janath has come to think of her as a valued friend whom she hopes to meet in the life to come.

22

"The Place for Us to Go"
Mildred Cluff Harvey
1866–1949

I was only 12 but I felt like a giant, towering over the small woman swaddled in white flannel blankets on the gurney that the ambulance men had deposited on the sidewalk in front of our house.

"Hello, Grandma," I ventured. The eyes in the wrinkled face looked at me, beyond me, seeming to see nothing. During the following two years that Grandma lived with us she never spoke to me or gave sign that she knew me. I met Mildred Cluff Harvey too early in my life, too late in hers, ever to know her as she was for most of her life. It remained for me years later to piece to-gether her story, to learn its lessons and appreci-ate her greatness. For greatness, said Eliza Roxcy Snow, is simply usefulness. And Millie Harvey was useful.

Millie Cluff's first memory, she had said, was of walking down a path through tall grasses, carrying a bucket of brown sugar to the thatch-roofed house where she lived. She was the daughter of Benjamin and Mary Ellen Foster Cluff, Latter-day Saint missionaries who ran the Church's sugar operations in Laie, Hawaii. Both Millie and her sister Ella were born there, in 1866 and

Mildred Cluff Harvey

1869 respectively, the Cluffs' fourth and fifth children. Millie was five before she ever saw more white people than the other missionary families on the island. Her strongest memory after the family returned stateside was of "standing at the fence and looking through just to see all the 'white mothers' pass."

One of those "white mothers" was Aunt Eliza, Millie's father's other wife, whom they rejoined in Logan, Utah, on their return. Even with husband and both wives working—he at carpentry and farming, they at spinning and weaving and keeping boarders—there was not enough to sustain both families at home in Logan. So, leaving Aunt Eliza there, Benjamin and Mary Ellen moved to less-populated Coalville, where there was more land, more opportunity. There, two more boys were added to the family. When Benjamin, the second child, was ready for higher schooling, Mary Ellen, leaving Benjamin Sr. on the farm, moved her brood into her parents' house in Provo and began for the family a long association with Brigham Young Academy, then a combined elementary and secondary school. Young Benjamin was later to preside over that academy when it made its official transition to Brigham Young University.

Even after the rest of the family had returned to Wasatch County, settling now in Center Creek, near Heber, Millie stayed on in Provo with "Bennie" as her guide and mentor. "Right nobly did he care for me," she remembered.

Meanwhile Mary Jane, the oldest daughter, who had been teaching school in Hoytsville, had married, and at term's end Millie returned to the mountain valley to care for her at the birth of her baby. Millie's work extended from house to classroom, and by age 15 she was assistant schoolteacher, then teacher. Alternating between Provo to learn and Center Creek to teach, Millie filled her teen years happily, as she remembered them. Across the street from "Aunt Margaret's," where Millie boarded for part of her time at school, "six girls were living and keeping house for themselves, and what good times we did have."

Meanwhile young Richard Harvey, son of one of the ecclesiastical leaders of the community, determined that "it was about time to make some arrangements for the future," as he later wrote, and therefore "I started my first courtship, with the Bishop's daughter." Richard and Millie were married in the Logan temple 15 December 1886 and moved into the four-room frame house Richard had built, "one of the best in the county," he later boasted.

A hundred years later my mother and I visited that little house, in which she had been born in 1900. Imagining away the lean-tos and shacks since added, I saw newly married Millie in 1886, arriving by train in Coalville, met by Richard's brother Will in a buggy on a disagreeable December day. "I thought I had married a king, a man among men," Millie wrote 30 years later. "And I have not changed." The Harveys felt the same enthusiasm about Millie. She recalled that Will's response to her apology for inconveniencing him was, "Gee, I'd go farther than this for a sister!"

That was the model I grew up with: The young couple, stars in their eyes and hard work in their bones, riding off into the sunset of bright promise. The young woman, as well prepared for a profession of community usefulness as she was for domestic life. Serious about her ecclesiastical duties but aware of her social responsibilities. Fun-loving—they spent their first New Year's on an outing to Coalville with two other young couples—yet home-loving.

Would I have exchanged my life for Grandma's? I wondered, looking those many years later at the sad little house and the weed-bestrewn yard. Many of her values I certainly shared—home, family, a life of productive effort: Even after her first children were born she continued teaching and attending school. Music was important to her mental and emotional well-being. The library she accumulated and passed on bespeaks her love of reading. Like me a bishop's daughter, she was at home in the Mormon community. As I have done, she loved parents and siblings, loved babies. More than I might have done, she supported Richard in filling a mission, leaving her behind with three children under four years old.

I found in Grandma's recollections one of my favorite stories told me by my mother:

One time in particular, Richard had written asking me to send him five dollars. At that time (it was winter) Howard was just out of shoes, and not one cent in sight. I did not know what to do except to ask God to open a way for me to get it. An evening or two after, my brother Foster came to spend the evening with me—he came so often and was such a comfort to me. Our evenings were spent singing, I at the organ. This evening he was looking for a particular piece of music, and in doing so emptied the place at the organ which held the music. The last time he put his hand in, when he pulled it out he said, "Is this where you keep your money?" and in his hand he held $6.25—just enough for five dollars for Richard and $1.25 for Howard's shoes. We were awed at it, and knew the time of miracles was not passed.

On Richard's return the little family of three children grew by two more, and with Millie's teaching and Richard's farming the family prospered. Two sorrows marred their contentment, however: the deaths a year apart of Millie's most-loved sister Mary and of Howard, their firstborn son. Barely eight years old, Howard had been trusted to ride his pony to bring in the cows at night. Stopping by his aunt's on the way, he promised to deliver her parcel to his mother, and tied it to the pony's halter rope and the rope to his leg to keep the parcel safe. The pony shied, throwing Howard off. But the rope held fast, and Howard was dragged homeward, his neck broken. "It was almost more than we could bear," Millie remembered 40 years and a thousand miles later.

Richard was becoming restless in the ever more populated valley with its limited potential for expansion for him or his children. "I decided to move someplace," Richard remembered. In February 1900 Lucile, the sixth child, was born. A couple of weeks later Richard, on his way home with a load of ice, picked up a pamphlet promoting settlement in Alberta, Canada. Thirteen years earlier Charles Ora Card had led a group of Utah polygamists fleeing prosecution to settle what was by 1900 a thriving group of Mormon towns just north of the Canada-USA border, and he and others were promoting the establishment of permanent communities there. "When I got home," Richard remembered, "I told Millie I had found the place for us to go." By April the couple had sold their farm and most of the cattle and were on their way north.

Richard went on ahead with the farm machinery and household goods, leaving Millie to follow three days later with the children, Elma Vere, age 12, John, nine, Foster, five, Mildred, three, and the baby, Lucile, just two months old. Leaving the lush beauty of Heber Valley must have been difficult for Millie. Did she share Richard's dynastic ambition? Or was she the "reluctant pioneer" historians see in many women following their husbands into the unknown? Did she feel the pull of father and mother in Provo or of two adjacent graves in Heber Cemetery? What fears did she have of taking her children so far from the Academy to a land where, so far as she knew, there was no opportunity for education? Putting myself in her place, I like to think she felt with Richard the call of a new land, the adventure of the unknown. Even so, when I later would have the opportunity to teach school on Lake Athabasca in what was then a similar frontier, I would decline in favor of further education in a known environment. I cannot know what fears Millie Harvey overcame in order to follow her husband's dream, but I admire enormously her love and her courage.

Millie and the children met Richard and his hand, Mormon Hort, at Great Falls. The men had already loaded the cattle and equipment on the northbound train, and since there was no passenger service that day the family accepted gratefully the trainmen's generosity and rode the rest of the journey in the caboose, bedding the children in the men's cots.

It was dark night and a storm was blowing when the train arrived at Stirling, the closest station to the Mormon settlements. Unloading the cattle, Richard and Mormon Hort would have to ride herd all night to ensure that they did not stray in the storm. A kindly stationmaster housed Millie and the children in the station house until morning.

The rising sun showed the southern Alberta prairie at its most splendid. To Richard, it revealed endless miles of greening grasses "and nothing to feed but my cattle. I thought this was paradise indeed." His account of going inside the station house and finding Millie "safe and even cheerful" says volumes to me, however. He must have known her doubts, her fears, her lack of confidence, to have been surprised at her smiles. But knowing my mother, and through her, her mother, I wonder at her control of the terror hidden beneath the surface of the smile.

The Canadian prairie is a magnificent experience. I fly often to Calgary and am no sooner on the road than I feel my eyes taking in the full 360 degrees of linear horizon. My smile broadens and my heart swells. I am home. I am back where nothing interferes with my thoughts, where my mind can expand to the very curve of the earth, where my soul partakes of eternity's expanse. But I was born there, was reared with the endless possibilities such landscape represents. Millie Harvey was a child of the mountains, nurtured and protected, at least from her fifth year, by friendly hills that walled in verdant valleys. Her mountains were bulwark against the malevolent forces attempting to eradicate Mormonism and its practices; my prairies invited me to expand my Mormonness into the world from which her people had fled. Two generations made such a difference—how can I judge? In any case, I do recognize that where for me the Utah mountains were initially constraining and oppressive, for Millie the Alberta prairies must have left her feeling unprotected and vulnerable.

Leaving Stirling for Mountain View, where Richard had purchased farm and house, the family created quite an entourage: Richard first, driving four horses hitched to a big double bed wagon loaded with machinery and furniture; then Millie, baby in arms, driving the covered wagon with boxes and bedding, the food, and two more children. Fastened on the back was a crate filled with clucking chickens, and following that a one-horse buggy in which Elma and John cared for two newborn calves. Trailing behind was Mormon Hort driving the cattle.

But it is the return journey a few discouraging months later that wrenches my sympathies. With faith in Apostle Amasa Lyman's recommendation, the little company was retracing its path toward Stirling, where they would take up new land on Etzicom Coulee. Not even the frame of a house would meet them there, and they would have to share the building of a home with the cutting of hay and the construction of shelter for the winter's care for the cattle. On the way, Richard, driving cattle this time, turned so suddenly that his saddle slipped under the horse and threw him to the ground. For a terrifying minute he felt himself dragged, until his foot eased itself from the stirrup. The horse trotted off to join the teams, leaving Richard herding cattle afoot. I can barely imagine Millie's anguish at the approach of the riderless horse; the haunting specter of another horse another time returning with its saddle empty. With what desperation did she run up the rise searching for Richard, and with what relief did she spot him walking toward her?

Arriving at what became know as Mammoth, the Harveys established themselves on the south slope of the coulee, one of those wrinkles on the prairie through which the spring runoff finds its way to the nearest river. For Millie and Richard there was little distinction between man's work and woman's work. Together they built the first house. An extant photograph shows the walls of uneven boards, the rickety porch, the rough shingles—the work of partners in the enterprise of survival. In front are the children, including Lucile, now about four years old, on her head the ubiquitous sunbonnet—always red, she used to tell me, so her mother could spot her where she played in the high coulee grasses, while Millie herself was plucking wild mustard from among the wheat.

The Harveys' nearest neighbors were the Keslers, a mile and a half to the east along the coulee. They, too, were LDS, but most of the rest of the settlers were not. But they shared the camaraderie of the coulee—the four bachelor farmers, the homesteading families, the schoolteacher Mr. Fitch, hired by the Harveys when the government proved too slow to provide a teacher. But with it all there must have been a loneliness for Millie, unacknowledged cabin fever, relieved by weekly Sunday School at the Keslers' and occasional Saturdays in nearby Raymond. Pregnancies carried the promise that after Hannah Russell, the midwife from Stirling, had delivered the baby, Mrs. Kesler would ride over daily to care for mother and child. Millie could return the service for her friend at her confinement. But the hunger for adult conversation must have been overwhelming, especially when Richard exchanged his cattle for sheep and supervised the older boys for weeks at a time on the distant ranges.

I have always known that Grandma Harvey was often "sick." A family story reveals how often Elma, the oldest daughter, was required to be surrogate mother: Lucile, complaining about having to bottle-feed motherless newborn lambs, asked innocently, "Why can't their mothers feed them?" "Their mothers are dead." "Then why can't their Elmas feed them?" The necessity for an Elma in the Harvey family came to me with a shock of recognition when I discovered a brief diary Millie had kept during a trip to Vancouver with Richard. By her description, her "sick headache" was a classic migraine. Pressing my mother, I realized that that malady often accompanied periods of depression which I have learned to recognize in my own life and in the lives of some friends. There is relief for us in a time when there are medications to relieve biochemical maladjustment. For Millie, there was only herself, the ever demanding work, and Elma, when she was home. No wonder, as my mother told me once, Grandma Millie used to take long walks over the prairie trails.

For all that, Millie was productive. She guaranteed her children secure, stimulating childhoods. The organ she insisted Richard bring with the necessities from Utah brought music into the family. And when one of the itinerant sheep shearers had a talent, the family would hear evening recitations of "Curfew Shall Not Ring Tonight" or "The Highwayman." There were Valentine parties, for the children one day, the adults the next. And birthdays and Christmas and conferences—highlights of the year, religiously observed.

Richard bred his sheep wisely to suit the Alberta climate, and eventually became quite rich. The new house—he would surely have described it as the best in the coulee—contained all the amenities he could provide: running water, ingeniously pumped into a cistern uphill and released under its own pressure into taps in the house; a huge oak dining-room table, around which the children, under Millie's direction, would study; and, after one particularly successful trip east, a piano. I had wondered how my mother, with her remote upbringing in the days before phonographs, ever developed the taste for opera with which she plagued us children every Saturday afternoon. As I learn about Millie, I am no longer surprised. And it takes little imagination to recognize the source of my mother's love of literature—I had to take university graduate work to be able to meet her knowledge, poet for poet.

For all that, Millie never, I think, found peace in the Alberta prairie, though I doubt that she complained. She was proud, and her image of herself as the proper and perfect wife and mother was demanding. Often repeated in our family is a retort she once made to my mother. As they climbed a hill together, Lucile wondered at her mother's lack of breathlessness. "I do not permit myself to pant," explained Millie. I wonder what other natural and needful urges she likewise suppressed. The retort does set in context her confession to her children that "if your father ever indicated a desire to live in Utah I should be most happy to go." What years of loneliness lie buried in that understatement?

It must have been to please Millie as much as to provide opportunity for their children that Richard eventually bought a house in Lethbridge, the nearest city. There Millie thrived. Her involvement in the Relief Society is evidenced by two artifacts I have: a recipe book, 136 pages printed and nicely bound, published under her direction about 1920; and a quilt, embroidered and pieced for her by the board who worked under her presidency in the Lethbridge Stake Relief Society. Logistically the work must have been overwhelming: The stake covered a radius from Lethbridge of 130 miles. Visits were generally overnight, and often Alberta's long winters and changeable weather would force the women to drive on treacherous roads. For 14 years Millie served in that capacity.

And yet, one of her daughter's most traumatic memories is of the morning in 1917 when she was preparing to leave for school, where she would take province-wide examinations. Coming downstairs, she discovered her mother in total emotional disarray, her mind wandering beyond recognition. Richard was out on the range, so Lucile called her sister Mildred to come home from the Galt Hospital, where she was in nurse's training, to care for their mother and the younger boys. Distraught, Lucile went off to take her exams. Bright though she was, she failed enough exams that she never returned to matriculate. Millie's "breakdown" passed, and life again resumed its normal activity.

Normal, that is, until Richard's sheep empire crumbled. His 45,000 head flock was ready for market as the market fell so low that he sold at a loss. Bank foreclosures cost him and his partner-sons their assets. The boys, now married men, left sheep ranching for salaried jobs, and Richard and Millie finally took their small remaining herd and moved to the Okanagan Valley in British Columbia. It was from there that my mother brought them back to live with us when they could no longer care for themselves.

And so I wonder. This volume is about heroines. Is Millie Harvey a heroine to anyone else besides me? How does the ordinariness of her life translate into heroic stature? I believe it is through her usefulness, as I noted at the outset, to family, church, and community. And her fortitude, another of Eliza Snow's values. Her persistence through the often tedious dailiness of woman's domestic duties. Her endurance to carry on through the maladies that beset her. Her faith, and faithfulness. Her leadership, and followership. Her thirst for learning, and the determination to find means to slake that thirst in herself and create it in her children. Her generosity and sense of social responsibility manifested to the neighbors on the coulee and the strangers who passed by her door.

I watched Millie and Richard those last years of their lives. Once Grandma realized that her sentences made no sense, she ceased to speak. She could no longer walk without my mother's strong arms under her arms, Mother's feet urging first one foot, then the other to shuffle forward. She epitomized Shakespeare's last stage, "Sans teeth, sans hair, sans eyes, sans everything." But not quite. In my aged grandmother's eyes I read her devotion to my mother, now her caretaker, and to her Richard. He was determined to outlive her, and after her death his loneliness was absolute. "To me he has ever been the lover, as he was when we were married," wrote my grandmother. Perhaps that is what I admire most: that after a lifetime together, because of or despite intimate knowledge of each other's virtues and faults, each received the other's unstinting adoration.

In this context of women of high achievement, of heroic dimension, I find none more praiseworthy than my grandmother, who did with generosity, good will, and stern self-discipline what was hers to do. I could ask for no finer model, no more splendid heroine than Mildred Cluff Harvey. For all her mere five feet height, she was to me a giant.

Note on Sources

In a mimeographed volume under the title *Four Leaves from History*, Lucile Harvey Ursenbach has compiled what few life writings remain of Richard Coope and Mildred Cluff Harvey. To their own dictations she has added photographs and biographical notes from her own knowledge and from letters and other family sources, which fill in some of the gaps. From this volume I have drawn heavily. Other sources include the autobiography of Lucile Harvey Ursenbach, typewritten and duplicated; oral histories of her sister Mildred Harvey Davies and her brother Robert Harvey, transcribed from interviews conducted by Charles Ursenbach; and the autobiography of Charles Ursenbach himself. Two small extant diaries—one of Mildred Cluff Harvey, beginning in 1910 and petering out into a notebook, and one of Lucile Harvey, also beginning in 1910 and diminishing in 1912—gave intimate insight into life on the coulee.

Two additional works have been useful: *How Beautiful Upon the Mountains: A Centennial History of Wasatch County*, compiled and edited by William James Mortimer (Wasatch County Daughters of Utah Pioneers, 1963), and *Cook Book*, compiled and edited by Lethbridge Stake Relief Society (Lethbridge, Alberta: n.p., n.d.). All are in the author's possession.

Maureen Ursenbach Beecher earned her bachelor's degree at Brigham Young University and her master's and doctorate degrees at the University of Utah. The mother of two college-aged children, she is a research historian and professor of English at BYU. Books she has authored or edited include *The Personal Writings of Eliza Roxcy Snow*, *Women of Covenant* (coauthored with Jill Mulvay Derr and Janath R. Cannon), and *Eliza and Her Sisters*. In this essay she wanted to depict how a woman's life can be lived nobly and well, however mundane or magnificent, private or public it may seem on the surface.

Index